NOVEL AND FILM

Bruce Archer Morrissette was born at Richmond, Virginia, 26 April 1911. He earned his B.A. at the University of Richmond (1931), his doctorat d'université at the University of Clermont-Ferrand (1933), and his Ph.D. at Johns Hopkins University (1938). From 1934 to 1938 he served as junior instructor in French at Johns Hopkins; from 1938 to 1962 he was assistant professor and then professor at Washington University; from 1962 to 1979 he taught at the University of Chicago, where he became the Bernard E. and Ellen C. Sunny Distinguished Service Professor (1974) and chairman of the Department of Romance Languages and Literatures (1967–70, 1973–76). In honor of his services to French studies, he was named Chevalier de l'Ordre des Palmes Académiques (1962) and Chevalier de l'Ordre du Mérite National (1980). He served at various times on the editorial boards of the *French Review*, *Symposium*, *Modern Philology*, and *Critical Inquiry* and taught as visiting professor at the University of Wisconsin (Madison), the University of Illinois (Urbana), the University of California (Los Angeles), and the University of Western Australia (Perth).

BRUCE MORRISSETTE

NOVEL AND FILM

Essays in Two Genres

With a Foreword by James R. Lawler

The University of Chicago Press
Chicago and London

The University of Chicago Press, Chicago 60637
The University of Chicago Press, Ltd., London

© 1985 by The University of Chicago
All rights reserved. Published 1985
Printed in the United States of America

94 93 92 91 90 89 88 87 86 85 54321

Library of Congress Cataloging in Publication Data

Morrissette, Bruce, 1911–
  Novel and film.

  "Bruce Morrissette: a bibliography": p.
  Contents: Post-modern generative fiction—Aesthetic
response to novel and film—The cinema novel—[etc.]
  1. Fiction—20th century—History and criticism—
Addresses, essays, lectures. 2. Moving-pictures—
Addresses, essays, lectures. 3. Robbe-Grillet, Alain,
1922– —Criticism and interpretation—Addresses,
essays, lectures. I. Title.
PN3503.M624 1985   809   85-995
ISBN 0-226-54023-5
ISBN 0-226-54024-3 (pbk.)

To the initiator of this book, James Lawler, and to my translator colleagues Françoise Meltzer, Charles Krance, and Gerald Honigsblum

B. M.

CONTENTS

FOREWORD

The twelve essays collected in this volume are the writings of a scholar who has brought fresh precision to the analysis of narrative techniques. By studying film in relation to the novel and, in particular, by discussing the experiments of recent French novelists, he raises questions of prime importance for contemporary fiction.

Bruce Morrissette's criticism is of wide range and varied nature. He has specialized in symbolist poetics, in Rimbaud, in the baroque novel, and in the life and work of an exceptional woman writer of the seventeenth century, Marie-Catherine Desjardins. But the main subject of his research over the past twenty years is the matter of these pages. Since the late 1950s he has stood as one of the most incisive explicators of the *nouveau roman*, of its past and present affiliations, of its interaction with the cinema. It has, indeed, become virtually impossible to dissociate his name from that of the novelist, filmmaker, and essayist Alain Robbe-Grillet, whose evolution he has followed with the sharpest of sympathies.

Robbe-Grillet emerged thirty years ago as one of the most brilliant authors of his generation. His audience, however, was small, his manner in great part misunderstood. What was required was a careful reading that took each novel in turn and showed its coherence within a developing project. This was achieved by *Les Romans de Robbe-Grillet*, which appeared in 1963. Bruce Morrissette had undertaken to study all the works published at that time with the respect one might apply to a classical text, and it proved rewarding. The new novel as practiced by Robbe-Grillet was not only "chosiste" or "objectal," but also a concerted psychological representation. This humanistic analysis threw new light: if it was not universally accepted, it demonstrated at the very least, with masterly finesse, that the novels were rigorous, that their techniques were richly innovative, that they could be seen to offer daring compositions of sign and sense. The success of the monograph was immediate; widely hailed, it went into second and third editions, which made room for discussion of subsequent novels and films by Robbe-Grillet and for consideration of the increased function of eroticism in the later works.

Yet at the same time, in the margins of this research, Bruce Morrissette was writing an important body of articles whose focus is a rhetoric of fictional modes. Here he shows himself, in the likeness of the authors he studies, to be a *criticus ludens* whose aim is to determine a "formalist schematics." Exploring modern and postmodern fiction, he reveals narrative freedoms that break decisively with conventions of time, viewpoint, and content. The approach is carried out in a style that is never self-indulgent; but pleasure quickens the search as precision combines with a characteristic openness to play.

The reader will find such qualities in this book. Although the essays as a whole do not elaborate a single argument, they can be said to maintain a consistent vision—that of a literary critic both analyst and engineer, who is unfailingly alert to original structures of fiction. This liveliness unifies the present volume and opens the way to Bruce Morrissette's latest work, *Intertextual Assemblage in Robbe-Grillet*, which demonstrates once more his art of unraveling complex texts.

Novel and Film is published to mark the retirement of Bruce Morrissette. It owes its origin to his friends at the University of Chicago who wish to celebrate an admired colleague, the holder of the Sunny Distinguished Service Professorship, Emeritus, and former chairman of the Department of Romance Languages and Literatures. At the end of the book a bibliography gives further proof of the vigor and breadth of his scholarly contributions.

James R. Lawler

ACKNOWLEDGMENTS

The material in this book has been included with the permission of the original publishers, having previously appeared as follows:

Chapter 1: "Post-Modern Generative Fiction: Novel and Film," *Critical Inquiry* 2, 2 (1975): 233–62. © 1975 by The University of Chicago.

Chapter 2: "Aesthetic Response to Novel and Film: Parallels and Differences," *Symposium* 27 (Summer 1973): 137–51. A publication of the Helen Dwight Reid Educational Foundation.

Chapter 3: "Problèmes du roman cinématographique," *Cahiers de l'Association Internationale des Etudes Françaises* 20 (May 1968): 277–89.

Chapter 4: "Roman et cinéma: Le Cas de Robbe-Grillet," *Symposium* 15 (Summer 1961): 85–103. A publication of the Helen Dwight Reid Educational Foundation.

Chapter 5: "International Aspects of the *Nouveau Roman*," *Contemporary Literature* 2 (Spring 1970): 155–68.

Chapter 6: "Topology and the *Nouveau Roman*," *Boundary 2* 1 (Fall 1972): 45–57.

Chapter 7: "De Stendhal à Robbe-Grillet: Modalités du point de vue," *Cahiers de l'Association Internationale des Etudes Françaises* 14 (1962): 143–63.

Chapter 8: "The Alienated 'I' in Fiction," *Southern Review* 10 (January 1974): 15–30.

Chapter 9: "Narrative 'You' in Contemporary Literature," *Comparative Literature Studies* 2, 1 (1965): 1–24.

Chapter 10: "Un Héritage d'André Gide: La Duplication intérieure," *Comparative Literature Studies*, 8, 2 (1971): 125–42.

Chapter 11: "Games and Game Structures in Robbe-Grillet," *Yale French Studies* 41 (1969): 153–72.

Chapter 12: "The Evolution of Narrative Viewpoint in Robbe-Grillet," *Novel* 1 (Fall 1967): 22–23.

1
POSTMODERN GENERATIVE FICTION

What was some years ago a highly contested critical view, that novel and film were not only thematically but also structurally interrelated, is now so widely accepted that to many it seems self-evident. Nevertheless, some scenarists and a number of novelists continue to argue the generic separateness of the two art forms and prolong theoretical distinctions and strategic differences that refuse to disappear. This essay explores some of these problems. It does not aim to investigate film novel relationships per se, although the fact that the two genres now share certain generative procedures may be further evidence that fiction in print and fiction on film lie to a great extent in a unified field both of diegesis and of structure.

A diachronic or historical approach to the theory of fictional generators would show that, with the shifts that have occurred in present-day aesthetic thought, much of what once was considered a static analysis of retrospective rules or established forms may now be regarded as the disguised beginning of generative theory. Aristotle's seemingly static doctrines of dramatic structure, involving such notions as peripeteia, discovery, or unity of action—to the extent that dramatists had consciously or unconsciously followed such doctrines—obviously served the *production* of their works, as well as their later analysis. In fact, any sort of artistic intentionality constitutes a kind of "generator," as does the deliberate adherence to outward forms such as rhyme schemes, stanzas, cantos, or chapters. As we shall see, it is not always easy to distinguish between generative formulas and self-imposed forms or limits, such as the sonnet with its fourteen lines, its quatrains, and its tercets. Although the most advanced practitioners of generative theory, like Jean Ricardou, seem to view their work as a radical break with the past and the discovery of an entirely new domain of fiction, literary history provides innumerable examples of precedents, from antiquity through the Grands Rhétoriqueurs,

1

the Gongorists and baroque poets, and many subsequent groups of writers down to and including the premodern and modern periods.

My object here is to present a synchronic, contemporary analysis of generative theory and practice in postmodern literature and film. Although the novel and the film of fiction are my chief interests, some excursions are required into nonfictional areas, especially in literature. This becomes apparent if we start by dividing types of postmodern generators into two main classes, linguistic generators and situational generators. The latter almost inevitably produce fictional structures, while the former may be limited to poetry or to texts of nonfictional prose. The most highly evolved generative works will contain both types.

Linguistic generators are primarily lettristic, syllabic, phonetic, or directly or indirectly anagrammatic. Early manifestations include rhyme, alliteration, assonance, acrostics, and a wide variety of exotic operations such as the lipogram, in which one or another letter is systematically omitted. One of the most striking illustrations from the past emerges from Jean Starobinski's recent study of Ferdinand de Saussure's "anagrams," which Starobinski terms "words beneath words."[1] According to the founder of linguistic science, the generative principle of many Latin poems lies hidden in systematically concealed words, or syllabic "anaphones," distributed throughout the poems and revealing the names of persons and places essential to the full meaning of the text. Thus Lucretius's poem starting with the Latin name Venus contains a series of syllables repeating the Greek form A-PHRO-DI-TE, and an oracular battle poem spells out in distributed syllables such references as APOLLO, DELPHI, and PHTHIA. That de Saussure lacked sufficient confidence in the objective reality of his discoveries to allow him to publish them is significant; as we shall see, the possible role of coincidence and chance in the proliferation of linguistic generators remains a problem.

The best handbook and account of nonfictional lettristic generation is the compilation *Oulipo: la littérature potentielle*, which represents the views and practices of the neo-Pataphysical group's updated version of their earlier Laboratoire de littérature expérimentale, then dubbed Ouvroir de littérature potentielle, or Ou-li-po.[2] The chief exponents of Oulipo were Raymond Queneau, Georges Lescure, Georges Perec, François LeLionnais, and Paul Enard. On close examination, Oulipo generators may be classed as either reductive or proliferative. Reductive procedures are illustrated in the Oulipo handbook by such operations as inventories of existing works (pp. 169, 183), in which nouns or other parts of speech

1. Jean Starobinski, *Les Mots sous les mots: Les Anagrammes de Ferdinand de Saussure* (Paris, 1971).

2. *Oulipo: La Littérature potentielle* (Paris, 1973).

are listed; "redondance," or the elimination of specified parts of poems, such as the first or last halves of lines (186); restricted vocabularies such as those of ALGOL or other computer languages (217); and lipograms (97). The lipogram, basically a reductive form (since one or more letters must be constantly suppressed), can nevertheless lead to expansion and thus function as a proliferative device, as witnessed by the most famous lipogram ever produced, Georges Perec's "novel" *La Disparition*, a full-length work without the letter *e*, whose story line involves characters derived from the alphabet, including the phantasmic Voyl (*e*) who mysteriously disappears.[3]

Proliferative generators exemplify the allure of what Leibnitz called *arte combinatoria*, as illustrated by innumerable modern and postmodern works ranging from serial music to Raymond Queneau's *Cent mille milliards de poèmes*, in which ten sonnets with identical rhyme schemes are so printed and arranged (with each line on a separate strip, and a set of blank pages used to keep the rearranged lines in place) that the reader may construct his own sonnets, to the incredible but mathematically exact number of 10^{15} or, as Queneau figures it, enough poems to provide uninterrupted reading matter to all of humanity for the foreseeable future. How recombinations may proliferate appears in the procedure called "noun plus seven," in which each substantive in a given poem is replaced by the one that follows it in seventh place in a specified dictionary; the resulting work is again subjected to the "plus seven" substitution, and so on (*Oulipo*, 143). Significantly, proliferation often follows an analytic process; thus a "generative analysis" of the detective story made by LeLionnais (66) may be used to produce detective stories ad infinitum just as Enard's "theatre tree" (281) gives combinatory dramatic structures leading to a proliferation of plots for plays. These latter examples, along with procedures of rearranged or spliced quotations and proliferative paraphrase (a technique used by baroque poets of the seventeenth century), lead to the conceptions of intertexuality and creation through rewriting and *littérature citationnelle* now finding wide acceptance among writers not only of poetry but of fiction as well.[4]

3. Georges Perec, *La Disparition* (Paris, 1969). Professor Colin Mayrhofer of Canberra sent me the following interesting note: "There is a beautiful example of the lipogram (*c'est le cas de le dire!*) in the seventh book of Daṇḍin's *Daśakumāracaritam* in which the first-person narrator, suffering from a love-bite on the lip, tells the entire story without using a single labial consonant."

4. The incorporation of texts from other authors is, of course, a classic procedure bordering on plagiarism and practiced by the greatest authors (e.g., Shakespeare's "borrowings" from Montaigne). A modern example, Thomas Mann's *Dr. Faustus*, illustrates the widest use of texts from elsewhere, most of them unrecognized until pointed out by critics (see Gunilla Bergsten, *Thomas Mann's "Doctor Faustus": The Source and Structure of the*

Patterns related to numbers, letters, syllables, and words—that is, linguistic generators—have played an important role in the evolution of generative fiction, serving also as producers or generators of situations, plots, and story lines. The most famous modern example is that of Raymond Roussel, who, when critics failed to uncover the syllabic-phonemic basis for much of his work, composed his seminal account entitled *Comment j'ai écrit certains de mes livres* (published posthumously in 1935). Several specific generative procedures are revealed: the first and last sentences of a text that are identical, except that one word or sound has changed, with the words themselves taking on alternative meanings, so that the "story" is engendered by the problem of joining the two homophonic phrases; the phonetic deformation of clichés, popular refrains ("j'ai du bon tabac . . ."), to create new phrases leading to invented episodes; and the regular paradigmatic operation of joining two nouns by a given preposition ("reître à dents") to arrive at previously nonexistent objects and decors. Most significantly for students of postmodern attitudes, more than fifty years ago Roussel insisted on the purely linguistic status of his fictional inventions: despite the exotic titles (*Impressions d'Afrique*, for example), nothing in his works, he wrote, came from outside reality; everything came from inside the text, from the words, their relationships, their interplay.

The contemporary novelist who is closest to Roussel in his theory and practice of *générateurs* unrelated referentially to outside social, geographical, psychological, or other "reality" is of course Jean Ricardou. Again, as with Roussel, the author himself has taken the initiative in revealing the processes that have engendered his fiction (James Joyce did not do otherwise in first disclosing the epic parallels of *Ulysses*). In *Problèmes du nouveau roman* (1967), *Pour une théorie du nouveau roman* (1971), and *Le Nouveau Roman* (1973), as well as in essays and lectures, Ricardou has presented a highly evolved and almost mathematical table of organization of possible generators, with illustrations from his own and other works. The most striking example is no doubt the title page of his novel *La Prise de Constantinople* (1965), as annotated and explained by Ricardou to show how the settings, characters, episodes, and descriptions all derive from or, as he prefers to say, are engendered by the letters, syllables, and typographical aspects of the title page itself. Ricardou goes beyond Roussellian generation, however, in at least one important as-

---

Novel [Chicago, 1969]). Georges Perec's novel *Un Homme qui dort* contains a large number of spliced-in citations. Creation of new fiction through rewriting older works is brilliantly discussed by Renato Barilli in the section on Calvino and Arbasino in *Tra presenza e assenza* (Milan, 1974), 252–67, "Calvino, Arbasino e la poetica della riscritura."

pect: while Roussel's nonreferential story also, like Ricardou's, derives from the text, it is not in itself an image or *mise en abyme* of the creative literary process, as is systematically the case in *La Prise de Constantinople* and in Ricardou's subsquent works, *Les Lieux-dits* (1969) and *Révolutions minuscules* (1971). A partial review of the interconnected generative elements found on the title page of *La Prise de Constantinople* would include the following: from JEAN RICARDOU, the numerical division into four and eight, as well as the principle of the half, the smaller, minor component (giving adults and children); the syllable AR-DOU, suggesting VILLEHARDOUIN, the chronicler of the seige of Constantinople (generating VILLE and IN, "dans la ville"); the CONST of Constantinople leading to the word and idea of CONSTELLATION (reinforced by the star in the Editions de Minuit's printer's sign) or referential "constellations"; the little *m* (for Minuit) by the star, from which emerges the section of the novel dealing with the "mystère dans les étoiles," the space travelers, and the like; and in Editions de Minuit itself the Ed of Ed Word, the Edith of the dedicatee, the *tion* of Sion (Jerusalem, the Crusades), the *mi* of demi or half, and the *nuit* of the novel's initial nocturnal scene. As Ricardou states in his notes, a book begins with its cover, its author's name, its title; the task is therefore to "déduire (produire) le livre à partir de sa couverture future." Since before there is nothing and after there is something, the book will begin with the word "Rien," and end with the thing produced, namely, "le livre." And within this text, all the elements will be linked and relinked, the oftener the better, according to the principle of redundant coherence that Ricardou calls "surdétermination." Even intertextuality in relation to other works comes into play: an eight-letter word derived from Claude Ollier's *La Mise en scène* (*abeilles*) "engenders" anagrammatically three sets of eight characters and a number of settings. Finally, the text becomes so self-contained that it bends back upon itself and repeats its own passages, becoming its own *mise en abyme*.

What is even more remarkable about Ricardou's generative fiction is that the author is able to set up for each new work a different system of organization: in *Les Lieux-dits*, a set of interrelated place names; in *Révolutions minuscules*, a series of fictional texts based on rhetorical terms and their definitions. In his role as critic, Ricardou has sought to apply his own methods to the analysis of works of past and present authors (Poe, Claude Simon, Robbe-Grillet), with interesting if sometimes questionable results. It is particularly in the generative analysis of others' works that Ricardou has had recourse to what is perhaps his most controversial principle, that of the "partial" anagram; obviously, if one is not obliged to find all, or even nearly all, the letters of a given word in its alleged transformation, the door may be opened to unlimited ingenuity of inventions. Another difficulty is the confusion between words as syllables and letters and words as *signifiants* having external reference or *signifiés*. In analyzing Robbe-Grillet's *Projet pour une révolution à New York*, for example, Ricardou proposes many whole or partial anagrams for the word *rouge*; Robbe-Grillet has answered that it was not the word *rouge* that became a generator in his novel, but the *color* red that engendered images of blood, torture, flames, and the like.[5]

Robbe-Grillet's objection to Ricardou's attempt to see in an often forced anagrammatic proliferation of the word *rouge* the generative basis for portions of the novel *Projet* emphasizes a crucial distinction between the lettristic-syllabic materials of the *signifiant* on the one hand and the semantic, or referential, materials of the *signifié* on the other. The visual, auditory, or other nonalphabetic aspects of the text may engender metaphors, serial patterns (like the figure eight in Robbe-Grillet's *Le Voyeur*), and, above all, situations or diegesis. Obviously, the graphic, phonic generators of the Roussel-Ricardou type are more prevalent in written texts than in film, where the situational generators tend to dominate (as they do in the novels of the chief exponent of the use of situational series, Robbe-Grillet). Nevertheless, phonetic transpositions or anaphonic reversals may occur as analogues or reinforcements within the photographic genre of film. For example, through rearrangements and use of radical reediting, Robbe-Grillet has created from materials made during the filming of *L'Eden et après* a second film entitled, through syllabic reversal or anaphonics, *N a pris les dés*. In addition, manipulations of phonemes, neohomophonic terms, and distortions of graphics are employed regularly in films by such divergent cineasts as Robbe-Grillet and Jean-Luc Godard; and Eugène Ionesco demonstrated two decades ago how syllables, refrains, clichés, proverbs, and various phonetic materials could proliferate, in the dialogues of *La Leçon* and *La Cantatrice chauve*, to generate scenes of absurdist farce.

Since linguistic generators may thus be closely involved in the production of situations and themes, we see that there is no hard and fast distinction between the linguistic and the situational types. Nonetheless, the situational generative technique may be isolated and seen to function in virtually pure form, without the need of linguistic reinforcement or phonetic accessories.

Situational generators, or fictional generators "proprement dits," are first of all not identical to what the critic Eugene Falk calls "thematic

5. See Robbe-Grillet's remarks in *Nouveau Roman: Hier, aujourd'hui* (Paris, 1972), 2: 160, in reply to Jean Ricardou's essay in *Pour une théorie du Nouveau Roman* (Paris, 1971), 211–33.

structures."[6] Themes, in the perspective of this essay, are considered as materials to be structured, and not as structures in themselves. Themes, to use an analogy developed by Robbe-Grillet in the preface to *Glissements progressifs du plaisir*, provide the "reservoir" from which the author takes his subjects and motifs; they are like de Saussure's *langue*, from which the novelist or filmmaker extracts the elements used to create his own indiviudal creative style or *parole*.[7] Fictional structures are not therefore thematic in any ideological sense (as, for example, the "thematic" structure of ambiguous, incoherent, open-ended scenes in the films of the Italian neorealists designed to embody and reflect a view of life itself as ambiguous and incoherent) but relate to, while going far beyond, such traditional structuring procedures as patterns of chronology, modes of viewpoint, intercalated narration, *liaisons des scènes*, analogues and *mises en abyme*, fictional patterns borrowed from epic or myth, and so forth.[8]

One of these structuring principles, interior duplication or *mise en abyme*, which I have studied at some length elsewhere,[9] not only is persistently fertile as a "generator," but also raises the fundamental question relating to generative procedures: namely, Are they designs that the author deliberately adopts as limiting the scope and contours of his work (i.e., does he *force* them into being), or are they truly generative or productive (i.e., do they *engender* or give rise to the text)? Certainly they cannot be spontaneous, or even always automatic; the program imposed by the author before or during the execution of the work cannot be equated with creative forces in the ordinary sense. If a generative *mise en abyme* exists unconsciously in the works of an author, what is its technical status? In a text on Shakespeare quoted by Ricardou in connection with interior duplication, Victor Hugo argues that in most of Shakespeare's plays the protagonist creates an inner duplication of his own dilemma in the situation of another character: "thus Hamlet creates beneath himself another Hamlet; he kills Polonius, putting Laertes in the same situation with respect to himself as he is in with respect to Claudius."[10] But was it by design? Coincidentally, André Gide, whose *Journal* of 1893 names and gives the first theoretical explanation of *mise en*

6. Eugene Falk, *Types of Thematic Structure* (Chicago, 1967).

7. Robbe-Grillet, *Glissements progressifs du plaisir* (Paris, 1974).

8. Epic and mythic parallels, or parallels to an earlier literary work such as the *Odyssey* or *Oedipus the King*, are related generatively to the "poetica della riscritura" studied by Barilli (see n. 4). Such generators may be used overtly (as in Butor's *L'Emploi du temps*) or covertly (as in Robbe-Grillet's *Les Gommes*) and give rise to a type of *mise en abyme*.

9. See chapter 10, "Interior Duplication."

10. Quoted in Jean Ricàrdou, *Le Nouveau Roman* (Paris, 1973), 49.

abyme, also uses the example of Hamlet but overlooks Hugo's point and focuses on the role of the inner play as a duplication of Hamlet's situation in terms of the characters of the play, "à l'échelle des personnages." This type of inner reflection of the main significance of a work in another work, explicitly or implicitly present, characterizes a great number of modern masterpieces, from *Les Faux-monnayeurs* of Gide himself through Joyce's *Ulysses*, Robbe-Grillet's *Les Gommes*, and Michel Butor's *L'Emploi du temps*, to such minor exercises in the genre as John Updike's *The Centaur*. What postmodern transformation of the *mise en abyme* has accomplished is to turn around the thrust of its significance: in the earlier period, duplication reinforced the psychological or referential meaning of the work by causing the characters of the fiction to become themselves aware of the same import that the author wished the reader to derive from the work, thus intensifying the centrifugal forces leading from work to reader, from fiction to life. In the postmodern theory of a Ricardou, for example, the *mise en abyme*, broadened in conception to include formal as well as thematic duplications, leads in centripetal fashion back into the work, away from the referential "outside," cutting the work off further from any lines or anchors that a reader may attempt to cast from the book to his real life or daily world. The work becomes self-contained, if not self-productive.

If the type of structure illustrated by *mise en abyme* may legitimately be termed generative, then so perhaps may other procedures affecting novel and film, such as "parallel montage," a technique that Eisenstein himself traced back to the fiction of Dickens and the early scenarios of D. W. Griffith. Sometimes parallel montage appears close to *mise en abyme*; sometimes it is ironic or contrapuntal (as in the *comices agricoles* scenes of *Madame Bovary*); in most modern works, it produces converging stories, either similar in nature or tied progressively to a unifying denouement, as shown in Griffith's *Intolerance*, Hitchcock's *Strangers on a Train*, and many novels ranging from Paul Bowles's *The Spider's House* through Durrell's *Alexandria Quartet* to Robbe-Grillet's *La Maison de rendez-vous*.

Setting many of these structural processes within a framework of generative theory may be considered in a sense a sort of "recuperation," within a new perspective, of old and familiar techniques. In the case of literary or cinematic serialism, however, we are faced with constructive methods that their authors avow to represent generators of fiction, and it is to these that I now turn. I am no longer dealing with principles that may have functioned only unconsciously, if at all, in the author's elaboration of his work but am addressing an intentional "deep structure" that the critic (or in some cases the author) may reveal. Whether such analyses and revelations are "proper" remains in some instances a debatable issue: Schoenberg, for example, seems to have rejected the value of discovering the underyling musical series on which he based his compositions, and Pierre Boulez has dissected such serial works as a Webern concerto while deliberately refraining from discussing the secret serial structure.[11] But when authors themselves draw attention to their structural processes, why should critics demur at discussing them?

Robbe-Grillet's constructional practices in his latest novels and films provide the most striking if not convincing demonstrations of postmodern fictional generators in operation. Basically, his theory is this: to choose popular, "ignoble," even worn-out fictional situations and "themes" from pornographic novels, detective stories, exotic action films, and Epinal engravings of sadoerotic tortures, and to structure these by means of generative metaphors, formal interrelationships, correspondences, and *mises en abyme*, subjecting this narrative field to topological manipulations such as reversal, infolding, turning inside out, and the like, to produce a radically new kind of novel and film.[12]

From the outset, series of similar objects (in form, at least) have served as controlling metaphors if not generators in the novels of Robbe-Grillet: the figure-eight images of *Le Voyeur* are not only quasi-identical geometric designs (two "eyes" on the doors, marks left by a swinging ring on the wharf, curling cigarette smoke, a coil of stout cord, etc.), but also part of the metaphor of Jacqueline's bound body that lies at the center of the protagonist's implied crime; the elaborate series of daggerlike forms in *Dans le labyrinthe* illustrates in images the generative power of an initial object, becoming a torch, a wallpaper design, falling snowflakes. In *Projet pour une révolution à New York*, the metaphoric color generator gives rise to many incidents: the revolutionaries act out a propaganda play in which the struggle between whites and blacks is resolved in a holocaust of revolutionary red, translated in the text by a series of scenes involving torture and blood, as well as engulfment by flames. The same work shows the evolution of the familiar *mise en abyme* of an inner novel (e.g., *La Jalousie*), which now not only "generates" an analogous reinforcement of the story line but, through the topological infolding mentioned earlier, turns the field inside out and replaces the original narrative level.[13]

The film *L'Eden et après* (1971) is based on a generative table of organization that clearly shows how Schoenbergian serialism has affected postmodern fiction. This table, which has appeared in the journal *Criti-*

11. See David Hamilton, "Musical Events," *The New Yorker*, 6 May 1974, 116.
12. See chapter 6, "Topology and the *Nouveau Roman*."
13. See chapter 6.

cal Inquiry (Winter 1975), consists of five columns headed as follows: Première série, sans ordre; scènes de l'Eden avant Duchemin; Deuxième série, ordre direct; scènes Eden dirigées par Duchemin; Troisième série, ordre direct; les rencontres dans le "parc"; Quatrième série, ordre inverse; tableaux composés par Duchemin; and Cinquième série, ordre inverse; événements de Djerba. In each column are briefly summarized seven incidents whose numbers are in the order indicated, allowing the correspondences and transformations within the various series to be collated and analyzed. Incidents in the various series bearing the same number reveal their common basis (a series related to blood, one to sperm, one to the drinking of poison, one to broken glass and cutting objects), while the forward movement of the story itself is seen to take place in the form of reordered reprises and disguised repetitions. Meanwhile, the film is generatively linked by a sort of systematic intertextual cross reference to earlier works by the same author: broken glass from *L'Année dernière à Marienbad*, labyrinthine scenes from *Dans le labyrinthe*. (Only the shoe fetish is lacking in *L'Eden* to allow the film to be included in the intertextual shoe or slipper series running from *Marienbad* through *La Maison de rendez-vous*, *L'Homme qui ment*, and *Projet pour une révolution à New York* to the 1973 film *Glissements progressifs du plaisir*.) In the latest manifestation of the incorporation of gratuitous thematics into generative metaphors, Robbe-Grillet has in *Glissements progressifs* converted the erotic metaphor of reciprocal sensual movement, accelerating to a climax, into a schematic of the overall structure of the film itself, so that even the ambiguous phrase "glissements progressifs" is used in the interscene text to describe the montage and visual integration of successive shots. Serial images, through gradual accelerated slippages, engender a rhythmic metaphoric structure whose concealed eroticism gives ultimate meaning to what we see on the screen.

Some critics have discerned in these generative practices only a continuation of the modern tendency to contest, attack, destroy ("abîmer," as Ricardou wittily puts it) such traditional fictional concerns as thematic causality, linear chronology, justified narrative viewpont, and the like, thus working at the aesthetic level for the revolutionary overthrow of bourgeois values. The neo-Marxists appear to believe firmly in this explanation. Postmodern critics prefer to view the situation differently; for them, generative structures isolate and protect the work of art and, by referring always back into the text (verbal or visual, or both), enable the novel or film to exist independently, aside from ideology or sociological issues and without serving even as an instrument of propaganda for any concept of avant-garde. Out of the outspoken antagonism of dada toward social and aesthetic forms there emerged, almost against the will of the dada artists, an art of positive construction. Out of postmodern fiction, behind a deceptive facade of rupture, chaos, and nonstructure, authors of contemporary novels and films are inventing new systems of coherency whose ultimate and problematic recuperation into one or another ideology is, to these postmodern artists, almost a matter of indifference.

2
AESTHETIC RESPONSE TO NOVEL AND FILM

Recent decades have witnessed, as I have pointed out, an unprecedented number of studies that attempt to define and analyze the relation between film and various literary genres, such as lyric poetry, drama, and above all the novel. These studies have taken opposing directions, some seeking to tighten analogies to the point of establishing complete equivalencies, others proposing radical separation of the genres to the point of denying the validity of all suggested parallels, cross-influences, convergencies, or analogies.

Any attempt to isolate the role of aesthetic response as a factor in comparing film and, say, novel quickly reveals the inadequacy of our conceptual system in dealing with a large, multifaceted problem in aesthetics. Intuitively, we feel that we know what we mean by aesthetic response; in practice, we discover that we cannot exactly place aesthetic response along the spectrum of reactions to film or novel ranging from the formal and structural, at one extreme, to the psychological, or even physiological and psychomotor, at the other. At one limit, the notion of the purely visual film image seems sufficiently remote from that of a word or a phrase, and of such a basically different order, that distinctions must be functionally possible; similarly, at the other limit of the neurophysiological response to film, it seems difficult to imagine a parallel among novel readers to the experiments using mass electroencephalograms performed on film viewers by Cohen-Séat and his group.[1] On the other hand, such a subtle critic as Roland Barthes applied to film images the same ideas of denotation and connotation, and of intellectual as opposed to emotional meaning, as those semanticists use in studying the functioning of language itself;[2] and projective empathy (which the EEG tests were

1. G. Cohen-Séat, *Revue Internationale de Filmologie* (January–June 1960): 37 ff.
2. Ibid., 83.

designed to reveal) has long been considered fundamental in reader identification, point of view in the novel, and the whole complex of reactions that, though as yet unmeasured by laboratory psychologists, could conceivably affect physiological response among readers in much the same way as film does among viewers.

Moreover, since the end of the era of silent films (even before, if we consider subtitles and similar verbal inserts), films have shared with literary genres a more or less highly developed use of dialogue, speech, and language, ranging from realistic conversational exchanges to commentary, soliloquy, voiced memory, and the like, all the way to filmed pages of books, posters, passages read aloud, telegrams held before the camera, and other devices yet to be tried, perhaps in the next films of Jean-Luc Godard. The most ardent separationists would be hard put to argue that these verbal elements change their character completely in passing from the printed page (of the scenario, say) to the screen or sound track. This is not to ignore the fact that being seen on the screen or heard as filmic sound can surround words with a different context; it is merely to insist on the common ground, the words themselves, underlying in such cases the visual as well as the auditory.

It may be useful here, before I attack directly the problem of film and novel, to review rather rapidly certain suggestions made in the past concerning film and poetry and film and drama. To the poets of the dada-surrealist period, film aesthetics constituted a logical extension of the search for unconscious imagery; unusual lighting, bizarre camera angles, strange confrontations of objects, sequences run backward or repeated, slow motion, all showed the film to be, in Yvan Goll's phrase, "visual poetry." Almost in the same fashion as automatic writing, the film was considered to be the cinematography of thought, even of the unconscious. Poetry is metaphoric; the film is, or can be, metaphoric; therefore film was poetry, and the aesthetic response to it was substantially the same as that evoked by verbal poetry, though perhaps more immediate or intense, since the verbal path was short-circuited, as in the pure poetic state recognized by the surrealists in dreams. An interesting consequence of this amalgamation of poetry and film was not only the production of poetic shorts such as Duchamp's *Anemic Cinema* and Man Ray's *Etoile de mer*, but also film-poems like Cocteau's *Les Hangars*.

With the advent of sound came a tendency to presume that film had at last discovered its true identity as a sort of conveniently recorded stage drama; the nefarious results of this assumption are well known in film history, which testifies to the flood of play adaptations that engulfed the early talkies. Even such a great cinematic theorist as Sergei Eisenstein at first viewed film and theater as closely related genres. Eisenstein's revised views, however, together with the acute analysis given later by Béla Balázs of the irreconcilable differences between the stage play and a film drama, rendered the theater-film analogy no longer tenable. Balázs's critique is perhaps the first serious attempt to see such generic differences as variations in form and technique as leading to necessarily different modes of aesthetic response. That his analysis could be applied to two versions of the same work, a play (seen and heard) and a film based on the play (also seen and heard) made it clear that fundamental differences in our responses must lie not in the plot, the theme, or even in the overall dramatic structure of the work (motivations, dramatic preparation, suspense, and the like), but in basic aesthetic aspects of play and film as separate genres.

Balázs established three formal principles of the theater: the spectator sees the enacted scene as a whole in space; he sees it from a fixed, unchanging distance; and he sees it from a fixed, unchanging point of view or angle of vision. (That more modern forms of staging have undermined the universal application of Balázs's principles of mise-en-scène may be overlooked at this point.) According to Balázs, the film contradicts these principles and adds a wholly new one: in a single scene of film the distance between the spectator and the filmed characters may vary; the scene may be divided into separate shots; camera angles and perspective may change within a single shot; and finally, montage or assembly of shots in a certain order, mixing long shots with close-ups and the like, creates a wholly new aesthetic effect, entirely absent from the theater. This effect is related primarily to the fact that the filmmaker may by these means place internal emphasis on details or aspects of each scene that "not only show but at the same time interpret" the picture.[3] The crucial point here is that whatever modifications may be found in later stage techniques, whether influenced by the film or not, Balázs's analysis appears valid for its historical moment. That such validity may prove temporary underscores the necessity for avoiding assertions of inherent or universal distinctions; the history of film criticism is strewn with the corpses of dead dogmas once considered living truths.

Obviously Balázs did not limit the aesthetic differences between film and drama to the presence in the cinema of internal interpretative modulations absent from the theater; what he sought to show was that, at the very least, film affects the spectator in a distinct fashion not to be confused with the effects of witnessing of a stage play. Beyond this, in Balázs's theory, the whole domain of filmic visual representation, the cinematic universe of a new kind of time and space, of objectified subjectivity and

3. Béla Balázs, *Theory of the Film* (London, 1952), 32.

visualized mental content, and above all, of psychological projection and identification experienced by the film viewer, made the art of the cinema specific and unique. From our contemporary viewpoint, the main value of Balázs's work is that it raised many of the fundamental considerations that must still be dealt with in comparing film with the other arts, especially the novel, and that it established as the true aim of the film the artistic creation of psychological or aesthetic effects made possible by the new cinematic techniques.

As soon as Eisenstein and his successors came to general agreement that the closest generic affiliation of film—that is, the fictional film, with which I am chiefly concerned—was with the novel, most of the prevailing arguments for and against this rapprochement were quickly proposed and discussed. Eisenstein sought principally to find in precinematic novels the formal sources for film techniques: close-ups in Dickens, parallel montage in Flaubert, and the like. The search for literary analogues to camera angles, such as *plongées* and *contre-plongées*, analytical scene cutting, flashbacks, dissolves, and most of the other recognized film effects (even speed-up and slow motion) led some critics back into history, from the nineteenth-century novel all the way to Homer and Virgil, whose *Aeneid* was studied by Paul Léglise in a book-length essay as an "oeuvre de pré-cinéma."[4] Almost at once, other critics reacted against the setting up of literary sources for film forms by arguing instead the influence of film on the novel. This idea, still strong, was in turn modified by the view that the true relation between the two genres is one of convergencies, or reciprocal interchanges, with film and novel sharing new ways of formalizing fiction. An outstanding example of this viewpoint is Claude-Edmonde Magny's *L'Age du roman américain* (Paris, 1948), with its development of the objective or behavioristic presentation of psychology as the main link between the two genres. A more specific illustration, limited to the role of point of view, comes from Alain Robbe-Grillet, who, after criticizing the Balzacian novel for its omniscient, godlike perspectives (descriptions of objects inside drawers, and the like) praises the phenomenological presence of *things* in the film and sees therein a lesson for the contemporary novel:

> Sur la pellicule les choses n'existent que comme phénomènes; elles ont obligatoirement une forme, et celle-ci se présente soit d'un côté soit de l'autre, jamais de plusieurs côtés en même temps; quant à leur intérieur, il n'a de réalité que s'il parvient à se montrer au dehors.
>
> Sous l'influence, ou non, de telles exigences du récit cinémato-

4. Paul Léglise, *Une Œuvre de pré-cinéma: L'Enéide* (Paris, n.d.).

graphique, le roman à son tour semble prendre conscience des mêmes problèmes. D'où est vu cet object? Sous quel angle? A quelle distance? Avec quel éclairage? Le regard s'y arrête-t-il longtemps, ou passe-t-il sans insister? Se déplace-t-il, ou bien reste-t-il fixe? Le romancier perpétuellement omniscient et omniprésent est ainsi réclusé. Même si ce n'est pas un personnage, c'est en tout cas un *oeil d'homme*. Ce roman contemporain, dont on répète volontiers qu'il veut exclure l'homme de l'univers, lui donne en réalité la première place, celle de l'observateur."

On film things exist only as phenomena; they have of necessity a form, and this form presents itself either on one side or the other, never on several sides at the same time; as for their interior, it has no reality except if it manages to show itself on the outside.

Under the influence, or not, of such requirements of cinematic narration, the novel in its turn seems to be aware of the same problems. Where is the object seen from? From what angle? At what distance? With what lighting? Does the glance stop for a long time, or does it pass on without dwelling? Does it change place, or does it remain fixed? The perpetually omniscient and omnipresent author is thus challenged. Even if he is not a character, he is in any case a *human eye*. The contemporary novel, concerning which we hear again and again that it seeks to exclude man from the universe, places him in reality in the central position, that of the observer.[5]

In the same spirit, Claude Simon replied to an inquiry of *Premier Plan* whose very formulation reflects the then-prevailing uncertainty over the relative priorities of film and novel. *Premier Plan* asked several new novelists these questions:

Les mécanismes créateurs de votre oeuvre romanesque
   —ne présentent-ils aucun point commun,
   —entretiennent-ils des relations de parenté,
   —manifestent-ils une convergence,
   —ou peuvent-ils être confondus avec les mécanismes créateurs du cinéma?

Do the creative mechanisms of your novels
   —have anything in common,
   —bear a relationship,
   —show a convergence?
   —Or can they be related directly to the creative mechanisms of the cinema?[6]

5. Alain Robbe-Grillet, "Notes sur la localisation et les déplacements du point de vue dans la description romanesque," *Revue des Lettres Modernes*, "Cinéma et roman," nos. 36–38 (1958): 129–30.
6. "Enquête," *Premier Plan*, no. 18 (n.d.): 25.

Of all the replies, Simon's is the frankest and clearest admission of a close relationship, if not an actual influence of film on novel. Developing ideas similar to those expressed by Robbe-Grillet concerning point of view, Simon proceeds to compare the whole associative structure of his novels to the principles of montage and scene linking. It is evident from his text that this most "verbal" of novelists sees himself, or saw himself at the time, working in forms closely allied to those of the fictional film, despite the fundamental difference between image and word, which, as he points out, prevents any *identification* or confusion between the two genres. Simon writes:

> Il est certain que la photographie et le cinéma ont modifié radicalement chez chacun de nous la façon dont il appréhende le monde. Il se trouve de plus qu'en ce qui me concerne, et sans doute du fait d'un esprit beaucoup plus sensible au concret qu'à l'abstrait, je ne peux écrire mes romans qu'en précisant constamment les diverses positions qu'occupent dans l'espace le ou les narrateurs (champ de la vision, distance, mobilité par rapport à la scène décrite—ou, si l'on préfère, dans un autre langage: angle des prises de vues, gros plan, plan moyen, panoramique, plan fixe travelling, etc. . . .). Même lorsque mon ou mes narrateurs rapportent autre chose que des scènes immédiatement vécues (par exemple des situations, des épisodes remémorées ou imaginées), ils se trouvent toujours dans une position d'observateur aux connaissances et aux vues bornées, voyant les faits, les gestes, sous un éclairage particulier et limitatif.

> It is certain that photography and cinema have radically altered the way each of us apprehends the world. Moreover, it so happens that so far as I am concerned, and doubtless because I have a mind that is much more sensitive to concrete images than to abstract ideas, I cannot write my novels other than by constantly defining the different positions that the narrator or narrators occupy in space (field of vision, distance, mobility in relation to the scene described—or, if you prefer, in another vocabulary: camera angle, close-up, medium shot, panoramic shot, motionless shot, etc.). Even when my narrator or narrators report something other than scenes that are immediately experienced (for example, imagined or remembered situations or episodes), they are always in the position of an observer with limited knowledge and views, seeing things, gestures, in a particular, limited light.[7]

It may be helpful here to list a number of the main issues in the many recent and current discussions of film novel problems, then to isolate and examine several that appear to illustrate best the question of comparative

7. Claude Simon, "Réponse," *Premier Plan*, no. 18 (n.d.): 32.

aesthetic response. Not necessarily in order of importance, the points most often raised include the following:

1. Objective viewpoint (phenomenology, behaviorist presentation, avoidance of interiority, etc.).
2. Subjective viewpoint (first-person narration, mental content, memory, hallucination, imagination, etc.).
3. Transitions (scene linking, associate or contrapuntal juxtapositions, *fondus*, superimpositions, overlaps, etc.).
4. Chronology (flashbacks, flash-forwards, "dechronology," tempo, real versus filmed time, absence of film "tenses," etc.).
5. Problems of film versus literary "language" (analogies of syntax, punctuation, metaphors, semantics, etc.).
6. Cinematic versus novelistic "universe" (cf. Cohen-Séat, Morin; questions of time, space, psychology, etc.).
7. Projection and empathy in novel reader and film spectator.
8. Verbal versus visual "description" (Are analogies possible or impossible?).
9. Presence or absence of the narrator in film and novel (effects of various modalities).
10. The "double register" (image and sound) in film versus the single register in the novel.

Nearly all of these items involve, on close inspection, aspects of both form and response to form. Let us examine at the outset a specific technique that has been called by some unique to film and by others common to both film and novel and that has been related in both cases to different or similar effects on viewer and reader. This device is the film *fondu*, or dissolve, which has been the object of pertinent comments by film theorists like Eisenstein, Balázs, and Resnais as well as by novelists and literary critics like Alain Robbe-Grillet and Arnaldo Pizzorusso.

The modalities of the *fondu* or dissolve are numerous; let us consider only its main form, in which one image fades out at the same time that the succeeding image gradually makes its appearance and replaces the original one. In film *fondu enchaîné*, as this procedure is called, image 1 begins to lose density and image 2, progressively superimposed, gains in density. At one point the images have equal presence, and both are seen; then image 2, becoming denser, takes over completely. It is well known that during the period when such transitions were considered to play the role of punctuation or syntactical articulation in film language, the dissolve was deemed the counterpart of such adverbs as "meanwhile," "elsewhere," "later," and the like. While the simple fade-out and fade-in signified a break, with passage of time or displacement of space, the dissolve meant, in Bela Balázs's words, a "deeper connection" between the two shots involved. Time, space, cause, and effect are thus synthesized by the time-lapse dissolve; Balázs cites an example of a series of dissolves of disintegrating boots and sandals in Joe May's *Homecoming*: in a real time span of a minute or two, "our consciousness accepts the suggestion that months, even years have passed in that time." In recent cinematic practice, the dissolve has evolved into a transition device that employs to an ever-increasing degree shared objects in the two images: telephone 1 fades into answering telephone 2; from this has emerged what may be termed the "solid" dissolve—there is no apparent film movement or change from telephone 1 to telephone 2, but when the camera angle rises we are in a different room, looking at a different actor.

To Eisenstein it was clear that film dissolves were an extension of literary techniques; he quotes from Dickens's *A Tale of Two Cities* a passage in which carts and other vehicles in postrevolutionary Paris are "rolled back" in time to become tumbrils taking victims to the guillotine.[8] When Balázs declared that "the technique of dissolve, which can change the scene and make time and space illusory, is eminently suitable for the presentation of the association of ideas and mental pictures in memory, in dreams or in imagination" (p. 150), he seemed to invite the identification of the procedure with many new novelistic devices, such as interior monologue and stream-of-consciousness passages, as well as sequences of objectified subjectivity. To bring this problem to a specific focus, we may look closely at examples of the dissolve in Robbe-Grillet's fiction (*La Jalousie*) and film (*L'Année dernière à Marienbad*).

In *La Jalousie*, a number of transitions, such as the passage leading from the crushing of the *mille-pattes* in the dining room to the scene of cohabitation of the narrator's wife and her presumed lover in a distant hotel room and later to the imagined crash of the couple in a flaming car, involve the author's introducing between two images one or more ambiguous words (*serviette, Franck accélère, cahots*, etc.) applicable both to the first and to the second scene.[9] Arnaldo Pizzorusso in 1958 had already termed the technique, using the example of a description of a photograph of the wife A . . . , which blends into a scene on the terrace with A . . . present in reality, an example of *dissolvenza* or *sovrimpressione* in the novel. When Robbe-Grillet, in a joint interview with Alain Resnais, was questioned about *fondus* in *Marienbad*, he discussed his early plan to include at the end of that film a series of *fondus* used to link "two

8. Sergei Eisenstein, "Dickens, Griffith, and the Film Today," in *Film Form and the Film Sense* (New York, 1957), 213.

9. The question of the *fondus* of *La Jalousie* is discussed in my study *Les Romans de Robbe-Grillet*, 3d ed. (Paris, 1971), 186–88.

pieces of present time," to contest the convention that viewed the *fondu* as linking different times. His interviewer interjected:

—*Pourtant, dans vos livres, il n'y a jamais l'équivalent d'un fondu.*
Robbe-Grillet: Ah si, je crois.
Resnais: Je ne crois pas non plus que ce soient des fondus. C'est une phrase que transforme l'image. Impression que ne donnerait pas un fondu.

—*However, in your books, there is never the equivalent of a dissolve.*
Robbe-Grillet: Ah, yes. I think there is.
Resnais: I don't think they are dissolves. It's a sentence that the image transforms. And that's an impression the dissolve would not give.[10]

We must admit that, in the case of the "classic" dissolve, Resnais is right: in film one is conscious of a second image replacing the first, whereas in the verbal passages it is only when the second scene has emerged, or has begun to emerge, that the reader becomes aware, *après coup*, that intervening terms may apply to either image. But the creation of the "solid" *fondu* referred to earlier, which is now practiced extensively by Robbe-Grillet in film (cf. *L'Immortelle*) and novel (cf. *Projet pour une révolution à New York*), has considerably modified the question, proving again that the bases of film novel analogies are constantly shifting. We are brought back, as always, to the difference between the visual and the verbal, which remains the great issue in the debate. Even the classic observations of Albert Laffay on the aesthetic failure of the "subjective camera" film par excellence, *The Lady in the Lake*, attribute the shortcomings of the film, by comparison with Chandler's novel, to a confusion between "fictive identification" (created through words) and "perceptive identification" (created by images). Yet Laffay himself argues elsewhere that perceptive identification ought theoretically to lead to psychological or fictive identification in more or less the same way in both genres (as it does in the novel *La Jalousie*, for example), quoting Merleau-Ponty's "Le Cinéma et la nouvelle psychologie" to show that the objective visual presentation of mental content possible in the film makes cinematographic art especially valuable as a demonstration of the phenomenological or existential links between the outer world and the individual.[11] It is an argument that in turn has served critics of the *nouveau roman* in their

10. "Entretien avec Alain Resnais et Alain Robbe-Grillet," *Cahiers du Cinéma* (September 1961): 16.
11. Albert Laffay, "Sujet et objet," in *Logique du cinéma* (Paris, n.d.), 94–95.

effort to link phenomenology, *chosisme*, and existentialism to the contemporary novel.

Leaving aside the linguistic issues affecting film/novel comparisons (as
treated extensively by Barthes, Metz, Cohen-Séat, and others), we may
state that the visual/verbal controversy, which forms the basis of the
strongest arguments for generic specificity and differentiation in aesthetic response, is centered on the question of *description*. Is a descriptive passage in a novel so inherently different from a cinematic "descriptive" shot that this irreconcilability of procedures and effects successfully
prevents any attempt to find equivalencies, convergences, or parallels? At
first glance it seems that an analysis similar to Balázs's differentiation between theater and film might help resolve the problem: words are less
specific than images; they are connotative, subjective; the one-by-one order of their reading differs fundamentally from the "global" perception of
a film image; they may be read with little if any visualization, savored for
their phonetic or even their typographical aspects; and so on. I once proposed an imaginary experiment to prove the nonequivalency of film and
verbal descriptions: let several filmmakers shoot the same descriptive
text, and note the stylistic differences; or let several writers put into
words a "descriptive" movie shot, then note the profound discrepancies
in the results.[12] I am perhaps less convinced now by this demonstration,
largely as a result of observing the effect of retrospective equivalency,
such as that which the reader of Robbe-Grillet's text for *Marienbad*
might discern between the verbal descriptions of scenes in the published
scenario and the images of Resnais's film, or vice versa. In other words,
that no necessary or inevitable parallel exists between a given set of
words and images does not mean that artistically or aesthetically satisfy-
ing equivalencies are impossible. George Bluestone's study of *The Grapes
of Wrath* in his pioneering work *Novels into Film* brought out many
such reinforcements in the case of Steinbeck's work and its film, some of
which even went beyond individual passages of the novel. All the theoretical objections that have been plausibly raised against equivalency
have not put a stop to the search for analogies and parallels; a case in
point is Visconti's search for film expression in *L'Etranger* that would exactly double Camus's literary effects, including that of an omnipresent
first-person narrator.[13]

One of the strongest statements arguing for a basic unity between film
and novel comes from Herbert Read, who, in the spirit of Joseph Conrad

12. See chapter 4, "The Case of Robbe-Grillet."

13. Brian Fitch has studied this question admirably in "De la page à l'écran: *L'Etranger* de
Visconti," *L'Esprit Créateur* 8, 4 (1968): 293 ff.

(with his precinematic doctrine of "My task . . . is to make you *see*"), as well as of the disciples of the "show, not tell" school, sought in the properties of the *visual* the ultimate objective of both genres:

> Those people who deny that there can be any connection between the scenario and literature seem to me to have a wrong conception, so much of the film as of literature. . . . If you asked me to give you the most distinctive quality of good writing, I would give it to you in this one word: VISUAL. Reduce the art of writing to its fundamentals and you come to this single aim: to convey images by means of words. But to *convey images*. To make the mind see. To project onto that inner screen of the brain a moving picture of objects and events. . . . That is a definition of good literature. . . . It is also a definition of the ideal film.[14]

Nevertheless, it is precisely the differences between the literary and the filmic "visual" that have been advanced by the author-critics like Claude Ollier and Alain Robbe-Grillet, despite the latter's apparent espousal of cinematic point of view in the new novel, to oppose setting up aesthetic parallels between film and novel. Ollier, for example, writes:

> Il semble parfois qu'il y ait certains rapports dans la construction, les développements, les enchaînements, mais cela est purement superficiel: ce sont de fausses analogies. . . . La notion de description, par exemple, n'a pas d'équivalent cinématographique. Ce que certains nomment "description" au cinéma est même l'opposé d'une description: les signes, les suggestions, et le sens ne fonctionnent pas du tout de la même façon, et bien sûr tout cela est très embrouillé. . . . Pour *Marienbad*, Robbe-Grillet, imaginant en fonction du cinéma, a écrit ses premiers textes non-littéraires.

> It seems sometimes that there are certain correspondences in the construction, the development, the transitions, but that is purely superficial: they are false analogies. . . . The idea of description, for example, has no equivalent in the cinema. What some people call "description" in the cinema is even the opposite of description: signs, suggestions, and meaning do not all function in the same way, and of course, all that is very confused. . . . For *Marienbad* Robbe-Grillet, imagining in terms of the cinema, wrote his first nonliterary texts.[15]

Although substantiating Ollier's conclusions, Robbe-Grillet's ideas lead in a somewhat different direction. In "Brèves réflexions sur le fait de décrire une scène de cinéma," this *romancier-cinéaste*, who certainly has what-

---

14. Herbert Read, *A Coat of Many Colours* (London, 1945), 230–31, quoted by Robert Richardson, *Literature and Film* (Bloomington, 1969), 13.
15. Claude Ollier, "Réponse," *Premier Plan*, no. 18 (n.d.): 26.

ever authority creativity in two genres can accord, bases his distinctions on the role of the model, or object described, in relation to the written or filmed text or image. Rather than argue the inherent differences between writing and filming, Robbe-Grillet states instead that while the models of objects in his films are necessarily "real," being chosen from material reality, those of his verbal descriptions are never real and correspond to no outside objects:

> Jamais il ne m'est arrivé, en écrivant un roman, de me placer devant un objet réel, ou devant son image, afin d'en donner une description plus précise. . . . Je ne cherche jamais de modèle pour le copier, et si, par hasard, je rencontre sur mon chemin tel objet que je suis justement occupé à décrire, j'en détourne aussitôt les yeux, pris de stupeur et presque de dégoût devant cette chose inutile, dérisoire, sans commune mesure de toute façon avec celle qui s'est formée dans mon esprit et à laquelle ma phrase est en train de donner le jour.

> When writing a novel, I have never placed myself in front of a real object or an image of that object in order to give a more precise description of it. . . . I never look for a model to copy, and if by chance I encounter on my path an object that I am trying to describe, I turn my eyes immediately away from it, stupefied and almost disgusted with the presence of that useless, derisory thing, without common measure in any case, with the thing that has been formed in my mind and to which my sentence is giving birth.[16]

In the case of films, on the other hand, the outside world indeed exists as a point of departure:

> J'ai, de toute évidence, un point de vue contraire lorsque je réalise un film: je n'aime que les décors naturels, et c'est leur observation directe qui me guide dans cette partie importante de *l'écriture* cinématographique que constitue le tournage. . . . Le vrai train T.E.E. Paris-Anvers . . . des maisons, des gens dans la rue. . . . Le film . . . restera . . . jusqu'au bout marqué par cette origine extérieure à lui-même du matériau qu'il façonne. Les deux langages—du film et du livre—ont en fait si peu de rapport que les éternelles discussions sur "le roman et le cinéma" ne peuvent prétendre à plus de précision . . . que si l'on parlait de "musique et peinture" ou "architecture et poésie."

> I have clearly a different point of view when I make a film: I like only natural settings, and it is the direct observation of these set-

16. Alain Robbe-Grillet, "Sur le fait de décrire une scène de cinéma," *Revue d'Esthétique*, nos. 2–3 (1967): 131 ff.

tings that guides me in that important part of cinema *writing* that is constituted by the filming. . . . The real train T.E.E. Paris-Antwerp . . . houses, people in the street. . . . Until the end the film will remain marked by the origin, external to itself, of the material it is fashioning. The two languages, film and book, have in fact so little in common that the eternal discussions on "novel and film" cannot claim more precision than if one were to speak of "music and painting" or "architecture and poetry." [17]

Perhaps the most significant observation to be made here is that Robbe-Grillet, seemingly arguing the impossibility of equating images in words and pictures, is in reality assuming that the real differences lie in the nature of the *object* as imagined, or as "seen" by the writer before or while writing, and the object as filmed from real life. Thus, presumably, nothing would stand in the way of a "realistic" literary description, just as nothing would prevent another cinematographer from "inventing" the objects of his films (as, indeed, many surrealists and others have done) so that they would correspond to no real models.

In fact, several basic assumptions made elsewhere by Robbe-Grillet lead to the conclusion that many of the effects he seeks (as well as certain of the structures and techniques he employs) in both novels and films are, at the aesthetic level, closely parallel. A specific case in point is the presentation in words and images of the mental content of the protagonist or another character. I have sought elsewhere to demonstrate that the special suppressed first-person narrative mode, or *je-néant*, or *La Jalousie* functions to create in the phenomenological transcription of the jealous husband's perceptions and sensations the objective correlatives of the subject's thoughts and passions.[18] Similarly, as the preface to *Marienbad* reveals, Robbe-Grillet considers the objectified subjectivity of the hero and heroine, in imaginary or hallucinatory shots, the equivalent of their mental content. Indeed, *Marienbad* could be cited against its scenarist's theory of cinematic realism: the overcharged versions of the baroque château bedroom as "seen" by the distraught heroine do not come from outside reality, except after elaborate arrangement, distortion, and manipulation, comparable to the implied changes in the objects Robbe-Grillet describes in the account of his method of creating prose descriptions, as quoted previously.

Implicit in the strict separationists' division between film and novel is the conviction that inherent differences between word and picture render true equivalencies impossible. To these critics, a statement such as

17. Ibid.
18. *Les Romans de Robbe-Grillet*, 112 ff.

Penelope Gilliat's declaration that Louis Malle finds in *Zazie dans le métro* "visual equivalents of [the] word-play" in Queneau's novel can only be based on false analogies and semantic confusion.[19] Logically, the separationists' position seems soundly argued; and if one considers the current philosophy of textuality prevalent among the avant-garde novelists and critics who seek the essence of literary art in relationships among words, syllables, and letters as well as in phrases, sentences, metaphors, and larger narrative units (as in the case of a Jean Ricardou, for example), it might appear that novel and film, instead of combining in a unified field of fictional structures, are moving even further apart. What this view ignores, however, is that a number of critics, readers, viewers, novelists, and filmmakers continue to hold, consciously or unconsciously, to the idea that there exists, beyond the words on the page and beyond the images on the screen as well, a common field of the imagination in which the work of art—visual, auditory, or verbal—takes on its effective aesthetic form and meaning.

Even Robbe-Grillet, who so eloquently espouses the "antinomy between film and novel," has argued, using the question of pornography as his pretext, for the priority of visual imagination, for which the visible image, or the words as read from the page, serve only as an accessory. His piece "For a More Voluptuous Tomorrow" begins with a long description of a pornographic book cover showing a naked girl attacked by rats. This, he points out, "belongs to an old literary tradition extending from the Marquis de Sade to Georges Bataille"; in addition, "it occupies a prominent place among the New York fantasies of my latest novel." The assumption here is clearly that the mental image evoked by verbal passages may be equated wtih or compared in one way or another to the illustration on the cover. A further development in this interesting short text shows that it is necessary to go beyond the naive visual inspection of a picture into the same imaginative realm wherein the provocative words of literary pornography create their images. Only man, says Robbe-Grillet, is affected by erotic pictures: "No bull, however deprived, will let its gaze be attracted by the photograph of a cow's rump." The questions raised have an importance that transcends the immediate matter of pornography. Robbe-Grillet writes:

> Which brings up further questions: What is an image? How does it function? What role does the image play in our civilization? Why does . . . man, who is free to perform an action every day, also need to contemplate its representation?
>
> Here, in short, is the whole problem of the imagination, which,

19. Penelope Gilliat, review of *Zazie dans le métro*, *The New Yorker*, 8 July 1972.

as its name suggests, constantly creates images and indeed requires them in order to sustain itself.[20]

What is suggested here, then, is that just as written texts have always been assumed to produce in the imagination an accompaniment of visual, or at least sensorial, images, more or less clear or confused, so the apparently "final" surface of the film image is quickly transferred into the imaginary realm, where it becomes productive of inner images, pseudomemories, associative, parasitic recalls, and conjectures. Film and novel, so different in their material aspects, in their psychological dynamics, in their technical modes (and yet so comparable), come together again on that "inner screen of the brain" of which Herbert Read writes, to form a unified field of inner aesthetic response.

Indeed, psychodynamics, yet to be fully explored by psychometrics, must certainly hold many secrets of deep response to novel and film, going beyond the intellectualized aesthetics of formal appreciation and critical analysis. Has the novel ever evoked, even in its most intense action sequences, the physical empathy affecting the muscles, the glands, the pulse and breathing rate that chase, suspense, and other extremely dynamic sequences in film bring about in most, if not all, viewers? Some thirty years ago Walter Pitkin of Columbia University argued against gangster movies, while accepting newspaper reporting of crimes involving gangsters, by claiming that in "psychic intensity" the picture version "is 1,000,000,000 times more effective than the printed." Merely as a "form of communication," Pitkin opined (that is, leaving aside psychological and aesthetic factors), the movies are "10 to 100 times more effective per unit of time" than printed matter.[21] Exaggerated or not, Pitkin's unscientific and unsupported psychometrics bears witness to a widely shared intuitive conviction that response to film is far more powerful than response to writing. Does this psychophysical activity serve only to reinforce basically similar feelings, differing largely in degree, or does it change the quality of aesthetic response so radically that it becomes unique in its nature? Is the kind of psychic projection experienced by readers of novels altered or only reinforced by seeing the protagonist of a filmed novel played by one or another specific actor? When spectators are "disappointed" to see a certain player take the part of a novel character into whose feelings and actions they have projected themselves on reading the book, it is difficult not to think that visual specificity has, instead of favoring self-projection, erected a barrier against projective iden-

20. Alain Robbe-Grillet, "For a More Voluptuous Tomorrow," *Saturday Review*, 20 May 1972.

21. Quoted by Andrew Bergman, "The Gangsters," in *We're in the Money* (New York, 1971).

tification. On the other hand, putting a charismatic actor like Humphrey Bogart into a role of mediocre projective appeal in its novelistic source may so transform a scenario as to create a near masterpiece of affective empathy: Raymond Chandler's *The Big Sleep* is a classic example. And what of the commonplace psychological differences in the active/passive roles of readers and film viewers? Certainly the spectator at the cinema, or watching a movie on a television set, submits himself in a special way to the scene, which, with its independent tempo, proceeds with little concern for his following or not following it, whereas the reader of a novel must at least work at comprehending the words and sentences, going through rather elaborate mental procedures in order to change ink marks on the page into thoughts, images, emotions, and the other components of aesthetic response.

Can this complicated relationship between film and novel, with its almost dialectic interplay of parallels and differences, ever be satisfactorily resolved? Is there a unified field of imaginative response beyond the page and the image? A more detailed investigation of the question would require careful analysis of all the points in the foregoing list, plus others, followed by a synthetic conclusion based on such a wide survey.

Admittedly, many problems remain. One is tempted time and again to say, watching some new effect in the movies, "the novel could never do *that*"; and vice versa. The stereophonic or stereoptic possibilities of non-synchronous sound and image, foreseen since the birth of the talkies, often appear to produce responses impossible to achieve in the novel. For example, a recent movie shows a couple entering a psychologist's office to learn the prognosis for their retarded child. When the door closes, we see the man and woman, depressed, moving about the kitchen of their house, while the sound track plays the interview with the doctor. How would the novelist handle this? Traditionally, by introducing guiding phrases ("Later, at home, they thought back over the interview," etc.); in more modern fashion, by mixing notations of kitchen and office, by producing the kind of text reviewers like to call "cinematographic." There is no doubt that the ready availability of two channels, picture and sound, has influenced cinematic structure, that narrative sound tracks in counterpoint with reinforcing or sometimes contradictory imagery seem to produce at the same moment in the viewers' consciousness synthetic effects that in written texts require at the least an effort at perception extending over many moments. Just as Eisenstein saw precinema in literature, critics now detect in many novels postcinematic effects; a joint evolution appears to be in progress. For better or worse, the two genres, novel and film, must look to a shared destiny.

3
THE CINEMA NOVEL

Novel and film not only have been studied in their formal interrelationships, they have also raised the question of amalgamation into the genre of the cinema novel, as opposed to the novelistic scenario of many traditional films. What is the cinema novel? From the outset the question runs the risk of being confused in the tangle of arguments surrounding the general links between novel and cinema: reciprocal influences, parallel techniques, transpositions, convergencies, and correspondences. In chapter 4 I write about this problem, sketching the history of the debates involved and trying to identify the many inconsistencies and contradictions found in the writing of cinema critics, on the one hand, and literary critics on the other.

My object here is to examine—particularly but not exclusively—a precise group of works, namely the contemporary cinema novels (which the French call *ciné-romans*) and published scenarios designed to be read by readers who have not necessarily seen the film in question, who are primarily readers of fiction and not spectators watching a film. It will doubtless come as no surprise to find that this rather limited group of works constitutes a microcosm of the wider area of cinema and novel in general, or that it sheds light on a "unified field" approach to the fictional structures and perspectives to be found in both novel and film. Naturally, any such research must admit certain fundamental, specific formal identities that to a greater or lesser degree separate the two arts (images and sounds in the cinema, words and phrases in the novel), and it must avoid the trap of total assimilation of the two genres.

The early period of the silent film was marked by the priority of written sources for scenarios; and even the few films not drawn from existing novels made extensive use of forms borrowed from the novel. D. W. Griffith himself attributed his "cinematic" close-ups to models found in Dickens and Eisenstein credited Flaubert with Griffith's parallel montages. At that stage the film drew attention to fictional or dramatic forms not previously recognized or identified, so that literary critics like Jacques Scherer could speak of the "découpage" or scene cutting of Molière or Racine plays, while Paul Léglise, as noted, called the *Aeneid* a "precinematic work." Once such resemblances were identified, some critics began to view novels as essentially cinematic: George Bluestone, for example, complains frequently in his excellent *Novels into Film* that Hollywood has failed to transfer into the script or the shooting all the "cinematic" effects present in a given novel by Steinbeck or Flaubert. The number of scripts of value written expressly for the screen had never been large, and when they did develop (as with *Citizen Kane*) they were structured like the novels that had already influenced the cinema.

Gradually, scenarios were composed specifically for films, especially for the avant-garde silent film. Some of these scenarios were published. They were silent film scripts with a few subtitles but without dialogues, as, for example, the text of *Un Chien andalou* by Dali and Buñuel. This scenario is a good example of the earliest attempts to use verbal descriptions to suggest to a reader the visual images of the screen. Had the sound film not come into existence at about this time, no doubt a considerable development of silent film scripts would have occurred; those that do exist in magazines of the era remain largely unstudied. The "pure" silent film, so regretted when it disappeared, was followed, as is well known, by over a decade of shallow "talkies" based largely on noncinematic popular plays with rigid decors and a plethora of wordy dialogue. Eventually, with the contemporary cinema novel, the novelized script made its appearance, and once more sound and image were mixed in written form.

An associated phenomenon has been the most parenthetical but instructive development of a new subgenre, novels created from films, "le roman tiré du film." This inversion of the traditional order, in which adaptations always went from novel into film, demonstrates the conscious or unconscious domination of the literary over the filmic, since the writers who take on the textualizing of these books from films (which are neither scenarios, cinema novels, nor genuine novels) feel it essential to restore to the narrative all the "literary" elements whose absence from the film itself may constitute its chief value. These writers invent for their readers all sorts of novelistic insertions found in the actual film only, if at all, by suggestion or implication: interior monologues, psychological analysis, even sociological commentaries. A good example is found in the novelized version of Godard's *A bout de souffle* (*Breathless*). The protagonist, played by Belmondo, stands for a long time in silence before a large photographic poster of Humphrey Bogart; the wordless effect is powerful. This scene of the inexpressive and silent Belmondo becomes in the "roman tiré du film" several pages of conventional interior monologue, beginning "Well, Bogey, old pal." Similarly, the famous final betrayal of the hero by the heroine, deliberately left ambiguous in the film, is explicated at length in the book in an archconventional passage of popular psychological analysis. Traditional novelistic forms and structures invade the film, revealing an absence of understanding of the new artistic and filmic values created by the screen genre.

One of the earliest works that may be called a true cinema novel, the deliberate creation of an author who composed his text originally to be filmed, is *Les Jeux son faits* of Jean-Paul Sartre. Despite the absence in this "novelized scenario" of any cinematic vocabulary (close-up, panoramic shot, and the like), Sartre nevertheless retains and describes a large number of scenic effects (the sun's rays falling on a hand, for example), even if he does not specify the camera angle or movement involved. (In fact, the camera moves about little in this not very cinematic film.) What makes the written narrative most similar to a film is the rhythm of the *découpage* or scene cutting, especially in the sequences of increasingly rapid alternating scenes of decreasing duration depicting the parallel stories of the hero and heroine at the beginning of the film. Here again we note that this parallel montage is only the prolongation and acceleration of a novelistic procedure pointed out by Eisenstein in the nineteenth-century novel such as *David Copperfield*, which films appropriated as particularly effective. To Sartre the film, like the novel and the drama, is only partially an artistic genre, finding its chief role as a vehicle of moral, philosophic, or political messages. Although Sartre criticizes the logical structures of conventional narrative genres, he freely violates his theoretical pronouncements in *Les Jeux sont faits*. In his famous attack on François Mauriac, whom he denounces for adopting a godlike point of view that focuses on both the exterior and the interior of successive characters, Sartre argues that in the post-Eisensteinian world the only logical or acceptable point of view must be a relative one anchored in the consciousness of an individual observer. But the Sartrian strictures of "François Mauriac et la liberté" are largely ignored in Sartre's own film (and in many of his novels as well). Far from trying to "justify" the various camera viewpoints of his film, and of his cinema novel, Sartre leaves them indefinite and arbitrary. Not only is the position of the camera not identified, its choice of visual subject or object seems to depend on no basic existential observational viewpoint. The result is a visual fiction subject to no relativistic controls, and about as godlike as that Sartre denounced in the case of Mauriac.

The question of justified viewpoints (that is, their correspondence to the perceptions of specific characters in the narrative or film) was destined to become a major concern in novelistic and filmic criticism. The great debates over "subjective camera," inspired by the well-known film *The Lady in the Lake*, shot by the actor-director Robert Montgomery with a camera attached to his breast, underline the importance of the use of the "first-person" film narrative, with most if not all of the visual angles justified through the implied eye of an observer-protagonist. At the height of the justified viewpoint movement, Robbe-Grillet published his "Notes on the Localization and Displacement of Viewpoint in Novelistic Description," not only attacking traditional Balzacian descriptive techniques (especially the use of an omniscient viewpoint that could see into closed drawers as well as into the minds of characters), but also praising the cinema as always showing its scenes "from a human viewpoint" of an active or passive observer. The novel itself, as well as the cinema novel, began to follow the principle of the "ciné-oeil," or observing eye. A few dissenters disagreed: Robert Champigny, for example, alleged curiously, in his theoretical study *Le Genre romanesque* (Monte-Carlo, 1963), that while the novel *must* practice the principle of justified viewpoint, the cinema does not do so. The statement by Claude Simon quoted in chapter 2 best illustrates the insistence on justification of point of view in the *nouveau roman*: "I cannot write my novels other than by constantly defining . . . camera angle, close up, medium shot, panoramic shot, motionless shot, etc."

Thus, for the typical author of the *nouveau roman* the novelistic narrative should emanate only from one or a series of individual consciousness, whose perceptions or images of the outside world are visually stylized in the manner of a film. According to one strict theory, there should be, in both novel and cinema, only "subjective" scenes. But both novel and film failed to adhere to these restrictions, and a number of principles of neojustification developed. Instead of purely subjective shots in which the camera, as in *The Lady in the Lake*, is substituted for the eye of a narrative protagonist, the cinema quickly showed a preference for scenes in which the camera is only *associated* with a character's viewpoint. This association can be of many kinds. A scene may be a short but fairly exact take of what a character would see through his eyes, as happens in each of the presumed observer's viewpoints in the kind of conversational exchange called in French *point-contre-point*: B as seen by A listening or speaking, and vice versa, from B's angle. Often the camera associates itself with a protagonist or other character by shooting his "view" from just behind his head, or off to one side, so that the viewer feels or understands that the camera is "looking" for the particular character. Total subjectivity becomes more and more restricted to scenes of memory (like the first quick flash scenes of the German soldier's hand in *Hiroshima mon amour*) or of hallucinatory pseudorecall (like many of the scenes in *L'Année dernière à Marienbad*). In the novel proper, the single fictional masterpiece to employ total perspective subjectivity, without the intervention of thoughts, speeches, or even pronouns referring to the narrator, was Robbe-Grillet's *La Jalousie.*

The written expression of visual or sensorial subjectivity has raised some vexing problems for the writers of scenarios and cinema novels. On the page, the printed text is called upon to describe or explicate what is only implied on the screen. If, for example, Marguerite Duras *writes* that suddenly the hand of a Japanese in a bed in Hiroshima is replaced by a flash shot of the clenched hand of a German soldier who died at Nevers during the war, the shock of the intuitive recognition of this as yet undefined *visual* memory by the spectator watching the film virtually disappears. A similar problem arises in the case of scene transitions involving *fondus* or fade-outs and fade-ins, in which an object or a decor is replaced abruptly or gradually by another, related to the first by a form, a psychological association, or some other diegetic linkage. Can descriptive prose create such an effect? A sort of flash shot may occur in prose when the text undergoes a sudden break in continuity; but is there, or can there be, a true written equivalent of the cinematic fade-out/fade-in?

I think that close equivalents do exist, but that they are of a somewhat different kind. The terms fade-out/fade-in or *fondu* may still be applied. Examples would include those passages in *La Jalousie* by Robbe-Grillet wherein a transitional phrase or word is inserted between two quite different scenes: when the text suddenly veers from a description of the heroine and her lover in a hotel-room bed as imagined by the jealous husband to the scene in which the lover Franck's car explodes in a flaming crash as it strikes a tree, the two separate incidents are linked by a phrase whose main element, "accélère," applies equally to the erotic acceleration of the first image and the acceleration of Franck's car in the second. The critic Arnaldo Pizzorusso points out other transitions of this kind, which he terms "fondus"—citing the passage from a text describing a photograph on the husband's desk to one depicting a similar scene on the veranda, using vocabulary elements applicable to either or both scenes. I have already noted that in a discussion of the possibility of textual *fondus* published in *Les Cahiers du Cinéma* (1961), the filmmaker Alain Resnais categorically denies the existence of literary *fondus*, while the novelist Robbe-Grillet vigorously affirms their existence.

The two films already mentioned, *Hiroshima mon amour* and *Marienbad*, are typical examples of the French cinema novel (in their printed forms). Both make considerable use of sudden flashbacks, false or imaginary scenes, even hallucinations. As cinema novels or scenarios, they illustrate several problems characteristic of the genre. For the filming of *Hiroshima* (directed by the same filmmaker as *Marienbad*, Alain Resnais), the author, Marguerite Duras, furnished a rather lyrical textual scenario, in a sometimes grandiloquent poetic style, with annotations of brief indications of the associated visual images and of accompanying, often in counterpoint, dialogues or sounds. The entire technical aspect (camera angles, distance of the framing, lighting, etc.), developed and added by Resnais, is absent from the printed script. If the greatest part of what could properly be called filmic is therefore lost in the book, we find on the other hand a whole file of accessory information completely lacking in the film itself. These are documents that served to impregante Resnais and his actors with the atmosphere and tone of the story or diegesis, before and during the camera work, and that are retained in the text as if to produce in the reader a feeling of the "reality" of the film, in a sort of cinematic equivalent of the convention of older novels (including some as recent as Sartre's *La Nausée*) presented as faithful transcripts of manuscripts found in a trunk, for example. This kind of scaffolding erected outside the film appears characteristic of the work of Resnais (who set up an elaborate chronological schema of *Marienbad* to guide his filming), and we find it in other scenarios used in his films, like his *Muriel*, with a text by Jean Cayrol. The published form of *Muriel* also illustrates what was at the time a relatively new technique in presenting the visual images seen on the screen: the edge of each printed page contains a series of photographs of the scenes covered in the adjacent text. Such a procedure also permits the author to reduce to a minimum the verbal descriptions of images. But the result no longer gives the impression of a real cinema novel and instead appears as an illustrated text, in the style of the Italian "photo novels."

If the printed texts of *Hiroshima* and *Muriel* are filled with such paranovelistic and nonfilmic accessories aimed at presenting the "depth" of character psychology and plot motivation, the published version of *Marienbad* represents, by comparison, a very different model of the cinema novel, one closer to the structures we associate with the *nouveau roman*. The emergence of the printed scenario from the script prepared by Robbe-Grillet is instructive. Alain Resnais, while making the film, stated that Robbe-Grillet had furnished a script so complete in every detail of dialogue and visual images that it could have been turned over to an "electronic robot" for the actual filming. The original script was typed (as was customary at the time) on facing pages, one containing the dialogue and sound effects, the other the visual angles, lighting, actors' movements, and the like. To compose the printed cinema novel, Robbe-Grillet took the two sets of pages, sounds and images, and melded them much as one might shuffle a deck of cards. Concerning the nondialogue parts of the final text, some critics observed that the language was "nonnovelistic," or nonliterary. Claude Ollier, himself one of the *nouveau roman* group, expressed his reaction as follows:

> Pour Marienbad . . . les textes en question ne sont pas organisés autour des mots et des descriptions, mais autour des sons et des images. Nul doute que si Robbe-Grillet avait commencé d'écrire non pas un film, mais un roman sur le même ciné-schéma, il aurait été amené bien vite à construire différemment ses phrases, et même probablement à concevoir autrement l'enchaînement des épisodes.

> In *Marienbad* . . . the texts in question are organized not around words and descriptions, but around sounds and images. There can be no doubt that if Robbe-Grillet had set out to write not a film but a novel using the same scenario, he would quickly have been impelled to construct his phrases differently, and even probably to conceive differently the arrangement of the episodes.[1]

But is the text of *Marienbad*, as Ollier states, indeed nonliterary? A close study of the style of the descriptions of scenes and camera movements shows not only the "literary" quality of the texts, but also a close similarity between these passages and the descriptive passages of the author's previous novelistic works, such as *Le Voyeur* and *La Jalousie*. Also, it is difficult to give much weight to an argument based on a comparison between an existing film/novel and a hypothetical "novel" the author never imagined or planned. If we look instead at Robbe-Grillet's established techniques of scene linking in his actual novels, we find, as I have mentioned before, the same types of "liaisons de scènes," subjective associations, psychological deformations projected against a pseudorealistic decor, and the like. If strictly speaking *Marienbad* is a cinema novel rather than a novel *tout court*, one must nevertheless admit that it is closer, in its published form, to the domain of the Robbe-Grilletian novel than to that of an "unprocessed" scenario.

The printed scenario of *L'Immortelle*, though it is designated by Robbe-Grillet as a "ciné-roman," seems, by comparison with *Marienbad*, something of a formal retreat, a return to an earlier format in which the genre made use of brief summaries of successive scenes. The scenes are spatially divided on the pages, and each bears a large numeral. These some three hundred identified parts or shots add to the nonliterary effect, as does the absence of the descriptive passages organized around sounds and images that characterize *Marienbad*. If the reading of *L'Immortelle* is

1. *Premier Plan*, no. 18 (n.d.): 26.

simplified, it is not made more cinematic, since the reader is deprived of the mental operation required by the text of *Marienbad*, which creates in that reader the impression that he is following the scenes in a film in quasi-visual fashion. In this sense *Marienbad* represents an unparalleled mixture of the two genres, film and novel.

Robbe-Grillet's difficulties in finding a suitable form for the publication of the scenario of his next film, *Trans-Europ-Express*, illustrate the problems of an evolving genre. For both *Marienbad* and *L'Immortelle* there existed before the filming a more or less complete descriptive script, with sounds and images, that could be transformed with comparative ease to the written page. What procedures should apply, then, when the author-filmmaker, as was the case for *Trans-Europ-Express*, used for the filming only a sort of *récit*, or narrative version, composed in a written style of almost schematized simplicity, mixed with fragmentary and approximate dialogue, all of which underwent constant modification and improvisation during the actual shooting, along with the insertion of new scenes and the reversal of the order of others? What could be the modalities of the novelistic form of such a film? The author, going over his notes and his primitive scenario, which may no longer correspond to the actual film scenes, is forced to return almost to zero; he could find it difficult if not impossible, even looking at this film on a Movieola viewer, to give *his* form and style to a valid text for his proposed cinema novel. The author indeed finally abandoned the problem, and it was not until many films later that he was able to construct the new scenic form used in the published version of *Glissements progressifs du plaisir*, which I have studied elsewhere. Intervening films, such as *L'Homme qui ment*, were made using the same sketchy, improvised shooting notes as *Trans-Europ-Express*, couched in a sort of utilitarian language directed at the actors and cameramen, at times using commonplace expressions and anthropocentric non-Robbe-Grilletian metaphors that the author would never tolerate in his *writings* (like "un soleil gai, sans souci," "a gay, carefree sunshine"). The conclusion is that if a film, at least in the case of a stylizing author like Robbe-Grillet, is not made with a scenario that already has a form permitting its adaptation in terms of the writer's own characteristic style, the cinema novel will fail to materialize, since writing it would constitute all the difficulties of composing an entirely new work, which not only would deform the existing film, but could also fail as a novel.

An important aspect of the cinema novels as well as those films themselves that deal with subjective and imaginary reality or truth, and in which memory and interior time come into play (an aspect closely linked to the writing or description of filmed scenes), is the controversial question of cinematic time as compared with novelistic time, and that of the tenses of verbs in written or spoken language. Does the film contain (apart from dialogue) the equivalent of the tenses of verbs? Since Béla Balázs, it has been customary to state that "films have no tenses" and to claim, perhaps too hastily, that a filmed scene always takes place in an eternal present, or perhaps in Alain Resnais's "zone atemporelle ou de tous les temps." Robbe-Grillet, in his preface to *Marienbad*, upholds the thesis that the film, existing physically (at least when projected) only in the present, is particularly suitable for expressing psychological reality, which always exists in a perpetual present. But cannot films also express, depict, or imply their own kind of past? After all, even a regular novel is always *read* in the present, and its "past," to which the film is accused of having no equivalent, is usually contained in a system involving the tenses of verbs. In reading a scene of the past, do we not mentally "see" it in the present? If we consider the simple flashback, inserted into the film to fill a gap in the narrative or to provide information about a certain character, it is perhaps true that the flashback scene appears to be taking place in the present. Suppose such a scene in a novel were written with verbs in the present tense (a style increasingly employed in the *nouveau roman* and elsewhere). Would it not also seem to occur in the present? And if the filmed scene evokes the past in relation to the present, as done first perhaps in the famous memory scenes of the film *Brief Encounter*, with fade-outs in the present (in the train) leading to recent events that only gradually "take over" the present? Does the film not thus acquire its ówn type of cinematic past? This effect is especially felt in those films in which the past is presented as an aspect of the present, in the "present" memory of a character or in a dynamic conflict between past and present, as in *Hiroshima* or *Marienbad*. A strong cinematic feeling of the past emerges from the confrontation, on the screen, of present and past. Even in the literary narrative, the tone of the tenses used (like the well-known present and *passé simple* of Camus's *L'Etranger*) is quickly converted by the reader into a conventional modality by which, as with a film, he "sees" in the present tense, except when the contrast between present and past gives rise to a true temporal feeling.

Authors of novels taken from films and the writers of film reviews and summaries in popular magazines such as *Midi-Minuit* and *Ciné-Revue* "narrate" the films, interestingly, more often in the past tense than the present; as disconcerting as this practice seems, it shows to what extent the conditioned mentality of certain would-be authors prevents them from truly grasping narrative time, almost automatically transforming filmic images from their cinematic present, or timelessness, into the kind of frozen *récit* of dead characters and complete events expressed, in French, by the *passé simple* or literary past tense. If the deepest feeling of the past always arises from a confrontation of two times, the film should no doubt be more successful than the novel in this respect, especially when it makes use of the two stereo channels available to it, image and sound, to create counterpoint effects such as past image against present sound, or vice versa. The innovative films of Robbe-Grillet and others continue to progress in this research for new forms.

If there is a metaphysical question even more serious than that of time hanging over film and cinema novel structures, it is no doubt what could be termed, following Diderot's title, the paradox of the narrator. Narrative modes in both film and novel have lost their relatively stabilized form of previous decades and continue to evolve rapidly, sometimes apparently without logical coherence. In this evolution the formula "camera equals narrator," sometimes held to be axiomatic, plays a fundamental role. During a relatively short period, the novel obeyed what has punningly been called "les règles du *je*," the so-called rules of pronominal expression (I, he, you, etc.) associated with the doctrine of justified viewpoint previously discussed. The entire content of the narrative, emerging under this system from the mind of a character, was structured according to his vision, thoughts, and perceptions. Films closely followed the same system. This doctrine of "realism of mental content" seemed to open up, for both novel and film, a large number of fictional perspectives, permitting a sort of stable narrative aesthetic that would end once and for all the dominance of the omniscient Balzacian author, which novelists, filmmakers, and critics denounced as an unwelcome survival if not of God, at least of a god from the machine. But first in the film and then in the novel, there followed a return to scenes not anchored in the consciousness of any character, or even in that of a possible or hypothetical human observer. The camera in particular seemed to discover once more the autonomic mobility and independence of the "camera eye" of Dziga Vertov during the heroic period of the Russian cinema. The camera became an "existence" that appropriates and *becomes* in the film a point of view outside any mental content within a character or narrator or neutral "third observer." The point of view passes in a way to the spectator himself, who becomes, with the aid of the camera, a new kind of fictional god: one who, if not omniscient, can nevertheless move about with seemingly magic powers, cut a path through the action, and react as an entity in the midst of the diegesis. This "personalizing" of the camera begins in the film version of *Marienbad*, probably under the influence of Resnais, since the cinema novel itself makes no mention of the famous "white scenes," for example, in which the camera itself seems affected by an emotional reaction. Even more striking is the scenario of *Les Abysses* of Vauthier, in which the camera becomes a character with its own text, moves through the action, and is knocked about and even thrown to the ground. In Samuel Beckett's *Film*, the film sequences depend entirely upon the opposition between a protagonist who tries to avoid the look directed at him by the camera and the observing lens that insistently seeks to approach and scrutinize the fleeing character. Could such effects resist or even replace literary descriptions or writing itself? Is a generic difference between film and novel becoming so specific that there will no longer exist the possibility of a viable cinema novel?

The question is further complicated by the fact that the novel itself is undergoing comparable developments and suffering a similar crisis that is affecting the doctrine "camera equals narrator" or its novelistic equivalent, the doctrine of justified points of view. With a freedom comparable to that acquired by the supermobile camera, the narrative viewpoint also moves from place to place, from character to character, to the spectator/reader, or even elsewhere. One must conclude that in such novels as *La Maison de rendez-vous*, Robbe-Grillet practices the very kind of displacements of viewpoint that he previously denounced as "Balzacian" errors. This coexistence and parallelism of film/novel structures, permitting a considerable extension in the field of the cinema novel, may be influencing criticism as well. Critics of the cinema are appropriating terms originally used for literary studies, such as narrative viewpoint, internal narrator, observation post, *liaisons de scènes*, or scene linkage by sight or sound (in the fashion of the Abbé d'Aubignac in the seventeenth century).

Literary criticism, at the same time, takes from the cinema not only a new vocabulary, but an entire conception of the organization of structural elements. Just as Claude Simon, in the passage quoted, confesses to constructing his novels according to cinematic criteria, so does a literary critic such as R.-M. Albérès introduce a procedure of textual reading and analysis explicitly in cinematic terms. If Albérès is right, the last fortress of literature—description—is now to be invaded by ideas and terms taken from the film; and such claims as that made by Claude Ollier that "the idea of description has no cinematic equivalent" have little validity. For, writes Albérès, Michel Butor's *Description de Saint-Marc* is basically nothing other than a form of "descriptive cinema." It is a work that employs the "rhythm, montage," and other filmic features of documentary films, forming a "total cinematic language." Anything in Butor's work that may appear gratuitous or confusing "would be perfectly comprehensible, once projected on the screen." Albérès continues:

> Butor emploie ici un langage que nous savons "lire" au cinéma et qui est la transposition écrite des panoramiques, des travellings et des séquences auxquels nous sommes parfaitement habitués lorsque

nous allons voir un documentaire sur les mosaiques de Saint-Marc de Venise. . . .

Nous habituerons-nous à "voir" en mots comme nous "voyons" en images? . . .

Cette ambition correspond aux besoins diffus et insatisfaits de l'homme de notre temps, qui est obscurément gêné et mécontent devant un roman qui n'est qu'un roman, un poème qui n'est qu'un poème . . . et que, à un niveau évidemment différent, la télévision, le mixage et le malaxage des arts font rêver d'un tableau-poème, d'un poème-film, puisqu'aussi bien existent déjà le drame radiophonique et le roman-cinéma.

Butor is using here a language that we have learned to "read" at the cinema and that is the written transposition of the panoramic shots, the *"travellings"* or dolly shots, and other kinds of sequences to which we are perfectly habituated when we go to see a documentary film about the mosaics of Saint Mark in Venice. . . .

Will we become accustomed to "seeing" in words the way we "see" in images? . . .

This ambition corresponds to the diffuse, unsatisfied needs of modern man, who is vaguely made uneasy and discontented by a novel that is only a novel, or a poem that is only a poem . . . and for whom, at a different level, television and the mixing and blending of the arts lead to dreaming of a picture-poem, a poem-film, since both radiophonic drama and the cinema novel are already in existence.[2]

In conclusion, it appears that the problems of the cinema novel, as I have tried to describe them here, are to a large extent the same problems as those faced by other contemporary arts: framing of scenes, structures, cutting and montage, *distanciation, liaisons de scènes*, formal series, motivated and unmotivated synchronicities, rotations and permutations within the work, repetitions and interior duplications, points of view, chronology and dechronology: all the elements that characterize present-day novels, films, music, and painting. It follows that criticism cannot entirely escape from this kind of syncretism, short of blindly taking refuge in out-of-date dogmas of sealed-off, inviolable genres, unless it wishes to turn its back on the most innovative and exciting forms of our time.

2. R.-M. Albérès, *Butor* (Paris, 1966), 94 ff.

4
THE CASE OF ROBBE-GRILLET

The study of connections between film and novel has inspired articles and books written by "cinema" critics on the one hand and by "literary" critics on the other. The "seventh art," film, was born with the twentieth century and has itself given birth to a set of technical and artistic processes that, say some, are invading all the sacred provinces of the traditional novel or, say others, are subject to the constant influence of literary art. Influence or convergence, transpositions or correspondences: the entanglement and reciprocity of the connections between cinema and literature (poetry, theater, novel) are reflected in commentaries that are increasingly embroiled, if not paralogistic.

The purpose here is not to establish a historical account of these connections. The reader wishing to know the rudiments of the question will find them neatly set forth (for the years 1920–40, in the two chapters devoted to this subject by Pierre Brodin in *Présence contemporaines III*, 93–97, 195–99). It should nevertheless be noted that it was, historically, "visual poetry" (to use the phrase of Yvan Goll) and the power of the cinema to express the *unconscious* (noted by Pierre MacOrlan) that primarily interested the literati. During the period of expressionist, dadaist, and surrealist films, what turned cinema into a "poetry of images" were trick photography, dissolves, superimpositions, "*travellings*," slow motion, free sequences, background changes, unusual lighting, point-of-view shifts, and new perspectives. If for this kind of film we speak of a novelistic process, it is only for the purpose of comparing the novel's *interior monologue* to this "cinematography of thought," or to *interior films*.

But this new art of cinema is not only poetry: it is theater. From its inception it struggles to free itself of that fixity before the filmed scene, which ties it to the theatrical tradition of the "fourth wall." If André Malraux is correct in saying that cinema became an art form on the day the camera discovered its mobility, it must be noted that studies of the earli-

40

est silent movies demonstrate that all the technical procedures mentioned above were developed with such rapidity that they were fully known by about 1905. Even the *process shot* (a scene acted in front of an already-filmed sequence) dates from the first era of cinema. At the same time, the conventional theater, for its part, multiplies its tableaux, abandons the division into acts, finds by way of revolving stages and other shortcuts the freedom of cinema's rapid transitions. Claudel's *Christophe Colomb* offered the public process shots on a screen; with his *Donogoo-Tonka*, Jules Romain wrote the first literary scenario; playwrights such as Pagnol turned themselves into filmmaking writers. Filmed theater was born, and alongside poetic films or free associations (*Le Sang d'un poète* by Cocteau, *Un Chien andalou* by Buñuel, etc.) one saw henceforth the diffusion of "plays for the cinema" written by Salacrou, Anouilh, Prévert, Jean Renoir, Marc Allégret, Marcel Carné, Truffaut, and others.

Film is poetry and theater, but it is above all the novel. As soon as stories and novels are brought to the screen, the problem of cinematographic adaptation is posed. This problem includes, if analysis is pushed far enough, all aspects of the novel-cinema connections, but in a fashion little suited to the concerns of this study. The aforementioned work of George Bluestone, *Novels into Film*, simultaneously reveals the importance and complexity of this aesthetics of adaptation and suggests methods for studying the comparative novel-cinema syntax—methods that promise interesting discoveries. But Bluestone focuses mainly on the translation into images of already-written works, and lengthily addresses preoccupations that for us would be side issues: the reduction of the novel to a possible duration on the screen; the invention of equivalencies of decor and such in order to reproduce the "style" of the novel; the restructuring of the plot to clarify and emphasize the story line; and so on.[1]

1. Until recently the "priority" of the novel over the cinema passed as a given: Did not all adaptations go *from* novel *to* films? This supposed priority is less staunchly maintained today. The success of a film like Marcel Carné's *Les Tricheurs* has given rise to a novelistic adaptation of this film, by Françoise d'Eaubonne, thus in turn offering critics material for interesting observations. The author of the novel adaptation, for example, feels compelled to reinstate in the narrative the conventional procedures of the novel (interior monologues, memories and thoughts of characters, indirect free style, and all the rest). But, as I note later, it is the *absence* of these elements in films that was to have constituted the modernity if not superiority of the cinema and that, according to most critics, had so greatly contributed to "cleansing" the new novel of these antiquated practices. The novelistic adaptation of films correlates with other mixed genres that comparatists will have to study someday: the written novel based on an entirely visual film (Jacques Tati's *Mon oncle*, "put into prose" by Jean-Claude Carrière); "novels" in the form of pictures and in comics; detective novels "with material evidence" in the form of envelopes of clues (objects like match tips, cigarette butts, hair, fingerprints, etc.); and photograph-novels in strips, born first in Italy, which with their close-ups, superimpositions, and "psychological" perspectives con-

When do we begin to find in the novel technical processes borrowed from the cinema, or comparable to those of the cinema? Thus posed, the problem already prejudges the questions of priority and of influence. Is it possible to identify as essentially cinematographic most of the processes mentioned? Do not the flashbacks of films have a literary origin? The example of Ulysses' narratives in Homer is a familiar one. Free transitions, background changes, unusual lighting, shifts in point of view, all of this "visual poetry"—do we not already find it in Rimbaud's *Illuminations* or in Lautréamont's *Les Chants de Maldoror*? Was Crémieux correct in 1927 (in *XXᵉ siècle*) in asserting that when Gide writes, in *Les Faux-monnayeurs*, "le visage de Laura se trouve donc tout près du sien; il la regarda rougir," he was using a *close-up*? May we establish, with Pierre Brodin, an equivalence or transposition of style between such a description by Paul Morand of a series of landscapes seen through the glass panes of the Simplon Express and the sequence of images (often of unbearable banality and accompanied by a ridiculous commentary) of a travelogue? We will have to deal with these tempting but dangerous analogies.

The example of André Malraux is well known. Claude-Edmonde Magny in particular (in *L'Age du roman américain*) has shown that *La Condition humaine* is based on a succession of scenes of cinematographic order, in which each scene is described from the point of view of a particular character, such as Tchen, of a camera eye. But if it is true that certain scenes (such as the one of the first meeting in Hemmelrich's store) give the strong impression of a filmed decor that is more or less conventional (the movement in the doorway, the lighting, and the chiaroscuro of the lamps and faces, notations such as "on the left," "behind," etc.), it is nevertheless inaccurate to say that these procedures are to be found throughout the novel or to make of them the very essence of Malraux's art. Even if we accept, with reservations, Magny's conclusion that nothing in the book exists independent of a character's observation, we could not establish this principle of novelistic structure as a criterion for proving the existence of connections with the cinema. Here as elsewhere, Magny strains too much to establish correspondences between the two art forms, especially when she attributes to the cinema too strict an adherence to the alleged rules of point of view.

In fact, the cinema constantly uses angles and points of view detached from all characters. Except in rare cases (see below), the camera never

---

stitute a type of frozen and portable cinema. It is equally interesting to note the surge of printed scenarios (cf. *Hiroshima mon amour*, *L'Année dernière à Marienbad*, etc.). Might this herald the birth of a new literary genre?

follows characters' consciousnesses in the manner Sartre requires in his famous article "Mauriac et la liberté" (*Situations, I*). Sartre himself, especially in *Le Sursis*, struggles to elaborate cinematographic transitions and ellipses. To produce the effects of simultaneity, which often are more reminiscent of unanimism than of cinematography, Sartre occasionally links in a single sentence actions taking place in Czechoslovakia, in Germany, in France, in Africa. Identical or analogous actions (characters sleeping or eating, for example) or even shared sentences create scene connections, or rather transitions, whose scenes seem less *interconnected* than *successive* or *simultaneous*. If it is true that some scenes in Sartre's novel are based on the consciousness of a single character, there are also, in the rapid textual transitions between distant places, many impersonal angles, just as there are for Dos Passos in the "Camera Eye" sections of *U.S.A.* The novelist, like the cinematographer, has the choice between a personal point of view and an outside, if not objective, angle. Moreover, a detailed examination of the so-called systematic usages in literature of cinematographic techniques remains to be done. It would not be surprising to discover that most of these parallelisms are based upon misapprehensions.

The importance of the connections between the novel and cinema can be measured by critics' constant concern to identify and analyze all eventual correspondences between the two art forms, in their ever growing wave of books and articles on the subject. In 1958 a historically significant issue of *Revue des Lettres Modernes*, entitled "Cinéma et roman," attempted to gather opinions in order to establish the state of the problem. This collection, without presenting a consensus or supplying guidelines for a definitive study in the comparison of the two genres, nevertheless constituted an important point of departure in the systematic attempt at clarification. While a real ordering of the often contradictory, if not incoherent, ideas to be found in the articles of "Cinéma et roman" would extend beyond the limits of this study, the volume can be of use in considering the particular case of Robbe-Grillet's novels during the period preceding his films. For it is the experiment of that author in his precinematic phase that gives rise, for the critics in the collection, to what G.-A. Astre calls in his preface "un insigne intérêt." For the critics of "Cinéma et roman," the heart of the problem of the connections between the two genres (as well as the most striking example, among then contemporary writers, of the very existence of these connections) was provided by the author of *Les Gommes*, *Le Voyeur*, and *La Jalousie*.

In approaching the problem, it is useful to examine some of the more salient ideas of the early novel-cinematographic critics, as delineated in the diverse articles of "Cinéma et roman." By bringing into sharper relief the common ground (or the shared ideas) within their specialized areas, one can better situate the argument of a given critic in the collection of opinions where, it seems, no recognizable voice leads to the *center*. Without such a general view, furthermore, no commentary on the individual situation of Robbe-Grillet can apply.

One can group the observations and discussions most often expressed in "Cinéma et roman" into three categories, for nearly all of the critics' arguments revolve around these three points or tend to synthesize them: point of view, the priority of the visual image, and the development of an externalized psychology.

As to their methods of attacking these problems, the novel-cinematographic critics generally combine two things into one: either the critic separates (in his opinion) what the cinema is "able" to do from what the novel is "able" to do, or else the critic discovers, in the procedures and techniques of the two genres, identities, resemblances, or comparisons of structure or of function that correspond (again in his opinion) to analogical or equivalent aspects of an identical artistic expression.

Occasionally what occurs is that a given critic, apparently without realizing the contradictory way he is proceeding, simultaneously employs methods of distinctions and of analogies (as is the case with Colette Audry). This spirit of contradiction is equally manifested in many categorical declarations by which two critics addressing the same subject affirm contrary conclusions with casual certitude: for Colette Audry, for example (p. 133), "it is certain . . . that Proust's universe . . . owes nothing to the cinema and cannot even be recaptured" by the cinema, so greatly is the evocation of objects in Proust "charged with analogies and correspondences." On the other hand, Jacques Nantet (179–84) thinks that the entire work of Proust, thanks to the analogical connections of the "revelatory madeleine," to the "travelings" of the bell tower of Martinville and the hawthorn bushes, and so on, reveals a "cinematographic vision" of the world. Confronted with such contradictions, the reader of "Cinéma et roman" finds it impossible to accept any given doctrine too quickly, since he may well find it refuted or contested elsewhere. The informed reader will adopt an attitude of skepticism and expectancy in the face of multiple opinions.

As to what directly touches upon the problem of point of view, Robbe-Grillet himself (in "Notes sur la localisation et les déplacements du point de vue dans la description romanesque," referred to earlier in this book), gives us the most precise insight into the question (previously addressed by Sartre in the article on Mauriac cited above). Robbe-Grillet notes, as I stated in chapter 3, that for most novelists preceding the modern period the position of the observer, in descriptive passages, was imprecise, ambiguous, blurred, often omnipresent and omnitemporal—and all of this without logical or structural justification. The eye of the writer was "everywhere at once." For Robbe-Grillet, it is "under the influence, or not" of the cinematographic narrative that the contemporary novelist tends more and more to specify the exact location from which objects are seen, at what angle, with what lighting, and so on. It is interesting to note that where Sartre advanced existential ideas to defend a similar opinion (a scene does not exist outside the character's *consciousness*, the omniscient author must disappear with the "death of God," etc.), Robbe-Grillet is rather guided by a concern that is at once aesthetic and practical. For him it is necessary that "the photograph be taken from a given place . . . that the camera be found somewhere." In the novel, observation must be done by the human eye, "even if it is not that of a character." Thus, for Robbe-Grillet it is less consciousness (of a character, of an observer) that must determine the point of view, as in the Sartrian system, than it is a geometric and visual perspective, "the absolute obligation" of the camera and of the eye of the novelist always to specify point of view, angle, lighting, and the like.

This idea, apparently clear or even convincing, immediately runs into difficulties. Is it possible to separate point of view in itself, as localization of a camera objective or of an authorial eye, from the *reason* or internal justification of this same point of view? Does this "observer," who for Robbe-Grillet (but not for Sartre) need not be "a character" in the narrative, have the privilege of randomly positioning himself almost any-. where, with no excuse other than the exactitude of these visual perspectives? Can he displace himself at will? What will then prevent such an eye of the camera or of the novelist from becoming, once again, an eye "everywhere at once," if not an eye that is perpetually omniscient and omnipresent like the eye of God? In abandoning the Sartrian idea of character consciousness as a justification for the narrative's point of view, Robbe- Grillet ran the risk of weakening his doctrine and at the same time brought it closer to the true techniques of cinema.

For in most films, the camera in fact wanders with as much freedom as the eye of the traditional author and displaces itself among filmed scenes with little or no "narrative" reason. The camera lens changes its location abruptly, assumes unexpected (even arbitrary) stances, shares the point of view of several characters in succession. Unattached to any consciousness, the camera lens positions itself above, below, alongside, or, like the "fourth wall" of the theater, opposite characters, behind them, or near a window. Then suddenly this same camera attaches itself to a character, to an observer, to a consciousness. And it does so in two ways: either it positions itself near a face in order to express a physical reaction, or it shares the glance of an observing eye and views the scene from its "human" point of view.

The result is therefore that the cinema often requires nothing with respect to point of view except perhaps the reproduction of a scene according to a given perspective. Here Robbe-Grillet seems to be correct. But if this perspective begins rapidly and arbitrarily to move (as often happens), nothing stands in the way of a return to the description given by an imaginary narrator who is positioned "everywhere at once," and the system advocated by Robbe-Grillet loses its theoretical value. Robbe-Grillet objects to Balzacian descriptions as being rendered without precision with respect to the position of the observer, especially when the latter tells us, for example, what is to be found in closets. The "logic" of this Balzacian system implies omniscience, and since the modern novel rejects such omniscience, the author of a novel will prefer a visual perspective whether or not there is a character to assume the point of view.

Yet if we grant to the camera an absolute liberty of movement, if we even go so far as to say (with Panofsky, for example) that the magical lure of the cinema arises precisely from the psychology of the spectators who become witnesses to all sorts of scenes, as if looking through a mobile keyhole—an omni-optique system is obviously created, the justification for which seems as difficult or arbitrary as in the case of the omniscient author.

Thus the camera in general follows a system of little coherence in points of view. Not only does it position itself almost anywhere, but it also runs up against enormous difficulties when it makes an effort to attach itself, as many cinematographic critics would have it do, to the consciousness of a character. As we shall see, the culmination of this effort in *The Lady in the Lake* not only fails as cinema, but also serves to elucidate several fundamental differences between the two genres.

Perhaps too much has been said about Sartre's criticisms of Mauriac, leveled against omniscient narrations, as if Sartre had advocated more or less exclusively a "cinematographic objectification" of novelistic techniques. For many critics it was not so much Sartre as it was the American "behaviorist" novelists and "objective" cinematographers who banished psychological analysis from the modern novel and demonstrated to modern novelists the necessity of *positioning themselves* in the world of the narrative and of giving the reader the coordinates of the point of view. But long before the behaviorist novel and before the invention of the cinema, novelists were already employing the techniques of point of view, often with an altogether "modern" subtlety. One need only read the elaborate studies of Auerbach and Georges Poulet on the subject, both of whom have analyzed, among many other classical and modern works, the art of Flaubert in *Madame Bovary*, where the point of view is at times handled in such a way as to make us *see* Emma (seated at the kitchen table in front of Charles, for example) just as a "camera eye" would do it, while the lighting of the scene emanates so to speak from the protagonist herself. It is a pure "Sartrian" process, a realistic description steeped in the subjective tonalities of the character's consciousness. Allan Tate, in a study on the same novel, exactly identifies the point of view in the scene in which Emma considers throwing herself out the window. According to Tate, this point of view is positioned somewhat next to Emma and slightly higher, behind her shoulder, and the entire scene is accompanied by an objective correlative of the heroine's confusion (the noise of Binet's lathe turning below). The question of point of view is thus not born with the cinema at all: it is probably as ancient as literature. But as with perspective in painting, an evolution can be traced: perspectives that are flat, linear, "renaissance," baroque, romantic, cubist, distorted, abstract, and so on.[2]

Let us consider the question of the *visual image*. Among novel-cinematographic critics, it is popular to assert that the modern novel has an unprecedented need to *visualize* its stories, to "rediscover" the image, and that it is under the influence of this need—created, they claim, by the example of the cinema—that authors of novels are increasingly occupied with the *object*, with geometric description, with "objectal" presence, and with surfaces. Most of the commentaries in "Cinéma et roman" go so far as to say that here the novel must always "surrender" its advantage to the film. For G.-A. Astre, "the novel barely attains these effects of an entirely significant reality" one finds in films. For Michel Mourlet, "Every time the cinema and the novel describe the same objects, the cinema triumphs over the novel." For A. S. Labarthe, the project of the modern writer who (to compete with the cinema) would create works by substituting objects for characters has led to the veritable "failure" of the contemporary novel.

It is admitted—albeit rarely—that a verbal description is, after all, a different proposition from an image on film or on the screen. But the import of such an admission seems hardly to be recognized, since there is a rapid return to the charge (as Mourlet and Colette Audry say) that "words are mere signs" of the image, or that "words serve only to give meticulous details of gestures and objects" when "no commentary intervenes outside of this *presentation*." It is recognized—but not often—that the visual property of film is neither an abstract nor an absolute realism. Let

2. It is fitting to add to the works cited the perspicacious article of Jean Rousset, "*Madame Bovary* ou 'le livre sur rien,' un aspect de l'art du roman chez Flaubert: Le Point de vue," in *Saggi e ricerche di letteratura francese*, 1: 185–203 (Pisa, 1960).

me note that many of the critics in "Cinéma et roman" seem to have abandoned the old idea that a photograph is a reconstitution of reality itself. Such a notion seems moribund but has not been entirely laid to rest. Michel Mourlet, for example, readily repeats that photography "has, to a certain extent, eliminated from painting the concern for resemblance."[3]

Mostly there is agreement in recognizing—and it is G.-A. Astre who emphasizes this—that "the camera is not a natural eye." Not only more sensorial than perceptive, the camera is first and foremost a *psychological* eye. Among the images projected on the screen, common sense continues to find "a necessary and unambiguous causal relation between the sentiments and their manifestations." This question of the visuality of cinema brings us directly to perhaps the most important question of all: that of filmic psychology. The external, "objective" psychology of film—in relation to the conventional novelistic procedures of psychological analyses and of characters' interior monologues—in turn immediately raises the question of the symbolic usage of objects, and even of mystical correspondences.

Where the cinema (by the comments of "off screen" voices or even of dialogue) is able to approach the novel or theater, cinematographic critics are quick to see a type of betrayal of the filmic genre. They tend to push such "techniques" back onto the novel or theater in order to reserve only "wholly pure" images for the filmmaker—or semipure images, since they admit, with Astre, that "the images on the screen are in large minority implicitly fashioned by the psychology of the theater or by the classical novel of analysis."

Nevertheless, the cinema attempts, following its "nature," to avoid dialogue. It prefers not to make use of interior monologues; it constantly strives (in the phrase of Michel Mourlet) to "speak with things themselves." Cinema is, according to Astre, "explicit and implicit at the same time." The novel, on the other hand, must follow the novelistic path foreseen by Nathalie Sarraute, the path of interior exploration or of verbal magic (both of which are, according to Mourlet, "the two passwords of the Novel of Tomorrow"). It remains to the cinema to occupy itself with *appearances*, with the surfaces of objects, verbal description remaining incapable of equaling the filmic image.

---

3. Even André Gide allowed himself such categorical pronouncements. "Les événements extérieurs appartiennent au cinéma; il sied que le roman les lui laisse," he wrote, exterior events belong to the cinema. And again, "De même que la photographie . . . débarrassa la peinture de certaines exactitudes, le phonographe nettoiera sans doute demain le roman de ses dialogues rapportés" (quoted in the *Dictionnaire des synonymes* [Paris, n.d.], 212, 375). Thus for Gide, instead of serving as an example for the novel, sound film purifies and delimits it.

And yet it is clear that these critics (for the most part) have in mind not so much those films in which we find cumbersome dialogues and plots laid out and explained by verbal language as an ideal cinema or a "visual cinema" such as may be found with certain filmmakers more preoccupied with images than with filmed drama. They dream of an abstract cinema, quasi-real (like those of a distant Chaplin), of filmic techniques that "work" only on events, or that would be based solely on analogies and symbols or on a syntax of the mute image—a syntax that would link the scene sequences, the "travelings," the shifts in viewpoint or lighting. It would be a cinema that, according to Labarthe, for example, would not use man as its measure, as the novel does (even the novel of Robbe-Grillet, despite the assertions of some critics). To Labarthe and his group, it is definitely the film, not the novel, that could become a truly *objective* art.

For it is indeed "objective psychology" that, in the view of most of the "Cinéma et roman" critics, constitutes the principal province of the cinema. It is true that certain critics admit that "American behaviorism" as reflected in novels of the twenties and thirties contributed to the emergence of *psychologie objective*. But it is even more likely, according to some, that this "behaviorism" derived mainly from the film, if indeed both literary behaviorism and objective cinema are not products of a certain "vision of the world" created by the effects on modern man of an increasingly technological society. Even if we cannot establish a priority in time, even if we must admit that literary behaviorism antedates cinematic objective psychology, or even if we accept the view that the two trends represent a convergence rather than an influence of one genre on another, it still cannot be denied, according to the critics of "Cinéma et roman," that the film wins out over the written novel, since only the film possesses, as G.-A. Astre argues, the ability to bring out "*meaning* at the same time as the object itself." It is an ability, Astre continues, that no novelistic technique, "even as skillful as that of a Faulkner or a Dos Passos," can match.

The literary critic may be surprised to read these articles by authors that seem to be unaware of, or to avoid mentioning, more recent works of analysis whose object is to trace in modern (or even past) novels a developed usage of objective correlatives (not to mention symbols) that function, or seem to function, more or less the same way in novels as do the props of filmic images. At most the critics recognize, here and there, the similarity between a Robbe-Grilletian fictional image (the blue package of cigarettes in *Le Voyeur*, for example) and that of a film (the child's ball in *M*). The authors of "Cinéma et roman" seem content to develop a supererogatory series of "contrasts" between what the film "can do" and what the novel "should do." Nowhere does their effort to examine the two genres in depth, to find in them equivalents of writing or, as Philippe Durand notes, "correspondences in the creative process," fail more completely. Either because of their prejudices or because of their ignorance on the subject of novelistic literature, the critics of "Cinéma et roman" disappoint us. If they are well versed in cinema, they seem in contrast to know very little of the novel.

Since it is the early Robbe-Grillet, as the author of the preface to "Cinéma et roman" informs us, that most obviously lends himself to the study of novel/cinema connections, we find in the remarks on these early novels by Robbe-Grillet the misunderstandings, miscomprehensions, and conceptual deformities already noted in their arguments.

In the first place, there is no consensus that Robbe-Grillet was influenced by cinema. Michel Mourlet sees in Robbe-Grillet the modern author who has par excellence imitated cinema. The novel of Mourlet's dreams would be nothing other than "the paraphrase of a film." On the other hand, Jean Duvignaud (*Arguments*, February 1958) asserted that Robbe-Grillet escapes a cinematographic influence, since he is seeking "a mode of literary expression which is absolutely pure, absolutely free of everything which might, from near or far, suggest the cinema."

Let me quickly retrace some early ideas on Robbe-Grillet and the cinema and briefly examine the critics' methods of connecting, or professing to connect, his work and the filmic universe.

As early as 1954, Roland Barthes, in writing of *Les Gommes*, noted a connection to be made between the technique of the cinema and that of Robbe-Grillet:

> les descriptions de Robbe-Grillet . . . se déclenchent spatialement, l'objet se décroche sans perdre pour autant la trace de ses premières positions, il devient profond sans cesser d'etre plan. On reconnaît ici la révolution même que le cinéma a opérée dans les reflexes de la vision.

> the descriptions of Robbe-Grillet . . . develop spatially, the object moves on without, however, losing track with its earlier positions, it acquires depth without ceasing to be flat. We recognize here the revolution that the film has brought about in our visual reflexes.[4]

Next, the critic finds an intentional analogy between the cinema and the scene in *Les Gommes* in which the gang leader Bona looks through a windowpane in an empty room. For Barthes, "la chambre, cubiforme, c'est la salle . . . et la vitre, c'est l'écran" (the room is the movie house

---

4. "Littérature objective," *Critique* (July–August 1954).

and the window is the film screen). There was no echo of Barthes's ideas in other critics of Robbe-Grillet's first novel: at best one finds here and there a few remarks tending to link the plot or the atmosphere of *Les Gommes* to *films noirs*, or to Hitchcock.

It was *Le Voyeur*, in 1955 (followed by observations on the cinema made by Robbe-Grillet himself in the influential 1956 *NNRF* article "Une Voie pour le roman futur"), that set off in nearly all the critics a wave of novel/cinema connections. The title *Le Voyeur*—so ambiguous, so variously interpreted—seemed to lend itself to the idea of the cinema. Everywhere in the collection "Cinéma et roman" the word *voyeur*, even when it is not specifically attached to the name Robbe-Grillet, hints that it is of Robbe-Grillet and his—alleged—theory of the novel that one is thinking. Thus G.-A. Astre can write: "Il n'est pire erreur pour le romancier 's'inspirant' des techniques du film que de vouloir transformer son lecteur en un simple *voyeur*" ("Cinéma et roman," 16). Astre here not only calls the transforming of the reader into a "voyeur" an error, but also reproaches Robbe-Grillet for relying on a theory of nonparticipation in the reader, all the while presuming in Robbe-Grillet a technique based on cinema. Adventuring even further, Michel Mourlet goes to the extreme of finding "preposterous" the effort he attributes to Robbe-Grillet of "trying to reproduce by means of language" the image of a film (of a film, of course, that did not exist!):

> Le résultat sérait dérisoire. Et pourtant nous voyons Alain Robbe-Grillet décrire le mouvement d'une vague ou de la série de gestes nécessaires à l'ouverture d'une mallette. . . . Un film . . . aurait enregistré le dit mouvement de vague, la dite série de gestes. Le roman tel que le rêve Robbe-Grillet est . . . la paraphrase d'un film.

> The result would be ridiculous. And yet we see Alain Robbe-Grillet describing the movement of a wave or the series of gestures necessary to open a suitcase. . . . A film . . . would have filmed the said movement of a wave, the said series of gestures. The novel that Robbe-Grillet dreams of creating is . . . the paraphrase of a film.
> ("Cinéma et roman," 29)

Nearly all the critics of "Cinéma et roman" also find *Le Voyeur* to be, in the words of Jean-Louis Bory, "un livre qui se voit plus qu'il ne se lit" (a book more to be seen than read). For Bory, the style of Robbe-Grillet "photographs." In fact:

> Robbe-Grillet ne pourra faire plus objectif que son roman, plus "en surface" que lui, sera ce roman qui, à la limite, ne sera plus qu'un album de photos. Ou un film.

Robbe-Grillet cannot be more objective than he is in his novel, more "on the surface"—without, at its limit, producing an album of photos. Or a film.

("Cinéma et roman," 125)

It is Colette Audry who finds the most to say about "Alain Robbe-Grillet's camera." For her the novels of Robbe-Grillet are—paradoxically—at once cinematographic and noncinematographic: a contradiction she resolves by affirming that the technique of Robbe-Grillet represents a particular manner of giving us, in a "typically cinematographic" way, stories that are themselves "noncinematographic." For Audry, the surfaces, backgrounds, and scenes of *Le Voyeur* would only render a film "mortally boring and incomprehensible at the same time." This is because the author, according to her, has eliminated from his novel all the *anguish* necessary for a good film, since even the crime that might add "the same plot as a detective story" can only be "deduced after a certain number of indications." Let us put aside for another study[5] the discussion of this false idea of the nondescription of the crime in *Le Voyeur* (or see the description of this crime in *Le Voyeur* itself, pp. 245–46). Let me frankly declare that it is equally false to say that Mathias's anguish is not communicated to us. On the contrary, the reader feels the effect of the objective structure of that anguish in the novel.

As to the demonstration of the existence of cinematographic procedures in *Le Voyeur*, the method employed by Colette Audry seems weak. She only describes a scene in the novel with the vocabulary and the technical preoccupations of a cinematographic scenario. Here is how Audry attempts to convince us that *Le Voyeur* presents itself just like a film:

> Il n'est que d'ouvrir *Le Voyeur*: l'Appareil placé quelque part sur le pont, se pose d'abord sur la foule des passagers dont les regards, tournés vers la jetée, signifient une impatience d'aborder. . . . [Mathias] s'aperçoit alors qu'une petite fille est en train de le dévisager fixement. A ce moment, commence un lent travelling-avant qui nous révèle progressivement la cale en pente . . . le quai perpendiculaire à la cale, tout un paysage géométrique . . . etc.

> One needs only to open *Le Voyeur*: the Camera stationed somewhere on the deck focuses first on the crowd of passengers whose eyes, turned toward the pier, convey their impatience to go ashore. . . . [Mathias] then notices that a young girl is looking at him fixedly. At this point a slow forward movement of the camera shows us pro-

5. See my chapter on *Le Voyeur* in *Les Romans de Robbe-Grillet*, in which the various possible meanings of *voyeur* in the novel are discussed. The real "voyeur" is in my opinion not the protagonist Mathias, but little Julien, who "sees" Mathias's crime.

gressively the angle of the hold . . . the perpendicular quay, an entire geographic landscape . . . etc.

("Cinéma et roman," 135)

This procedure could obviously become an easy game. No doubt screen-
writers in Hollywood proceed no differently in "adapting" a best-seller to
the screen.

What pains Colette Audry the most is why Robbe-Grillet struggles "la-
boriously to sketch . . . this collection of images, in cinematographic aspect, of which the cinema, with the aid of a real traveling shot . . . could
give us in a few moments an infinitely more exact and complete vision."
And yet as an answer to this quandary, Audry is able to find only one
rather unclear idea: the author, she writes, is not really trying to "compete" with the cinema but can find no other way of "attaining literary
existence"!

What does this mean? Are we to assume that the critic is beginning to
perceive the fundamental difference that separates a verbal description
from a film image, to recognize the specificity of the two categories of
artistic creation? Audry does not explain herself further. An interesting
theoretical question immediately arises: What would be the results if several authors "presented" verbally the images of the same film? Would
there not be as many "cinematic methods" in the descriptions as there
would be authors? Are we to imagine that all these authors, by virtue of
the very fact of describing filmic images, would produce "Robbe-Grilletian" prose? Nothing cold be more absurd. Even if they began with the
intention of imitating that author, only those who had already felt his verbal influence could achieve an approximation of his style. The art of
Robbe-Grillet (like that of any artist) does not depend upon the *thing
seen*; it depends upon the complexity of internal processes—vision, language, habits of thought—that constitute his manner, his style. Such a description of a wave's motion is so in no sense. It is an entirely *literary*
structure: a verbal wave or billow that is Robbe-Grillet-like, whose reality
in no way resides in some presumed realist-scientific exactitude, since
that reality resides nowhere other than in the total effect—*literary* effect—of the words, sentences, and arrangements of structural parts. The
image remains at most an epiphenomenon that accompanies, valorizes in
accessory fashion, a manifestation that is, first, in the realm of language. If
another—Claude Ollier, for example—manages to create descriptions
very close to those of Robbe-Grillet, he is undertaking neither cinema
nor photography but rather, in his slightly different manner, using the
style of Robbe-Grillet. And why not? Are there not paintings by Braque of
a certain period that can pass (without the one harming the other) for
Picassos?

With the appearance of Robbe-Grillet's *La Jalousie*, in which the narrative is presented to us in the form of a withheld first person narration (what I have termed the *je-néant*), the critics were quick to make comparisons between the "point of view" of the narrator in that novel and that of the protagonist in Robert Montgomery's famous film *The Lady in the Lake*. Already in *L'Age du roman américain* (Paris, 1948), Claude-Edmonde Magny had praised this film: "The most remarkable, the [film] that really uses first-person narration in hyperbolic fashion . . . in which the camera is constantly in the hero's position and shows us things as they appear to him, without ever allowing us to see him, unless he is looking at himself in a mirror" (p. 33). In reading *La Jalousie*, critics were reminded of that film. Jacques Howlett, well aware of the nuances of the phenomenological novel, immediately made this distinction: "in *The Lady in the Lake*, the camera took the hero's place, but in *La Jalousie* there is no hero. The gaze of the narrator is one that is unaware of itself" (in *France-Observateur*, 30 May 1957).

Colette Audry takes up Howlett's idea, to draw an even sharper contrast: "Whereas Robert Montgomery makes a character of his camera, Robbe-Grillet makes his character a camera. The former humanizes the lens or objective; the latter *objectifies* the human personage." This view, despite the various difficulties of logic it may raise, at least has the merit of emphasizing the endless chatter of the narrator in *The Lady in the Lake*. That narrator (a facet Claude-Edmonde Magny ignores), far from being absorbed in what he sees or does (as behaviorism would have it), never stops *commenting* upon his actions, his thoughts, or giving us analyses and monologues (in a very banal verbal style), reminding us each instant that he is the one who "sees" what we see. He spends an exaggerated portion of his time conversing with others in front of the many mirrors (in which we see him even too "normally"); he constantly shows us his cigarette, held in his excessively visible fingers. He even appears before us conventionally seated at his desk, to explain to us that we are about "to live what he has lived." In other words, the entire mechanism of this first-person camera seems poorly conceived, if not simply awkward in execution.

There is more. We quickly realize that, technically, the differences that separate the wide-angle optics (of the human eye) from the very limited visual field of the camera render the substitution—even if illusory—of a camera for a person almost impossible. This difficulty, of a visual nature, does not touch very closely upon the fundamental question of the cinema with respect to the novel, but it nevertheless warrants a scrutiny, since the failure of this film in the sphere of psychological transfers provides a general lesson in the analysis of points of view. *The Lady in the Lake*, far from establishing the prescribed identification between the human eye and the camera lens, has demonstrated the near impossibility of such an identification.

The experience of *The Lady in the Lake* leads us mainly to conclude that the "conventional" points of view—detached from characters and variable in position—of regular cinema (including over-the-shoulder shots, traveling shots, and all the rest) are more adept in producing an *identification effect* of spectator/character than are the views of an "objective" camera moving in the guise of the narrator's eye. Moreover, the cinematographic critics who most admire *The Lady in the Lake* admit that the film was a failure, and that what might have, or ought to have, passed for the very essence of filmic development in "point of view" simply did not do so.[6]

Would the situation have been different had Montgomery deleted his narrator's endless commentary that reaches us from behind the screen— had he made it more "objective," limiting his hero's verbal-mental aspect to dialogues with other characters, for example? In such a case, at any rate, the film would have been far more comparable to Robbe-Grillet's *La Jalousie*. In its present form, *The Lady in the Lake* has almost nothing to do with that novel. Further worth noting is the total absence, between the film and the novel, of parallels in the use of time or of chronology. There is nothing in the film but a linear or literal chronology, with no effort to have the chronological interior of the hero's psychological universe felt, or to penetrate the spatiotemporal dimensions of a narrator situated at the heart of the narrative.

Montgomery's film and Robbe-Grillet's novel both initiated new directions, each in its own genre, in first-person technique: and there ends almost all similarity between *The Lady in the Lake* and *La Jalousie*. Indeed, a close look reveals that these new directions are in fact opposed. Montgomery gives us (and rather badly) monologues, verbal observations, pseudo-"tough" commentaries in the American style, which, instead of creating an identification of the spectator with the narrator, prevent it. The filmmaker increasingly imprisons himself in an optical system that is mechanically awkward, if not impossible to accept. Robbe-Grillet

6. The film *The Lady in the Lake*, played an important catalytic role in France with respect to examining point-of-view problems in the cinema and the novel. In addition to the texts referred to, especially worthy of note are Albert Laffay's "Le Cinéma 'subjectif,'" *Les Temps Modernes* (July 1948); C. M.'s "L'Imparfait du subjectif," *Esprit* (September 1948); and Georges Blin's remarkable book, *Stendhal et les problèmes du roman* (Paris, 1954), 118–19.

gives us in *La Jalousie* nothing but what his narrator sees, does, and imagines, in a *sensorioverbal* system or unlimited angle, remaining free in the space and time of the protagonist's psychological universe.

What is surprising about cinematographic critics like Colette Audry is that they readily level against *La Jalousie* (but apparently without realizing it) the same reproach found among certain purely literary critics (such as, for example, Bernard Pingaud): that Robbe-Grillet (in the words of Audry) wants "to forbid to his reader any effective participation." I have tried to show elsewhere the utterly groundless logic of this idea so contrary to the real intentions and structures of Robbe-Grillet's work.[7] It is nevertheless difficult to comprehend how and why those who are quick to praise the "objective" yet emotionally expressive effects of an Eisenstein or an Astruc refuse to see in Robbe-Grillet anything other than the "gaze . . . dehumanized, desensitized, in a word 'objectal,' of a simple lens or glass, or pure objective" (Audry, p. 136). On the one hand accusing him of producing cinema in a novel, these same critics seem to be asking the author to produce a conventional novel, complete with psychological analysis, interior monologue, and the like. Here is another proof that, with respect to *La Jalousie*, readers seem clearly divided into two camps: those who, with Colette Audry and Jacques Brenner, think that "the reader, put in the place of the jealous husband, feels no passion" (Brenner in *Paris-Normandie*, 19 April 1957)—those who, in other words, either do not understand or reject what Robbe-Grillet does—and those who, like Jacques Howlett, for example, clearly see that the reader manages not only to "valorize" the jealous husband's narrative but to enter as well, by way of the "aesthetic reduction," into a new literary universe.

Robbe-Grillet's novel *Dans le labyrinthe* could no doubt have furnished the critics of "Cinéma et roman" with the material for many identifications between film and novel. The variations of the shape of objects in the closed room of the narrator, the "dissolves" at the moment of the picture on the wall's animation or penetration into the scene, the perspectives on the crossroads seen as if in a mirror, the decreasing series of streetlamps, the alternating play of blackness/light in the halls of the building, the modalities of the falling or trampled snow, and the "cinematographic" end of the narrative when the narrator turns away from the town's labyrinth with the rapidity of a zoom lens shot backing away at full speed—all this offers tempting analogies. It is disconcerting that a work such as *Dans le labyrinthe*, on its face resembling no existing film, can pass for having been composed in imitation of the latter. It would be of

7. Cf. the chapter on *La Jalousie* in *Les Romans de Robbe-Grillet*.

great interest to see how the novels (or "techniques") of Robbe-Grillet would translate onto the screen. But though he moved on to write and produce a large number of films, from *Marienbad* to *Glissements progressifs du plaisir* and others, Robbe-Grillet has never adapted any of his novels to the screen.[8]

The various early discussions of novel/cinema connections, especially between the first novels of Robbe-Grillet and films of that period, tended to lose themselves in the same misunderstandings that elsewhere encumbered the study of the novelistic genre in general, and of the then current work of the novelist of *La Jalousie* and *Dans le labyrinthe*. Most of the debates on point of view, the visual image, and the so-called objective psychology of films merely furnished more or less ingenious variations on preoccupations already all well known in literary criticism.

It seems likely that at the base of all this is the fact that when there is a suppression of the *commentary* (Balzacian, Stendhalian, Proustian, or other) or of the interior monologues of the conventional novel, without any substitution of some other "personality" speaking to us (like, for example, the "hard-boiled" narrator in the novels of Cain or Hammett, or even Hemingway), that is, without any recognizable bridging voice between the protagonist and the reader/viewer, the difficulties start to appear. The reader (or the critic reading for him) sees in the absence of the bridging voice either—as Sartre did for *L'Etranger*—simply the "absurd," or a series of purely visual, objective images like those of a film. No longer hearing the author's familiar voice, the reader feels himself transported to the cinema.

This superficial idea, however, will not sustain analysis. If essays on film aesthetics have for a long time emphasized the need to substitute for authorial explanations purely visual scenes, the authors of movie scenarios have in fact invented many devices to replace the missing commentaries. These include "emotional reaction" scenes (such as tears in the eyes of an observer), key objects associated like leitmotifs with actions, themes, or characters (such as Orson Welles's sled in *Citizen Kane* or the child's balloon in *M*), voices from off screen, montages, fade-ins, and all the innumerable variations in camera viewpoint when it associ-

8. Alain Resnais, the film director of *Hiroshima mon amour*, announced in the June 1960 issue of *Esprit* that Robbe-Grillet was preparing a film script for him that would soon be made. The film was, of course, *L'Année dernière à Marienbad*. The questions treated here were, of course, studied again, but from the new angle of Robbe-Grillet as *cinematographer*. While speaking to me of his cinematographic work (as early as the summer of 1960), Robbe-Grillet emphasized at length the fundamental difference that separates a scene in a *written* novel from a scene in a visualized and annotated scenario, but in an *entirely different* style, almost "without writing." Cf. the preceding chapter.

ates itself with the visual field of almost any character (like the patient looking up at the surgeon bending over him with his scalpel, or the person about to fall from a height, who looks down at the ground), or the camera that takes the point of view of no one at all (installing itself on a car hood to film the couple in the front seat). In contrast to this, the *nouveau roman* has created more original and more daring extensions of fictional viewpoint.

It seems clear that an effective analysis of the possible influences of the film on the novel, or vice versa, would require some solution to the problem of stylistic equivalencies between the two arts. The question is analogous to that of the equivalencies once worked out to relate literary forms to the pictorial baroque forms of Wölfflin. When Jean Rousset, in *La Littérature de l'âge baroque en France* (Paris, 1953), developed an operative system for studying baroque literature, it was not by borrowing, with minor modifications of terminology, the famous categories of Wölfflin, but by creating, within literary forms themselves, new baroque categories, designed to fit written structures.

It becomes necessary to admit, finally, that a novel, being first of all a linguistic phenomenon (a narration of a certain length, related in a certain manner), is not a film or even a series of visual images, and that comparative novel/film studies must reject false analogies and parallels, or contradictions and blind alleys, and concentrate on the serious study of the relations between the techniques and creative modalities of the two great arts of expression.

5
INTERNATIONAL ASPECTS OF THE
NOUVEAU ROMAN

As its title implies, the *nouveau roman* is a novelistic, not a cinematic development. Fascinating as its relation to the film continues to be, its major importance and influence lie in the domain of the contemporary novel. Some years ago, at the time when it began to be recognized as potentially the most important stage in the contemporary evolution of novelistic form, most critics stressed the absence of coherence and unifying principles to be found in the new movement. "Il n'y a pas d'école Robbe-Grillet," wrote Roland Barthes in an article by that title; others called the term *nouveau roman* itself "une notion fourre-tout," a catchall term, whose disunity was emphasized by the proliferation of designations such as "antinovel," "roman du refus," and even, in Claude Mauriac's ingenious coinage, "alittérature." A presumption arose that the new novels not only lacked connections or common features among themselves, but were also cut off from and independent of the literary past, both French and international. With the passage of time this conception of an isolated or fragmented novelistic phenomenon has undergone great change. The new novel of the fifties and sixties is seen now as having deep roots attaching it to soils fed by many and diverse predecessors and at the same time as producing fertile seeds that have flourished in many places more or less remote from its native locale.

It is now possible to identify the role of a number of international factors in the formation of the conception of the *nouveau roman* held by certain contemporary French writers, as well as to point out and examine the penetration of some of their basic ideas and characteristic forms not only among novelists of other countries but in international novelistic criticism as well. While specific examples are plentiful, one cannot be exhaustive in a brief space; in fact, each passing year sees the publication of works related in one way or another to the *nouveau roman*, and it may well be that the influences involved will become so generalized that their origins will be lost sight of. Meanwhile, it seems appropriate to make an initial stocktaking of this somewhat complicated situation.

One of the oddities of the international or comparative literary scene is that influences from "foreign" sources often turn out to have their actual origins in the very literature on which they exert their effect. Such was the case in the cycle leading from Edgar Allan Poe through French symbolism back to the imagists and early-twentieth-century American poetry in general; and such is the case for one of the most fundamental of modern novelistic techniques, that of interior monologue or stream-of-consciousness writing, which James Joyce by his own admission, and even insistence, had found in the writings of Edouard Dujardin (especially *Les Lauriers sont coupés*, 1887) and had then modified to create an essential mode of presenting the thoughts and mental content of characters in the post-Proustian novel. Among the most obvious influences of interior monologue on the *nouveau roman* are those affecting Michel Butor, Claude Mauriac, and Claude Simon, ranging from passages in normal syntax, including modes of self-address (or of didactic *you* forms with which the narrative voice speaks to and for the character), to neo-Joycean or Faulknerian stylized "inner voice" syntax designed to create the illusion of verbalized conscience at a subvocal level. Even more interesting from the theoretical standpoint is the evolution of interior monologue in the works of Nathalie Sarraute in the technique she calls "sub-conversation," an attempt to suggest in words psychic "tropisms" and other manifestations below the level of any vocabulary or syntax. In another direction, Robert Pinget piles one upon the other long series of more and more extensive interior monologues recapitulating and widening one small incident until it encompasses virtually the entire mental existence of the protagonist, as in the "accumulation" novel *Quelqu'un* (1965), or weaves a complex pattern of alternative and contradictory inner narrations taking place in an unidentifiable central character, as in *Le Libera* (1968). Basically, the entire novel *La Jalousie* of Robbe-Grillet (1957) may be considered a special case of interior monologue in which the protagonist's mental content, converted into pseudo-objective descriptions of objects from the "real" world around him, expresses his personal universe in what the French critic Bernard Pingaud has aptly called a long "exterior" monologue. The existence of international modalities of interior monologue is witnessed by the numerous studies of the subject in many countries, such as those of Melvin Friedman and Rolfe Humphries in the United States and R.-M. Albérès in France. Albérès, indeed, uses interior monologue in his *Métamorphoses du roman* as his main base for a comparative study of the international novel of today. The technique has become so widespread that further comment seems unnecessary.

The example of Joyce is evident in the wide adoption of another organizing principle to be found not only in the *nouveau roman* but in the contemporary novel outside France: the structuring of the plot on the basis of a myth, usually classical, whether hidden within the work (as in *Ulysses* or Robbe-Grillet's *Les Gommes*) and thus tacit or unacknowledged, or openly identified by the author or his characters (as in Butor's *L'Emploi du temps*, 1956). So much has been written about the use of myth in modern literature that it may appear superfluous to add anything; one may, however, point ou that the myth functions as a structural support in the modern novel in two ways. It may, as in *Ulysses* or the works of Butor, Updike (*The Centaur*), and Hershey (*Too Far to Walk*), link the novel's contemporary characters and situations to ancient or archetypal models, or it may, as in *Les Gommes* (1953), form in addition to an "unconscious" parallel a sort of ironic counterpoint between the humanistic pattern of myth and the chance arrangements of "unmotivated synchronicities" that create the perhaps illusory links between a modern action and its archetype. In any event, and whatever the "intentionality" of the novelist (serious in the case of Joyce, perhaps ironic in the case of Robbe-Grillet), mythic parallelism poses the question of structural fictional "models" and their evolutionary changes and underscores, as T. S. Eliot noted in writing of *Ulysses*, the transition from modalities of "plot" to those of structure.

Myth, in turn, suggests a similar, if smaller, novelistic device: inner duplication, which André Gide long ago called a sort of "construction en abyme," comparing the interior duplication to the central or inner shield on certain coats of arms, which he believed (perhaps wrongly) often reproduced exactly the main or outer heraldic pattern. (See my chapter 10, "Interior Duplication.") Like inner plays or like mirrors in certain paintings, the duplication process permits the novelist to confront his characters with an image of their own situation, but within the work, where they may react to it at their own level, thus heightening and reinforcing the theme by multiplying its perspectives. From the inner play of *Hamlet* to the "roman africain" of Robbe-Grillet's *La Jalousie*, the inner duplication provokes reactions (as with the king or the jealous husband) even when these reactions are left unanalyzed and treated only through depiction of their objective effects (dialogue and action in *Hamlet*, distorted versions of the plot of the inner novel in *La Jalousie*). More important, the inner duplication creates models that augment for the reader the full meaning of the novel, and the characters themselves, as in the case of some mythic parallels, may remain unaware of the counterpoint. A well-known international example mixes interior duplication with rotating viewpoint, first in Gide's *Les Faux-monnayeurs* and then in its English imitation, Aldous Huxley's *Point Counter Point*, where one of the characters speculates on a system of ten novels placed one within the other, like Chinese boxes, each constructed from the point of view of a different character. The extent to which these early-twentieth-century ideas have reappeared in the new novel may be illustrated by a brief and partial list of novels that have employed inner duplications, in forms ranging from inner pictures and drawings to related incidents and novels read or discussed by characters in the work: Nathalie Sarraute's *Portrait d'un inconnu* (1956), Michel Butor's *L'Emploi du temps*, *La Modification* (1957), and *Degrés* (1960), Robbe-Grillet's *La Jalousie, Dans le labyrinthe*, and *L'Année dernière à Marienbad*, Claude Ollier's *La Mise en scène* (1959), Jean Ricardou's *La Prise de Constantinople* (1965), the Spaniard Jorge Isaac's *María*, and the Italian Italo Svevo's *The Conscience of Zeno*. If one may say that the novel of courtly love Paolo read to Francesca in Dante's *Divine Comedy* was perhaps the first literary example of interior duplication, it is also fair to state that the technique seems to have lost none of its effectiveness in later times and other countries.

The influence of Franz Kafka remains strong in the Western literary world, from Ransom and Rex Warner in the United States to Agnon writing in Hebrew in Israel. The French new novel has felt the spell and has, especially in the case of Robbe-Grillet, at times conveyed a similar metaphysical malaise emanating from a meticulously described milieu in which ambiguous or apparently meaningless actions evolve without explanation. Robbe-Grillet not only rejects Kafkaesque "allegory," he denies allegorical intent in Kafka himself, admitting at most that if Kafka's stairways "lead somewhere," they are, in the work itself, simply *there*. The stylized simplification of the central characters, their reduction to mysterious initials (K., A., N., or at most a given name, Mathias), the absence of knowable "truth" in their motives and situations, their innocence or guilt of implied crimes, the realistically but neutrally described backgrounds: all these relate Robbe-Grillet to Kafka. If the city of *Dans le labyrinthe* appears Kafkaesque (when it does not evoke de Chirico's paintings, often called pictorial parallels to Kafka), it is no more so than the haunting vertical hospital of Dino Buzzati's *A Clinical Case*. From Kafka, in great part, come the many new novel characters who appear vague, imprecise, empty, without social "dossier," even without a known past, in the pages of Robbe-Grillet, Pinget, Beckett, Sarraute, or Musil (*The Man without Qualities*). It is under the sign of Kafka, rather than of Pirandello as some have suggested, that we must place the contradictory, lying, unreliable protagonist, with his undetermined or variable features, who has come to represent the opposite pole from the Balzacian character (against whom Robbe-Grillet and Sarraute especially have conducted scathing attacks) whose personality is completely inventoried and whose place in the social world is fully defined. It is now the Kafka-derived character who has become, not only in the novel but also in the theater from Ionesco to Pinter and the cinema from Robbe-Grillet to Godard, the typical protagonist.

The new novelists have, in general, made important modifications with respect to narrative mode and point of view as compared with the techniques of the earlier novel. The tendency begun with Henry James and his disciples that called for placing the observational center inside the novelistic field rather than outside (usually in an omniscient narrator who while ostensibly looking on from outside nevertheless retains the privilege of intruding at will into the ideas and emotions of his characters) becomes accentuated with André Gide and especially with Jean-Paul Sartre, who developed for the theory of the narrator-within-the-field a supporting existentialist argument in his well-known attack against omniscient narrational polyvalence directed, as pointed out elsewhere, against François Mauriac. The Sartrian relativist narrational theory was followed by a large number of novels organized around a pattern of rotating viewpoints, presenting multiple perspectives of the same events, wherein characters and their actions are shown from many angles and the angles of perception of the characters themselves, like so many searchlights placed in different locations, attempt to illuminate a central "truth" that is rendered, in the process, increasingly uncertain, ambiguous, and contradictory. Among the numerous possible examples, the following are perhaps the most typical and striking: Robbe-Grillet's *Les Gommes*, Michel Butor's *Degrés*, Nathalie Sarraute's *Le Planétarium*, Claude Mauriac's *Dîner en ville*, Claude Simon's *La Route des Flandres*, and, on the international scene generally, Lawrence Durrell's *Alexandria Quartet*, Paul Bowles's *The Spider's House*, Camilo José Cela's *La colmena*, Francisco Ayala's *Muertes de perro*, and, of course, in an earlier period, the stories and plays of Pirandello. It should be noted that subsequently the point of view in the French new novel appears to have undergone a shift that, if misinterpreted, might seem to constitute a sort of return to the omniscient author. In Robbe-Grillet's *La Maison de rendez-vous* (1965), an extremely mobile first-person pronoun attaches itself in succession to a variety of characters, in such a way that the reader himself becomes, as it were, the narrative center. It is almost as if the omniscient narrator, driven from the house of fiction by Henry James, had returned through the back door of *La Maison de rendez-vous*. In any case, there is a crisis in the theory of the "justified" viewpoint, situated inside the fictional frame and logically responsible for all the narrational angles of the work. A similar experiment is found in Robert Pinget's *Le Libera*, whose first-person *je* narrator is a phantomlike double of a number of characters present in the small village where mysterious crimes against children have been committed and yet remains different from any of them, a sort of immaterial guilt figure embodying a narrational conscience but lacking corporeal presence.

The question of justified viewpoint is crucial not only to the international contemporary novel, but to films as well, and it constitutes a convenient bridge to a short survey of the field of cinematic fiction in its relations to the novel. Historically, the cinema served at first to reinforce the current of objective representation going back to the theories of Maupassant: suppression of analytical penetration, accompanied by descriptions of gestures or expressions of face and tones of voice, with the exclusion of direct or indirect attempts at expression of thought processes or emotions. Thus the first serious treatment of the subject, the chapter "Cinéma et roman" in Claude-Edmonde Magny's *L'Age du romain américain* (1947), saw the film as an example or lesson for the novel in methods of eliminating "outworn" psychological analysis or authorial commentary, leading to a type of novelistic structure she called "behaviorist," limited to external observations. If there is indeed a "behaviorist" fiction (the term has never been extensively used in criticism written in English), it seems it would include not only Hemingway, Dos Passos, Dashiel Hammett, and Raymond Chandler in the United States (examples studied by Magny), but also in certain important respects portions of the works of Camus and Malraux in France as well as those of Goytisolo and Ferlosio (*El jarama* in particular) in Spain. Comparison of the way Raymond Chandler's protagonist Philip Marlowe (in such novels as *Farewell, My Lovely*) uses the "I" pronoun and Camus's technique using Meursault's *je* in *L'Etranger* reveals that in both cases a considerable degree of suppression occurs "behind" the pronoun, concealing most of the narrator's thinking and especially his emotions and leading the reader into his own projective reinforcement or reconstruction of the implied psychology of the hero.

Without foreseeing the possibility of the interior or subjective cinema, that was to appear with *Hiroshima mon amour* (1960) and *L'Année dernière à Marienbad* (1961), Magny clearly anticipated the Italian film of the early neorealist period, and even to some extent the complex mode of intermingled reality and fiction in which elements borrowed from the outside world (newspaper stories, historical personages, documentary materials, and the like) would take on increasing importance in both films (those of Godard, for example) and novels called variously "nonfiction" or montage novels. Again, literary history provides many examples *avant la lettre* of such mixture problems: the *fait divers* behind the plots of *Le Rouge et le noir* of Stendhal, Flaubert's *Madame Bovary*, or Gide's *Les Faux-monnayeurs*. In his *Doktor Faustus*, Thomas Mann (as stated earlier) follows a conscious procedure of montage construction, using passages from texts on music, extracts from current magazines, and a hundred "real" sources whose identification has become a minor scholarly pursuit in itself. John Dos Passos had already "fabricated" documents to give to *U.S.A.* a similar appearance of "real" stuffing: the newsreel passages, the biographies of Ford and other men of the time, newspaper headlines, and the like. The most striking example of novelized reality or "nonfiction novel" is, of course, Truman Capote's *In Cold Blood*, based on a "researched" crime first known to the author from a newspaper report. Despite the impression often given by critics, Capote was by no means the inventor of the genre, which has been practiced widely by writers on celebrated criminal cases (see *The New Yorker*'s "Annals of Crime" series) and in at least one instance by no less a novelist than André Gide himself (in *La Sequestrée de Poitiers*). What is interesting in the case of *In Cold Blood* is that to "fictionalize" his materials (on whose absolute realism and veracity he so strongly insists) Capote employs most of the chief techniques of the *nouveau roman* and of *découpage* as found in the cinema, including reversals of the chronology of events, parallel or alternating sequences, flashbacks, and the like. It is now obvious that not only in the novel, as ordinarily understood, but also in so-called objective or nonfictional presentations of reality, modes and models derived from the cinema have deeply conditioned all writers' ways of seeing the world and organizing it for verbal expression. An earlier-quoted text by Claude Simon in *Premier Plan*, no. 18, makes the point quite thoroughly for the novel, and Capote's "novel" proves the case for fictionalized reportage, since *In Cold Blood* constitutes a sort of cinematic novel based on its author's questionable guarantee that he has invented nothing. This guarantee, in turn, while suspect in some important details, hides the more important fact that in giving *form* to his materials, in his recourse to techniques of novel and film, Capote has, in reality, invented everything. One may see in this a clear proof of the assertion often heard from practitioners of the *nouveau roman* such as Robbe-Grillet and Butor that it is always the form that gives a literary work its true meaning.

In any list of contemporary "problems of the novel," such as point of view, modes of interior presentation of thoughts and feelings, manipulation of objective descriptions, and the like, the question of chronology and "dechronology" must figure prominently. Unfortunately, the best-known studies of novelistic time (Pouillon's *Temps et roman*, Mendilov's

Time and the Novel) were written before the most important contemporary developments, and the subject will require book-length treatment
by skilled critical analysts to explore its full extent and significance. Although the "prehistory" of literary dechronology, from the flashbacks of
Homer through the complicated time relationships among the intercalated stories of the seventeenth-century baroque novel (like *L'Astrée*)
and the meanderings of such "time-free" writers as Sterne, is interesting
and relevant to modern developments, it is apparent that a far more radical evolution in time structures has occurred that sets twentieth-century
authors apart from their predecessors and will require new analytical
procedures. For the contemporary novel often makes of temporal or
atemporal structures the very basis of its fictional form, and the nonlinear
time found therein (involving circles, spirals, labyrinthine squares or corridors of time, and the like) no longer corresponds to external time and
exists solely in the fictitious universe of the individual work. One may
speak of three phases in the evolution of nonlinear literary time: that of
the flashback or the intercalated story, in which past events are brought
into the present through retrospective narration; that of associative time,
in which memories are revived in a much freer style by the shifting affective states of a narrator or character (from Proust to the Robbe-Grillet of
La Jalousie); and finally, that of completely restructured time no longer
commensurable with a virtual or real time, in which the narration makes
"impossible" loops in time, as in Robbe-Grillet's *La Maison de rendez-
vous*. It is important to distinguish here between artificial time-shifting
arrangements (such as that of Huxley's *Eyeless in Gaza*), having the aspect of a jigsaw puzzle and allowing the entire figure to become visible
only when all the pieces are in place, and the new fictional topology in
which actions bend back upon themselves, narrations pass imperceptibly
from person to person, in structures whose closest analogies seem to lie
with music rather than with previous literary time patterns. While the
nouveau roman has gone further in this direction than the novel outside
France, a few examples of related dechronological experimentation may
be cited: Vargas Llosa's *La ciudad y los perros*, and *La casa verde*, Alejo
Carpentier's *Vuelta a la semilla* (an attempt at time reversal), Cortazar's
Hopscotch, many stories of Borges, Eduardo Sanguinetti's *Capriccio ita-
liano*, and no doubt others. It may be noted significantly that when the
nouveau roman adopts a temporal arrangement that ostensibly should
lead to a series of events susceptible of replacement into linear time, as
for example in Michel Butor's *L'Emploi du temps*, wherein the narrator
starts a diary for the year six months after the "beginning" date of the
diary, attempting to record both the past six months and the six months
that ensue, the events are never successfully merged, and it is this very

décalage or incommensurability that becomes the basis of the ambiguity on which the novel rests. Of all contemporary writers, it is probably Robbe-Grillet who has progressed furthest in time dislocation, from the false time circle of *Les Gommes* through the "time hole" form of *Le Voyeur* and the sets of *impasses chronologiques* of *La Jalousie* to the contradictory starts, stops, and reversals of *Dans le labyrinthe*, the two self-annihilating "years" of *L'Année dernière à Marienbad*, the conflicting repetitions of sequences of *L'Immortelle*, and the last phrase of tangled "reentrant" time lines of *La Maison de rendez-vous*, *Trans-Europ-Express*, and *L'Homme qui ment*. By contrast with these later novels and films, the time schemes of Pinget, for example, with the accumulations of repetitions of *Quelqu'un*, or even the anonymous free narration of *Le Libera*, appear almost conventional, though to readers unaccustomed to contemporary dechronology they still seem (if one may judge by reviews) strange to the point of incomprehensibility. Time, the most stubborn of vectors, with its "arrow" hitherto always pointing forward, is at least yielding to the pressure of new tendencies that bend it, twist it, turn it back on itself, tie it into knots. The cord that bound literary time to "real" time, already strained, becomes more and more frayed.

One international phenomenon that was considered by many critics to be an invention of the French *nouveau roman* but was soon revealed to have much older origins and to be far more widespread than at first thought is the use of "unusual" pronouns as the basis of the narrative mode. The best-known case is that of the narrative "you" (*vous*) employed by Michel Butor in *La Modification*. Examples continue to turn up, and after the publication of an article on the subject friends and colleagues added to the specimens I quoted (including such books as John Ashmead's *The Feather and the Mountain*, stories of Mary McCarthy, and the like), furnishing enough material to warrant the assertion that the "you" device in one form or another is one of the prevalent contemporary narrative techniques and suggesting the need of a book-length study comparable to that of Bertil, *The First-Person Novel*. (See my chapter 9, "Narrative 'You'.") Among the works not mentioned previously may be cited Edouardo Mallea's 1940 novel *La bahía del silencio* (which begins with "You entered the flower shop"; "Usted entró en la florería"); Carlos Fuentes' *Cambio de piel* and above all his short novel *Aura* (1962); the Norwegian novelist Peder Sjögren's *The Man Who Tried to Flee* (1949), in which, as Richard Vowles has pointed out, an anonymous narrator addresses a woman seated in a train compartment, relating her story to her (or inventing it), in the "you" mode, uttering the pronoun "I" only at the beginning and the end of the novel (as in Robbe-Grillet's *Dans le labyrinthe*); and William Styron's *Set This House on Fire*, which has been studied by both Michel Butor and Melvin Friedman under the sign of the *nouveau roman* (including the use of the Oedipus myth) and which contains a long section related, by the "normal" narrator, *on behalf of* the protagonist and in the "you" mode.[1] The device of narration *for* another, apparent in the Mallea and Styron novels, was of course used extensively by William Faulkner in *Absalom, Absalom!* Certain examples of *vous* from Balzac and Flaubert pointed out by Frederic St. Aubyn suggest that direct address to the reader, as well as the more indirect "dative" *vous* in French (cf. Flaubert, "La voix de M. Lieuvain se perdait dans l'air. Elle *vous* arrivait par lambeaux de phrases") may figure in the origins of the narrative "you." Even the familiar second-person pronoun *tu* has been used by Georges Perec (*Un Homme qui dort*, 1967), and Monique Wittig has experimented with a mode using *on* very close to the "you" form (becoming "you," in fact, in translation into English) in her *L'Opoponax* (1966). In each case the task of critics is to examine the aesthetic justification of the mode, which without such structural relevance would degenerate into cliché and sterile mannerism.

Another new trend, which does not seem as yet to have influenced the novel outside France (unless one may see certain aspects of John Barth's work as constituting a parallel development), but which may well spread further, is what may be termed, in honor of the French novelist Raymond Roussel, who set the example more than forty years ago, the Rousselian production or generation of narrative form. (See chapter 1, "Postmodern Generative Fiction.") As Roussel revealed in *Comment j'ai écrit certains de mes livres*, the basis of most of his stories and novels is to be found in relations between homophonic phrases and words whose proliferation by phonetic deformation and extension gives rise to all the important elements of plot and scene in *Parmi les noirs*, *Impressions d'Afrique*, *Locus Solus*, and other bizarre but beautiful works whose sources had mistakenly been thought to be purely "gratuitous" or to depend on the release of unconscious imagery by recourse to surrealist methods of automatic writing. The neo-Rousselian movement, while not yet truly international, is significant in that it represents the extreme limit at present of novelistic formalism and as such may point toward the future of contemporary fictional innovation. In a sense, Vladimir Nabokov may be said to have followed Rousselian principles in creating, for example, the interior poem of *Pale Fire* as well as the general plot structure of others of his novels. We encounter once more an aspect of the more general doctrine of *determining form*, which in the most advanced neo-Rousselian experi-

---

1. Cf. Melvin Friedman, "William Styron et le nouveau roman," in *Configuration critique de William Styron* (Paris, 1967).

ments almost succeeds in substituting itself for content. The outstanding example is Jean Ricardou's previously discussed work *La Prise de Constantinople* (1965), in which *everything*—characters, plot, descriptive developments, the order of events, repetitions, variations—arises from *language* alone and, quite literally, from letters, syllables, homophonic forms, and the like grouped according to sound and geometric forms that give rise, for example, to three sets of eight characters whose names and the initial letters thereof are connected by internal relationships, as well as to parallel stories and levels of time (the Middle Ages, the present, a science-fiction-like future). The novel is also, as I stated earlier, its own literary manifesto and bears on the back cover a second title, *La Prose de Constantinople*.

Other aspects of the *nouveau roman* have international parallels, not only among novelists, but among composers and painters, whose writings often bear a close resemblance to the declarations and manifestos of writers and critics of the new novel itself. I refer, for example, to the attention devoted to *things* or objects (often called *chosisme*) in world literature and painting, to doctrines of repetition, suppression or erasure, fortuitous series, and improvisations found in the works of John Cage (whose rhetorical devices themselves are worthy of careful stylistic analysis), in those of the painters Rauchenbach and Jasper Johns, and in the prose commentaries and also the music of a Lukas Foss and a Pierre Boulez. Not only the vocabulary but the style and repertory of ideas used in catalogs of modern exhibits of painting and sculpture, as well as in the program notes of concerts of avant-garde music, are often an almost exact image of what one may read in the essays of Roland Barthes, Michel Butor, Robbe-Grillet, or any of a number of cinematic critics writing for *Les Cahiers du Cinéma*. These materials call for attention from a new breed of specialist in *structures comparées* and offer exciting opportunities for the development and application of fresh analytical techniques.

A word of caution may be appropriate to call attention to the emergence of careless, clichélike allusions in critical writings to certain aspects of the *nouveau roman*. Setting aside the comments of more or less well-informed French critics (Barthes, Abirached, Genette, Pingaud, and the like), it may be first pointed out that in Spain the new novel, especially in its early phases, has been intelligently studied by both Juan Goytisolo (*Problemas de la novela*) and José-María Castellet (*La hora del lector* and particularly his study of Robbe-Grillet, *De la objectividad al objeto*), and that in Italy Eduardo Sanguinetti and Renato Barilli have both written astutely of the *nouveau roman* (which has influenced Sanguinetti himself, as well as such writers as Buzzati, Testori, Calvino, and Vittorini). In England, on the other hand, some critics, like John Wain and

John Weightman, have exhibited considerable resistance to the French innovations and have only begrudgingly admitted the obvious worldwide interest in the *nouveau roman* as compared with the relatively tepid attention currently paid to the traditionally thematic novel still popular in Britain (as exemplified in the works of the angry young man group). In the United States, popular book criticism has made it chic to suggest, whenever possible, connections with the *nouveau roman*. *Time* has specialized in this type of criticism; speaking of the novels of Virginia Woolf, June Arnold, John Fowles, Peter Israel, and the like, *Time*'s critic referred to their use of "shifting symbolic identities" (*Time*, 10 March 1967), which he attributes to the influence of Robbe-Grillet's *La Maison de rendez-vous*. Elsewhere the same critic or a colleague writes of the uncertain locales and ambiguous characters of a James Saltar novel as existing in a purely mental space-time continuum à la Robbe-Grillet and speaks of a narrator split in two "in a hazy New Novel fashion" (*Time*, 14 April 1967). The danger is that, like the term surrealism, the phrase new novel may be used to designate anything that seems to differ substantially from the ordinary or conventional. Even the French agree that of all countries the United States seems to have become the country par excellence of the new novel; let us hope that journalistic hackwork will not make the observation a sardonic joke.

In conclusion, it appears that we currently are faced with two associated phenomena: a progressive internationalization and at the same time a more and more widespread mixing or melding of art forms, from the literary to the visual, the auditory, the filmic. The problems of artistic creation take on closely similar forms in nearly all countries and in almost all spheres of creative activity. New forms appear everywhere, often geometrical or topological, with their circles, spirals, labyrinths, Möbius strips or whatnot; series or sets of objects emerge, whether symbols, objective correlatives, or merely phenomenological particulars, just as serialism in music chooses arbitrary, chance, or "acausally" related sets of notes. In the novel and in the arts generally we encounter symmetries and asymmetries, reciprocities, doublings and interior duplications, the artificial generation of forms (whether through Rousselian word permutation or the use of I Ching or tarot cards), repetitions, accumulations, erasures, ellipses, negations, interrogations and multiple responses thereto, more and more radical displacements of the narrative or perceptive center, structures that rotate about themselves, reversals and entanglements of time sequences, multiple dénouements and alternative resolutions, as well as many other forms and techniques whose rapid evolution in contemporary art constitutes perhaps the most fascinating and fertile materials for the comparatist of today and tomorrow.

6
TOPOLOGY AND THE *NOUVEAU ROMAN*

Mathematical analogues in fictional structures, from Lewis Carroll's *Alice* to Cortazar's *Hopscotch*, have appeared to some as mere ludic performances and to others as indications of deep parallel structures with implications that go beyond trivial games, especially when the analogies are discovered by critical study and not identified more or less openly by the author. When I first proposed (in 1972) the use of topological forms in the reading of Robbe-Grillet's novels, I did not foresee the writer's later adoption of the term itself in *Topologie d'une cité fantôme* (1976).

With the emergence of new forms of fictional structure in the French *nouveau roman*, many of them paradoxical and baffling at first sight, a number of corresponding new critical approaches appeared, ranging from those applied by the practitioners of "human sciences" (linguistics, communications, and the like) to the proposals of those who seek in sociological concepts the ultimate meaning of the works of such novelists as Robbe-Grillet. Critics like Roland Barthes and his structuralist colleagues point out the use of codes and messages, syntagmatic and paradigmatic structures, norms and infractions of norms, to explain such novels, with occasional reversions to phenomenological or "objectal" use of things, in greater or lesser proliferation, while Lucien Goldmann, Jacques Dhaenens, and the "philological sociologists" find in the *nouveau roman* implicit reflections and effects of liberal capitalism, in its late-twentieth-century state of autoregulation and government intervention. Dhaenens in particular proposed to read Robbe-Grillet's *La Maison de rendez-vous* as a "mediated expression of the new working class" and of its future members, university students![1]

---

1. Jacques Dhaenens, *"La Maison de rendez-vous" d'Alain Robbe-Grillet: Pour une philologie sociologique* (Paris, 1970).

Other critics have attempted to develop systems of novelistic analysis that, instead of leading outside or away from the text, lead into it in a new or deeper sense. The outstanding example of this group is Jean Ricardou, whose demonstration of verbal interlockings in Claude Simon's *La Bataille de Pharsale* and Robbe-Grillet's *Projet pour une révolution à New York* rivals for these works—which are not ostensibly based on puns, anagrams, syllabic transfers, semantic interchanges, and the like—the erudite findings of critics of novels in which such principles have in fact been proved present, such as Joyce's *Finnegans Wake* and, especially, the works of Raymond Roussel, whose importance as an early inventor of generative fictional procedures has become increasingly apparent.[2] In addition, critics like Julia Kristeva have expanded the notion of the text to that of the *intertext*. This intertext may come from two main sources: from the ensemble of an author's works (which may increasingly, as one sees in the novels of Robbe-Grillet, Claude Ollier, and others, contain elaborate self-references and reintegrations of elements from earlier works by the same writer) or from the interlocking between the text of one author and that of another (as in Ricardou's use of the eight-letter word *abeilles* from a novel of Ollier as a "generator" of innumerable elements in *La Prise de Constantinople*).

Having from the outset of my work on Robbe-Grillet attempted to delineate the various fictional *forms* found in his novels and films, I was led at an early stage to use, in a manner somewhat similar to that of Jean Rousset dealing with baroque literary structures, analogies from mathematics and geometry. The notions of circles, spirals, figure eights, Y and T forms, labyrinth boxes and corridors, and comparable figures proved, I thought, not only useful in discerning the actional structure of this or that novel but also necessary in arriving at a correct abstract statement of the author's own compositional intentions.[3]

Geometric patterns indeed appear to offer striking formal analogies to the structure of innumerable important modern works: cycloid displacement, ellipses, *vrilles* or double circular-staircase movements, chessboard designs and arrangements, and other more or less complicated figures may be discerned in, for example, such novels and films of Robbe-Grillet as *Les Gommes*, *Le Voyeur*, *L'Année dernière à Marienbad*, *Projet pour une révolution à New York*, and *Trans-Europ-Express*. At times

2. Jean Ricardou, *Pour une théorie du Nouveau Roman* (Paris, 1971). For Roussel's penetration into Anglo-American criticism, see Rayner Heppenstall's *Raymond Roussel* (Berkeley, 1967).

3. Clear proof of the geometrical-mathematical nature of Robbe-Grillet's novelistic planning is given by the projected use of the alchemistic number circle of the tail-biting Ouroboros serpent as discussed in my book *Les Romans de Robbe-Grillet*, 3d ed. (Paris, 1971), 38n.

these forms closely resemble game structures, in a conjunction that suggests a fertile relationship between games and literature.[4]

On closer examination such works as *La Maison de rendez-vous* and *Projet pour une révolution à New York* seem to invite analogies from a domain beyond, or different from, that of simple two- and three-dimensional geometry, since what is involved is structural relation among contiguous and interpenetrating textual surfaces. This domain may be called fictional topology. A rudimentary illustration would be the comparison of the overall structure of *Finnegans Wake* to a Möbius strip. Considering the written text of Joyce's novel as an uninterrupted, continuous band of words (since the last words are actually those that precede and lead into the first words of the book), we may say that only the Möbius strip (a "twisted" band that has only one true surface) could contain in space the unbroken continuum that for practical reasons has been printed on the successive pages of Joyce's novel. Or again, in topology the problem is frequently that of discriminating between adjacent areas or surfaces: in a novel like Robbe-Grillet's *La Jalousie*, different time areas lie side by side in the chronological or dechronological pattern. The formal solutions arrived at by the author (two different times separated by an ambivalent phrase, for example) constitute devices of fictional and verbal boundary construction.

Topology represents the primary intellectual operation capable of revealing the modalities of surfaces, volumes, boundaries, contiguities, holes, and above all of the notions of *inside* and *outside*, with the attendant ideas of insertion, penetration, containment, emergence, and the like. All these conceptions may be identified in recent fiction, especially in the novels and films of Robbe-Grillet. The question inevitably arises as to the legitimacy of introducing paraliterary systems, including topology, into fictional analysis. Proponents of the procedure may use two lines of defense. The first and more conventional argument in favor of "injecting" a nonliterary discipline like topology into the study of novel forms would be that the similar structures thus revealed must result from inherent intellectual categories, à la Kant, or deep mental structures, à la Lévi-Strauss. Comparable arguments have been advanced for analogies between literature and art or literature and music, or the manifestations in various arts of general stylistic tendencies such as the baroque. It is a point of view that, however strongly denied by many critics, reappears continually and probably lies at the base of much of the current thought that goes by the loose name structuralist criticism.

The second defense of a topological approach would, by insisting on

4. See chapter 11, "Games and Game Structures in Robbe-Grillet."

the analogical, metaphorical use of nonliterary thought in textual analysis, bring topology (in this instance) into the realm of literature itself, by conferring upon it through the metaphorical process the status of a self-contained literary operation. In the examination of new, paradoxical fictional texts, this method would argue that the use of external systems can lead to clarification and fuller understanding, on condition, of course, that the provisional assimilation into the texts of metaphoric forms from outside the diegetic frame or fictional field be held in strict control and never confused with the fiction itself. Viewed in this way, topology may serve to define "demonstrable" analogical structures in the novel and thus form a legitimate extension of textual analysis.

Some examples may be cited to illustrate the procedures involved. Let us first consider the function of the *hole*, or structural opening, and later the *reentrant forms* found in relations between container and thing contained. The two will, of course, be ultimately linked; it is through a hole that structural reentry must occur. Since the novels of Robbe-Grillet furnish the most convincing illustrations of these operations, I shall refer almost exclusively to them.

No doubt the evolution of the *ellipse* in narrative structure forms an important background for the contemporary use of fictional holes. Without retracing the long history of the ellipse, we may note the proliferation of ellipses in the influential novels of the American thirties (the "undescribed" rape of Temple in *Sanctuary*, Dos Passos's deliberate lapses in the reported careers of his characters, and the like) and in many French novels written more or less in their wake. As I mentioned earlier, Claude-Edmonde Magny in *L'Age du roman américain* has written brilliantly of the transfer of such elliptical structures (reinforced by the example of the movies) from the novels of Hammett and Hemingway to the works of Camus, Malraux, and other writers. Magny—indeed, as a chapter title indicates—argues that the whole objective or, as she calls it, the "behaviorist" novel of the immediate pre–World War II period is based on the "Art of the Ellipse." The detective story, subjected in France to more intellectualized analysis than in England or the United States, proved a fertile field for investigating the fictional ellipse, and certain minor but ingenious novels in this genre (Dorothy Hughes's *In a Lonely Place* or Agatha Christie's *The Murder of Roger Ackroyd*) now appear definitely as precursors of the narrative hole or *trou* as found in the works of Robbe-Grillet, Simon, Pinget, or other new novelists who employ the device.

While the hole per se is not exactly a topological figure, it becomes one upon the passage through it, or the establishment around it, of groups of elements that have been suppressed within the hole or that are used to fill it with true or false "content." The hole of *Le Voyeur* is a case in point: basically, there is a hole or ellipse in the action or time scheme of the novel (the hour around midday during which the protagonist, Mathias, may be presumed to have committed the sadistic murder of a young girl whose body is thrown over the cliffs into the sea). This hole is first of all present analogically at many levels: a large blank in the printed text; a "blank" in Mathias's memory; a hole burned by a cigarette butt in the pages of his notebook; the vanishing point of the two branches of the figure eight that outlines countless images of the novel, at the intersection of two loops, which is the geographical point at which Mathias leaves the eight-shaped road around the island to seek out and (presumably) kill Jacqueline. All of these reinforce the hole, which in the author's own words, "finally engulfs everything." Into this hole Mathias attempts to stuff his various alibis (the imaginary visit to the Marek farm, for example), creating a virtual content that is further complicated by the "confirmation" of his false account by the young Julien (probably the true "voyeur" of the novel). Gradually the events of the murder begin to emerge from the hole in Mathias's memory, when repeated attempts to prevent their upsurge (conveyed through word blockages and the like) yield finally before an almost complete reconstruction of these events hidden within the hole. In a sense, the narrative attains completeness only because of and through the hole. The hole functions to permit a tremendous release of creative energy at various levels (implied psychology of the protagonist, resolution of ambiguous plot, stylistic tensions, and so forth). A paraliterary analogy from astronomical observations: the curious doctrine of black and white holes in the matter of the universe, as described by Penrose and Hjellming (see *Time*, 21 June 1971). According to their view, matter disappearing into a "black" hole may emerge elsewhere through a "white" one, resulting in a powerful release of energy. Certainly the aesthetic tensions of *Le Voyeur* are created in large measure by first suppressing "matter" (i.e., plot or action) in a black or hidden hole, then allowing it to escape later through a sort of "white" hole in Mathias's consciousness, thus to return, with great energy, to the diegetic universe from which it had been made to disappear.

The hole in *Le Voyeur* (Jean Ricardou derives the title itself from the word "voy[ag]eur" by making a "hole" in the middle of the word) is a single and central gap at the heart of the novel. A subsequent novel, *Dans le labyrinthe* (1959), uses repeated disappearances and emergences of scenes as well as passages through analogues of the hole, both positive and negative. At times the image of this hole is itself hidden, as in the many transitions between the narrator's room and the street outside that occur as the descriptive movement leads to the implicit word "window," hidden behind another word, "curtain," whose mention leads imme- diately to the transfers from inside to outside. Thus the hole itself be- comes a sort of virtuality. In other examples, the negation "No!" surges up in the text, leading to the immediate disappearance of a scene, which may emerge elsewhere in time or space. *Dans le labyrinthe* contains, moreover, a kind of scientific analogue of hole structure that the author himself has incorporated into the novelistic field. In the narrator's room stands a lamp whose shade is pierced by a small hole that causes the im- age of the bare lamp filament to be projected, through the well-known principle of the camera obscura, on the ceiling. This "white hole" is doubled by its "black" opposite: a fly, walking around the edge of the same lampshade, functions as a sort of "antihole" that paradoxically (but in scientifically exact fashion) causes the same filament to be projected, in movement this time, on the walls of the room. As this counterimage approaches the hidden window and falls upon the curtain, the text passes through the concealed "hole" to emerge as a description of an analogous lamp filament burning in a streetlamp below, against which the soldier- protagonist (the double of the narrator-in-the-room) materializes. The narrative content, expelled from the interior through a double hole im- age, emerges elsewhere in the fictional field, outside, in the labyrinthine city (*Dans le labyrinthe*, p. 14).

It is in Robbe-Grillet's *Projet pour une révolution à New York* (1970) that the principle of the hole is advanced furthest beyond what in *Le Vo- yeur* may be called two-dimensional techniques of the ellipse surrounded by more or less ambiguos boundaries in the fictional field. In *Projet*, the notion of the hole leads into multifold topological areas wherein passage into and out of the hole involves relations between container and thing contained. An independent parallel to these topological manipulations of novel structure may be cited from an interesting, if relatively unknown, journal, *Radical Software*. In one of several articles applying topology to new systems of viedotape programming, John Lilly uses the analogy of the locked room problem:

> Mathematical transformations were next tried in the approach to the locked room. The concept of the key fitting into the lock and the necessity of finding the key were abandoned and the rooms were approached as "topological puzzles." In the multidimensional cognitional and visual space the rooms were now manipulated without the necessity of the key in the lock.
> Using the transitional concept that the lock is a hole in the door through which one can exert an effort for a topological transforma- tion, one could turn the room into another topological form other

than a closed box. The room was in effect turned inside out through the hole . . . leving the contents outside and the room now a collapsed balloon.

Most of the rooms which before had appeared as strong rooms with big, powerful walls, doors, and locks now ended up as empty balloons. These operations were all filed . . . under the title, "the key is no key."[5]

Projet illustrates various modalities of the passage of inner contents of houses or rooms through a keyhole into a narrational conscience on the outside. Once established there, what was interior or contained is then treated as exterior or uncontained or, in other terms, as the primary narrational field. One of the agents in this operation is the locksmith-*voyeur* (the word at the same time refers back to the novel *Le Voyeur* and forward to the new type of lock-penetration structure of *Projet*) called Ben Saïd, who becomes at various times a first-person narrator and who "penetrates" closed areas of the story by looking through a keyhole. The incidental fact that the keyhole of a New York Greenwich Village house, such as that described in *Projet*, would hardly be of the old-fashioned open type implied in the novel is irrelevant: once the *idea* of the keyhole appears, the transformation from closed Yale lock to open keyhole to abstract hole through which the narrative may pass becomes structurally or transformationally correct. At other junctures in the story line, windows (broken or unbroken), doors (to rooms, between subway coaches, etc.), or even poster representations of such openings serve to channel the narrative flow.

Thus the hole must be treated as a mechanism of transfer from inside to outside, related to the interplay of interior duplications whose evolution in Robbe-Grillet's *Projet* is from the separate or independent inner model illustrated by the "African novel" being read by the characters of *La Jalousie* (in accordance with the Gidian *mise en abyme*) to inner texts, both visual and verbal, whose contents not only mirror the primary story line but emerge from the confines of the interior duplication itself to blend with or to constitute the main narration. A first step in this procedure occurred with the café-scene engraving of *Dans le labyrinthe*, whose description becomes animated and moves out into the main fictional field. The cover of the Chinese illustrated magazine in *La Maison de rendez-vous* (1965) serves as an opening for passage between sectors of narrative. Inner duplication, having served as analogy (in *La Jalousie*), as point of departure (in *Dans le labyrinthe*), and as a liaison device (in

5. John Lilly, "Programming and Metaprogramming," *Radical Software*," no. 3 (Spring 1971).

La Maison de rendez-vous), now evolves into an unfolding of the narrative line, with ever more complicated entanglements of container and thing contained that make *Projet* a fictional "topological puzzle."

The main vehicles of topological manipulation of the fictional field in *Projet* are, besides the keyhole discussed earlier, a paperback detective novel, its gory sadoerotic cover illustration, the auditory text of certain tape recordings, and the oral or written "reports" made by one or more character-narrators. In the case of each of these, the narrative line (the exterior, or "uncontained" line) penetrates the duplicated field (inner novel, illustration, recorded material, report) in such a way that it becomes impossible to distinguish between container and thing contained. The procedure bears a close resemblance to the topological figures of the well-known Klein bottle and the more recently described Klein "worms." The paradox of the Möbius surface, mentioned earlier, is reinforced in Klein forms by paradoxes of contained and uncontained volumes, offering more exact and more illuminating analogies than does the Möbius strip for the multidimensional interpenetrations of narrative fields in such a novel as *Projet*.

Referring to the illustrations (fig. 1), we may follow the analysis offered by Warren Brody:

> The Klein form is different [from conventional geometric forms such as the doughnut or sphere]. There's no inside; there's no outside. Instead, you have a contained tube and an uncontained tube, a contained hole and an uncontained hole from which you can make interlocking Klein forms in a chain. . . . Any part of the form can touch, contact, communicate with, flow with any other part, and the parts, the whole, in time flow through each other in a way the doughnut and sphere cannot. We have a quality of continuousness in the form and at the same time intracontainment or infolding. . . . [The Klein form] is permeated by context. It has no walls. Yet it uses its structural infolding for maintaining itself changing in a sufficiently regular way to find new relations.[6]

These new relational modes appear strikingly in *Projet*. We may consider the narrative analogues to be: main narrative line as "part uncontained," mirror image of the narrative line within an inner duplication as "part containing," and inner narrative line no longer distinguishable from the duplicating text as "part contained." In *Projet* (p. 91), the *je-narrateur* "takes refuge" in the paperback crime novel his sequestered "niece" is reading. As he pages through, seeking the passage illustrated on the cover (which the heroine, Laura, holds behind the keyhole through which Ben

6. Warren Brody, "Biotopology," *Radical Software*, no. 4 (Summer 1971).

Saïd peers), he becomes caught up in the inner fiction that parallels, down to names, events, and places, the established situations of the novel. Not only this, but the main action now progresses within the pages of the inner novel: as the narrator pursues the interrogation of JR, the subway sequence of Laura and her little gang of boys is developed. The reader loses sight of this ambiguity of container and thing contained until the narrator suddenly states "I close the book" (112). Since the events that are ostensibly "read" in the inner book form an integral part of the remaining narrative, one can no longer regard the paperback as a simple analogy to the main novel, as in *La Jalousie*, or as a generative or transitional technique, as in *Dans le labyrinthe*. In a sense, the later appearance in the "main" text of references to events developed in the secondary text suggests the mode illustrated by panel 5 of figure 1, "deliberate anticipation of containing." An analysis of the way the sound track of Laura's tape recorder makes an "impossible" bridge between different times and places (cf. 69, 133), while erasing distinctions between them, would show similar modes of containment, anticipation, and infolding.

Much of the complicated Kleinian infolding of a work like *Projet* represents a predictable or at least logical extrapolation of previous literary structures, ranging from inner plays, Pirandellian ambiguities, shifts from one plot level to another, and the like to confusions between superimposed stories as, for example, in Roger Leenhardt's film *Le Rendez-vous de minuit* wherein the cinematic heroine watches a film (in which she also plays the heroine) whose visual frame, as it disappears beyond the edges of the real cinematic frame, no longer permits a distinction between separate sections of the plot. The shock of recognition produced by comparing the structural forms of certain new novels with those of recent topology seems to suggest that forms of the imagination, on which the novel must depend, tend to undergo an evolution very similar to that affecting the abstract thinking of boundary mathematics. That such comparisons have been made by the young video programmers of the *Radical Software* group, who have found in Klein forms models for their multilevel video recordings, shows the wide applicability of topological constructs to creative art forms. Without proposing a structuralist view of innate mental configuration as the underlying explanation of such singular coincidences, we may nevertheless find in them, if only at the metaphoric level, suggestive reinforcements of the belief in a possible or eventual "unified field" theory of the arts as systems of thought.

A final word may be added concerning the topological aspect of game structures in the novel. In *Projet*, the flamboyant finale occurs on a vast chessboard on whose squares reappear varous scenes and elements of the fiction. Complicated rules govern the movement from one square to

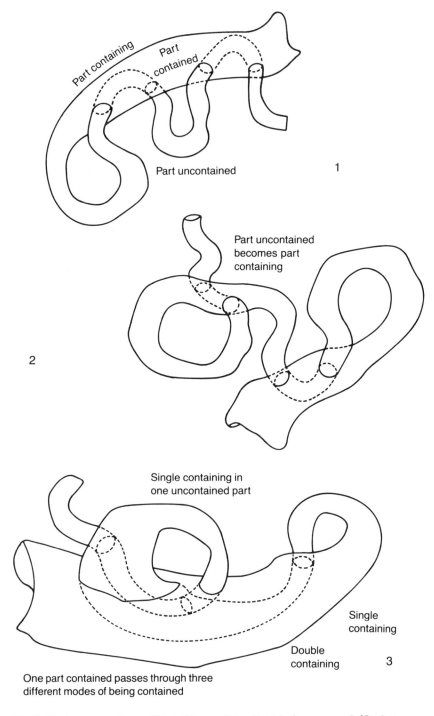

Fig. 1. Klein worms. From "Klein Worms," *Radical Software*, no. 3 (Spring 1971): 2.

Inspin—part contained continues containing itself ad infinitum

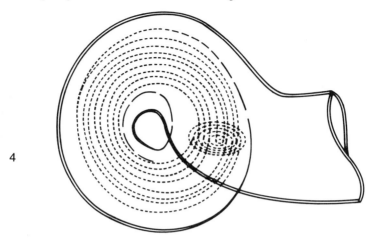

4

Deliberate anticipation of containing

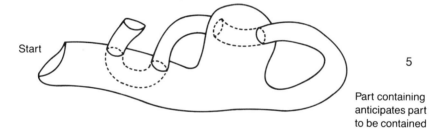

Start

5

Part containing
anticipates part
to be contained

Anticipation—part to be
contained anticipates the
containing

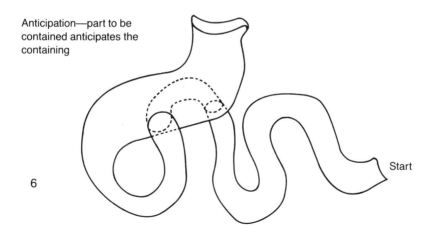

Start

6

another. One senses that Robbe-Grillet as *scriptor ludens* is creating, once more, an inner analogy of the creative fictional process. Inner duplications and games rejoin topology.[7] New forms foreshadow each other in expanding series of container, part contained, and part uncontained, until the primitive image of the legendary serpent Ouroboros biting its tail, with which Robbe-Grillet began as an incipient novelist in the 1950s, yields to the multiple twists and turns, entries and reentries, of Klein worms or more elaborate forms, as yet scarcely discernible. The novel, like the other arts, writes Robbe-Grillet in *Pour un nouveau roman* (p. 143), may anticipate systems of thought. If this is the case, then the critic is justified in going outside the novel, even into domains as seemingly remote as topology, to put new forms of fiction into a wider perspective.

7. See chapter 11. For inner models, see chapter 10, "Interior Duplication." Early examples of literary prototopological infolding may be found in the medieval narrative structure of *entrelacement*, used by Chrétien de Troyes and others: cf. Eugène Vinaver, *A la recherche d'une poétique médiévale* (Paris, 1970).

7
MODES OF "POINT OF VIEW"

Since the dawn of the art of narration there has existed either consciously or unconsciously the problem of the "point of view" adopted by the author, the narrator, or the storyteller, just as by analogy there has existed the question of the perceptive order that determines or organizes forms of painting, music, and architecture. A narrative, like a painting, always originates from a point of view (at times even multiple or ambiguous) that ostensibly justifies it and gives it value. From time to time there occur in one art form or another modifications, indeed upheavals, in techniques that cannot be otherwise accounted for, such as the revelation brought about in painting by the invention of linear perspective. Each great style contains its own system of point of view: the baroque, realism, impressionism, cubism, abstract art. The novel could not escape this law: each novelistic style is characterized by a set of procedures that allows the novelist to situate himself with respect to his work and to situate his characters with respect to one another. With the invention of the cinema, in which problems of pictorial and narrative genres overlap, we witness the development of an entirely new vocabulary that has but one purpose, to express accurately the point of view of the camera (and therefore of the author) in every filmed scene: close-up, dolly shot, downward and upward perspectives, forward and reverse camera angles, and so forth. Film thus becomes a veritable testing ground for point of view where the confrontation of visual and narrative aspects serves to shed light on many a problem heretofore exclusively associated with the novel.

It is always useful to provide, however briefly, some historical background for a problem. I do not know who first spoke of "point of view"[1]

1. A colleague pointed out to me that Victor Hugo (in *Préface de Cromwell*, 1827) wrote: "Le théâtre est un point d'optique." In fact, Hugo also added that the critic should place himself "au point de vue de l'auteur" to judge a literary work. Obviously, Hugo's ideas,

(perhaps an anonymous critic in the *British Quarterly Review* of 1866); but in any case, it was Henry James who gave this term its definitive meaning, namely, "post of observation" from which a narrative is built and which can occasionally, thanks to a clever rotation of viewpoint, shift from one character to another. Set forth about 1890, this seemingly simple idea (whose aesthetic ramifications have yet to be exhausted) was picked up in the United States in 1920 by Percy Lubbock in his treatise *The Craft of Fiction*. Lubbock codifies the elements of a system of well-defined categories of possible points of view and, to paraphrase, argues that a narrative can be structured:

1. In the first person (a *persona* narrating and who is only rarely the nominal author);
2. in the third person (an omniscient author who knows all the thoughts of his characters and who can intervene and comment on the action, or who tries hard to remain "absent" or "neutral"); and
3. using variable points of view whereby the author can shift from one mode to the other, employ flashbacks, have a particular character tell the story, limit his omniscience to a single character or to several, stay outside the thoughts of the characters (in order to act objectively), mix interior monologues with objective descriptions, express himself alongside or behind a character, and so forth.

Of course Lubbock lists only processes and techniques known in American novels of the time; namely, those that can be found since James, Faulkner, Hemingway, Dos Passos, and others. With the evolution of the contemporary novel, Lubbock's list seems increasingly inadequate. But critical analysis always depends on creative action; and since Aristotle the spelling out of literary principles always takes place *after* the fact.

With James and his followers, the principle of point of view stems especially from a consideration of a structural or aesthetic order, whereas in France it seems that this principle stems from questions of a moral or philosophical order. It is in the name of "freedom," ironically enough, that Jean-Paul Sartre, in his crucial article of 1939, attacked Mauriac for violating his own principle in *La Fin de la nuit*.[2] It was also Sartre who linked point of view to metaphysics, which, he affirms, always underlies novelistic technique. Sartre turns to Einstein's theories on relativity of "frames of reference" in order to deny the possibility of a privileged observation point that would allow the expression of "absolute truth." In

though perhaps anticipatory, are not yet the modern conception of point of view as the optical/verbal position of the author or of a narrative personage.

2. Jean-Paul Sartre, "François Mauriac and Freedom," *Situations*, I (1939).

Sartre's existential aesthetic system, which seems to lead to a phenomenology of the novel, a narrative text can contain only the immediate information needed for a sudden awareness of the world on the part of one or more "existing" characters.

The debates on point of view were late in coming to France, but after arrival they multiplied rapidly, especially when the cinematic example took its place next to novelistic techniques. The period following World War II saw a burgeoning of studies of point of view in film and literature, as well as comparative studies between the two genres. Albert Laffay, Jacques Doniol-Valcroze, Jean-Pierre Chartier, and others published (in *Les Temps Modernes* and *La Revue du Cinéma* in 1947 and 1948) articles that deal at length with analytic techniques of point of view in film and novel. The works of Claude-Edmonde Magny on the American novel and on the relation between the novel and film (especially the earlier quoted *L'Age du roman américain*) made possible, thanks to the principle of point of view, ways and means not only to explain the works of Faulkner and Dos Passos, but also to better understand the post-Sartrian novel, which today is referred to as the new novel or *nouveau roman*.

One single, rather second-rate film, *The Lady in the Lake* by Robert Montgomery, inspired about 1947 a string of essays on point of view. Among the critics were people as diverse as Chris Marker, Albert Laffay, Claude-Edmonde Magny, and Georges Blin. To gain a full measure of the importance suddenly acquired in France by the idea of point of view as an essential element of novelistic structure, one need only note that in the three principal works on the novel that appeared in 1941–43 there is not one reference to the question. I refer to *Paradoxe sur le roman* by Kléber Haedens, *Puissances du roman* by Roger Caillois, and the famous issue of *Confluences* titled "Problems of the Novel." Today, on the other hand, there is hardly a critic who does not know the requirements and the systems of point of view; and one can witness, just as in the case of the film critics, the development of an impressive vocabulary capable of expressing its nuances.

Whereas the analysis of point of view is recent, the problem, as I stated earlier, has existed since the beginnings of the art of narrative. Fairy tales always begin with "Once upon a time"; it is only in the twentieth century that the child interrupts his mother (as Nathalie Sarraute says) to ask, Who's saying that? Back in the era of the live storyteller (ancient Greece, the Middle Ages, etc.) it was not thought paradoxical to have a professional storyteller tell the tales. His narrative nonetheless contained all the elements of the problem of point of view (dialogue, analysis of the characters' thoughts, intervening stories, flashbacks), for every narrator takes on the point of view of a fictitious witness or an imaginary character.

Starting with the very first novelistic forms, the quest for verisimilitude triggered a set of artificial processes: alleged "sources" (rediscovered manuscripts, letters, etc.), the narrator's remembrances, stories told by someone else, narratives in an imaginary first person—in a word, all those modes of presentation that Robert Brasillach illustrates in his ingenious novel *The Seven Colors*, and others still.

Before discussing systems of point of view among more recent novelists, it is fitting to examine quickly certain significant processes that can already be found in earlier authors, starting with Stendhal. As Georges Blin has eminently pointed out in *Stendhal et les problèmes du roman* (Paris, 1954), we know that Stendhal was working from both sides of the fence in his novels. In spite of the objections Sartre makes with regard to such a process, Stendhal was both within and outside his characters; as Blin put it, he would at the same time engage in restricting the field and intruding on it. According to Blin, even those parts of *Le Rouge et le noir* that appear at first to be written from a point of view other than Julien's (Mathilde's, for instance) are as if filtered through the observing consciousness of Julien, the protagonist. The reader penetrates the consciousness of Mathilde, so to speak, only *as if Julien were looking in.* And just like Sartre after him, Stendhal consciously based his technique on an essentially metaphysical theory of sensations. Since outside the realm of sensations nothing can exist, Stendhal assigns to narrative a wholly modern relativism of perception.

The case of Balzac, who it is generally agreed represents the "omniscient" narrator par excellence, seems to point to a regression in the development of point-of-view techniques. Not only does Balzac situate himself inside and outside his characters, but he hopscotches from one character to another as the spirit moves him without any worry about "posts of observation." His descriptions are the result of some abstract or nonexistent point of observation that allows us to see everything at the same time, even inside closed bureau drawers. Whereas Stendhal brings us the world of Julien (despite the author's intrusions, which do not destroy the illusion of the point of view of the hero), Balzac brings us only the world of Balzac; we read the thoughts of a Balzacian character as if *Balzac were looking on.* At most, a deeper quest might reveal in Balzac a very limited, virtually unconscious effort at sharing the viewpoint of some of his characters; these techniques, like those of Dickens, have remained at a fairly primitive level.

It has been pointed out that Dickens, who overwhelms us like Balzac with detailed descriptions and exaggerated characters, did become preoccupied with modes of presentation that tend to restrict the visual field to one privileged character, as illustrated by his use of the first-person narrative in *David Copperfield*, for instance.[3] In fact, research proves that several preoccupations with modern novelistic structures and terminology were already in evidence among English writers well before the first essays of Henry James in 1888. The term "point of view," as I mentioned above, appears as early as 1866, as do other phrases such as "point of sight," "standing point," and narrative "through" a character.[4]

It would take too long to give a full account of the research done on Flaubert in the area of point of view. Flaubert, who insisted on being impersonal and objective to the point where he would include in his narrative only what a third-party observer could witness, turned out to be, perhaps in spite of himself, the innovator of techniques of interior perspectives: the "discours indirect libre" or free indirect discourse (which often functions as an interior monologue); the "participating" vocabulary that allows the author to filter the world through the consciousness of a character, all the while maintaining the third-person mode (she was thinking, she was delighted, she convinced herself, it seemed to her, she would have liked, she recalled, she perceived, she fancied, she would have desired); and what Jean Rousset calls the "modulations" of point of view to allow passage from one character to another.

These elements are discussed in studies by Léon Bopp, Erick Auerbach, Allan Tate, and Georges Poulet, as well as in the article by Jean Rousset, "Madame Bovary or the 'Book about Nothing,'" which concentrates on one aspect of the art of the novel in Flaubert: point of view.[5] In 1944 there appeared in the *Philological Quarterly* an original article, virtually unknown in France, entitled "*Voir* as a Modern Novelistic Device." In it Anna Hatcher picks out several passages from *Madame Bovary* among them, for example, *Emma le vit qui disparaissait . . .* , "Emma saw him disappearing") in order to demonstrate that sentences of the type "A sees B leaving" function in Flaubert so as to *detach* the reader from character B in order to draw him closer to character A, thus allowing the reader to remain on the scene with A without following B, who is leaving. (And this is precisely the case for the statement mentioned, taken from the scene with Emma and Bournisien, where the reader has just accompanied the latter into church without Emma.) But Jean Rousset, in his fertile article, points out that this technique can work for Flaubert in just the opposite way. "When [one] has to step away from the heroine," Rousset writes, "how does one do it without breaking the thread? By

3. See Fred W. Boege, "Point of View in Dickens," *PMLA* (March 1950): 90–105.
4. See Richard Stang, *The Theory of the Novel in England, 1850–1870* (New York and London, 1959), especially the parts entitled "The Disappearing Author" and "Point of View."
5. "Madame Bovary ou le livre sur rien," in *Saggi e richerche di letteratura francese*, vol. 1 (Milan, 1960).

using Emma's glance; . . . carried off by Emma's stare, the reader leaves her for the object of her stare, and accompanies the other character from that moment on." Of course, both critics are right; the *regard* (glance) in Flaubert can work both ways. Besides, the study of the perspective structures in *Madame Bovary* is far from exhausted. One can find in this novel overlapping devices involving simultaneous or double points of view (such as "they did not bother sharing their feeling about it [il ne songeaient pas à s'en raconter la sensation], so engrossed were they in their all encompassing reverie [trop perdus qu'ils étaient dans l'envahissement de leur rêverie]."

The works of Maupassant (that frequently underestimated author, whose theories on implicit psychology and objective representation herald certain aspects of the new novel) offer an interesting illustration of a technical process involving the aesthetics of point of view. In *Bel-Ami*, through the sequential use of *mirrors*, the protagonist Georges Duroy can read on his own face the outline of his psychological state, every time he looks at himself in the mirror, while the reader also looks on. Without relinquishing the point of view of his main character, it would have been theoretically impossible for the novelist to furnish us with the description of the progressive changes Bel-Ami's face undergoes, unless Bel-Ami actually sees himself either in the mirror or through some other means.

E. D. Sullivan in *Maupassant the Novelist* (Oxford Press, 1954, 87 ff.) and Martin Turnell in *The Art of French Fiction* (New York, 1959, 216 ff.), study meticulously the development of the mirror theme in *Bel-Ami*, but without mentioning the significant role mirrors play in the notion of point of view. For Sullivan the presence of the looking glass used by Bel-Ami forces the hero to take stock of himself and of his "progress" in the world; for Turnell, the reflected images even facilitate his progress by "encouraging" Duroy. But with the exception of the initial description of Duroy (made by the author before the text definitively espouses the point of view of Duroy the protagonist), we have no information on Bel-Ami's face other than what Georges himself gathers while looking in the mirror. If Maupassant had not been preoccupied by the idea of furnishing us with a novelistic universe observed from the hero's *affective* center, he could, of course, have drawn up a series of physical portraits of Georges without having recourse to secondary images provided by mirrors. Besides, nothing stands in the way of the mirror's working simultaneously toward psychological ends (as seen by Sullivan and Turnell) and technical ends (objective pretext for self-observation). It should be added, however, that in two places at least in *Bel-Ami*, Maupassant changes point of view in order to adopt that of Mme Walter (in the scene of her meeting with Duroy in the church and in the scene where she learns that

Duroy wants to marry her daughter). There is also a short scene (the one preceding Duroy's second marriage) presented from a completely impersonal angle. Very much like Flaubert, Maupassant has his own "inconsistencies" of method, despite his otherwise systematic use of the unique point of view.

In order to trace the development of the new novel in terms of point of view, we should also examine in summary form a number of techniques and theories of the novel before World War II. André Gide's reflections on the relations between the novelist's intentional field, or even that of his double within the novel, and the perspectives of a character "with" whom a particular scene is described or unfolds—either in the novel itself or in the fictional writer who situates himself within the novel—these relations are already of a complexity that reminds one of the *nouveau roman*. As I have mentioned elsewhere, the example of André Malraux (especially in *La Condition humaine*) illustrates the development of an aesthetic of point of view closely tied to that of films, with its shooting angles, optical perspectives, and scenic ties usually associated with the transitions among the characters to whom the author successively ascribes a point of view.

The modalities of a style or a technique always emerge out of precursors' attempts and examples; but once they acquire a past, the new styles seem free to take on new faces, unanticipated aspects, complex and sometimes surprising forms and structures.

We can safely say that no one could have anticipated not too many years ago the sudden wide and varied uses of narrative pronouns. The choice available to novelists seemed to limit itself more or less to a third-person "he, she" (objective or participating) or the first-person "I" (of a character or pseudocharacter within the text). Here and there an occasional "we" (such as at the beginning of *Madame Bovary*), which generalizes the narrator, an occasional *on* (French personal but indefinite pronoun approximately equivalent to the English "one"), which dilutes its presence as an ostensible observer, or for that matter a "he," which disguises an "I" identified only later on (as in Camus's *La Peste*), a rather daring development at the time. But all of a sudden the so-called *règles du je* (the pun is Jean Pouillon's and refers to the *règles du jeu*, or "rules of the game," which is virtually identicial phonetically to *règles du je*, or rules of the first-person "I") turn out not to be such hard-and-fast rules after all. Critics discover even among the novelists of earlier periods (Proust, for instance) certain uses of a *je* either double or multiple, with several levels of significance, as well as uses of *il* with which the reader can identify as much as if not more than if he were reading a text in *je*. Then, following a number of innovations in the new novel, critics made a concerted effort to explain the use of a pronoun that seemed new—namely, the narrative *vous* ("you"). Aspects of this phenomenon are more fully dealt with in chapter 9, "Narrative 'You.'"

Are we dealing here with an "artifact of form," a tour de force, as is the *vous* in Butor's *La Modification* according to certain critics? It does not seem so. On the contrary, this effort to get rid of all pronominal references to oneself seems to allow for two things to happen at the same time: the creation of a means of escaping conventional systems of narrative pronouns, systems long since weakened, and also the development of a new and powerful psychological realism. For the various pronouns (*il, on, vous, je*) were becoming cumbersome and at times intolerable from the point of view of what Sartre calls the metaphysics of the novelist, or incapable of eliciting the sympathy or empathy of the reader with respect to the protagonist or the storyteller. When the latter kept on saying to us *je*, "I," we progressively ceased to identify ourselves with him, just as in real life we almost always refuse this identification with those who tell us about their adventures or their troubles, constantly saying "I," "I," "I." The tendency of the supposedly impersonal pronouns "he, she" to appropriate for themselves, by means of self-projection, the reader's point of view made the choice of the narrative pronouns even more difficult. A strict behavioral objectivity seemed undermined by the uncertainty regarding the point of view that would be adopted by the reader within narrative texts, in spite of the pronominal system used by the author. As far as the effects of the first person are concerned, the failure of the "I" contaminated the narrative in its very essence. Furthermore, the attempt to eliminate the "I" from narrated texts proved remarkably true to life (do we say to ourselves "I" when we live out and think out our lives?) and capable of expressing the presence and the vision of the world of a central storyteller in such a way as to appear to effectively constitute a true discovery in the realm of the modalities of point of view. Without the word *je*, which in fact tends more and more to *prevent* self-identifications, the reader of a Robbe-Grillet text like *La Jalousie* is forced to adopt the point of view of the narrator and follow him in his thoughts and movements. An important corollary to this principle is the elimination from the narrative of all the analytic apparatus or commentary that besets the conventional novel; instead of receiving from the author a series of psychological principles already worked through, the reader creates in himself the motives, the reactions, the emotions for which the text supplies him with objective support.

When the point of view within a novel shifts from one character to another, the structure becomes very complex. The problem of different fields, or different camera angles in a film, was already raised by such authors as

André Gide (we can even refer to the intertwined relations between the author and characters such as Edouard of *Les Faux-monnayeurs* with his novel within a novel, a kind of *je de miroir*, to use another pun based on the phonetically similar expression "jeu de miroirs," or game of mirrors).

In his novel *Degrés* (1960), Michel Butor set out on several familiar paths: reconstructions of one day in the past, setting up of a certain "volume" of already experienced actions (by presenting them under various focuses), yet another attempt on the part of a narrator, as is almost always the case with Butor, to confer upon the events of his life a structure, if not a meaning. The originality of the work does not, therefore, rest with its themes but emanates almost entirely from the mechanics of the points of view as developed in the course of the three parts of the novel. In part 1, a high-school teacher named Pierre Vernier addresses to his nephew Pierre Eller (the coincidence of the first names is intentional) "notes on our class . . . which are addressed to you for when it would be impossible for you finally to read them." Wishing to emphasize the uncertainty of a limited point of view "by multiplying the references . . . by shedding light . . . on the fields of probabilities," the narrator in part 2 yields the pen to his nephew, who apparently becomes the storyteller. However, the hidden "author" comes through from time to time in the consciousness of this new persona, so that we read, for instance: "In the evening you began to put together this text which I am continuing, or more exactly, which *you* are pursuing by using me, for, in reality, it is not I who am writing but you. . . . You try hard to see things my way." This point of view undergoes a final modulation in part 3. Henri Jouret, who is also Pierre Eller's uncle, now has the floor, but this time to stand in for a sick and dying Pierre Vernier. Jouret, like Vernier at the beginning, addresses his nephew by saying *tu* to him, but he keeps for himself a *je*, which occasionally causes textual gaps between countermovements of real and fictitious *je* pronouns. It is no surprise to hear the dying Vernier whisper at the end of the book, "Who is speaking?" For "Qui parle?" is the very password of point of view.

One will note in *Degrés*—as well as in *Le Planétarium* by Nathalie Sarraute and *Dîner en ville* by Claude Mauriac, two other new novels composed according to the principle of orbiting bodies or observation stations of points of view—a disturbing uniformity of tone in the diverse characters, especially if we compare these works with one such as *The Sound and the Fury* by Faulkner, where the styles of Benjy and Quentin, for instance, in the portions written from their points of view, are extremely differentiated. French authors seem to refer almost exclusively to the *content* of what is being said, rather than to verbal modalities of style, in order to situate the inside shots within the mosaic of the text or the plot. This prismatic effect produced by the points of view reflected within a work is closely related to the problem of the use of repetition or reflection in its entirety or reduced, partial, diminished, disguised, and deformed in its perspectives. André Gide in his *Journal* of 1893 was delighted to find in a work of art, "thus transposed at the level of the characters, the very subject of that work," a process he compares to that of the blazon, "which consists of placing within the first a second one *en abyme*." My chapter 10, "Interior Duplication," examines the examples in painting and literature cited by Gide. Examples from his own works (from *Narcisse* to the interior novels such as *Les Caves du Vatican* and *Les Faux-monnayeurs*) are well known.

The use of inner duplications in fact led in several directions. Gide apparently saw the connection between the interior drama in *Hamlet* and his own use of inner novels. Aldous Huxley, in *Point Counter Point*, as discussed elsewhere, extrapolated Gide's process to project an interplay of ten novels, one inside the other, and constructed from different points of view, with differing angles: medicine, mathematics, and physics. One would think it was an effort to develop the idea expressed by Goethe when he wrote that images repeated and reflected in mirrors, far from fading, reaffirm themselves in a "more intense and truer view."

The plays within plays,[6] closely tied in literature to new techniques of ambiguity (stage narrators, confusions among actors and spectators, real/unreal Pirandellian characters, parodic or burlesque repetitions of scenes in Beckett and Ionesco) bring up the question of *aesthetic distance*. Since Bullough, Ortega y Gasset, and Bertold Brecht, critics have been arguing about the power of *distanciation* in the function of a play. For some, the inner duplication works as a way of *destroying* aesthetic distance, while for others it only underscores the artificiality of the theatrical allusion and increases the so-called *Verfremdungseffekt* (Brecht) or the "dishumanization" (Ortega) that separates the spectator from the work and pushes him to a moral judgment.[7]

Among the new novelists, we can point to numerous examples of duplications of subject matter within the work. These reflections or partial summaries are always related to the question of point of view; namely, they represent at the level of the characters the same set of meanings (or

6. See R. J. Nelson, *Play within a Play* (New Haven, 1958).

7. See Oscar Büdel, "Contemporary Theatre and Aesthetic Distance," *PMLA* 76 (June 1961): 277–91; P. A. Michelis, "Aesthetic Distance and the Charm of Contemporary Art," *Journal of Aesthetics and Art Criticism* 18 (September 1959): 1–45; Jacques Howlett, "Distance et personnes dans quelques romans d'aujourd'hui," *Esprit* 7–8 (July–August 1958): 87–90; Jean Carta, "L'Humanisme commence au langage," *Esprit* 6 (June 1960): 1113–32; and the interview with Alain Resnais in the same issue of *Esprit*.

ambiguities or even nonmeanings) as does the novel as a whole for the reader. In a quasi-allegorical rather than symbolic fashion, these inner structures enhance the general meaning of the work by reflecting it.

Each novel by Robbe-Grillet contains one or more illustrations of Gide's techniques of *mise en abyme*. In *Les Gommes*, objects (statues, curtain patterns, etc.) and other references to the Oedipus legend reflect the story of the protagonist. In *Le Voyeur* we read the legend of the island where the story takes place, which expresses in mythical form the essentials of the plot. The title and poster of the film *Mr. X on the Double Circuit*, as well as other details in the same novel (the statue in the square, the painting on the wall), have similarly something to do with the story of Mathias. The narrator's wife in *La Jalousie* perhaps first considers cheating on her husband while reading a novel, lent to her by a neighbor (her lover?), that relates a story of infidelity and jealousy. (Not the first time since Paolo and Francesca that a novel has served to seduce a woman!) *Dans le labyrinthe* is organized around a painting representing a key scene in the novel that either moves or freezes successively when the action passes through this "opening" in the labyrinthine structure. This tendency by Robbe-Grillet to seek duplications within his works reaches a higher point with each successive novel and film.

One last aspect of the problem of point of view needs to be pointed out. In the new novel, we often witness what might be called the breaking down of allegedly realistic barriers that in the consciousness of the protagonist or of the reader separate the "real" from the "unreal." By refusing to explicitly "frame" one or another scene as "really seen" by one character or "imagined" by another, the author tampers with the linear perspectives (chronological, etc.) of conventional point of view and arrives at a new psychological realism. The meticulous descriptions of objects and movements found in authors like Robbe-Grillet do not in any way have a "photographic" or naively realistic purpose; they are, as I have frequently pointed out, rather *supports* or objective correlatives of a tacit psychology that endows them with implicit meanings. Each character of the novel *projects* upon the world his emotional and mental content in a way commensurate with his perception of this world. The best example is still that of Mathias in *Le Voyeur*: under the guise of a seemingly "impersonal" text we see unfolding hallucinations regarding false visits, nonexistent conversations, a sinister interplay of objects all in the shape of the number eight—the entire "world" of the protagonist, who without these visions would have no way of relating to us because, ontologically speaking, he would not exist.

If the point of view of a novelistic character must be changed into a sort of image-thought (all thought projects upon the world in a sequence of images more or less deformed depending on the character's level of desire, fear, and feeling, we may witness a series of profound changes in both genres, novel and film. The role of dialogue, for instance, is becoming problematic since it can easily be replaced by an "exchange of views" in the literal, visual sense of the term. If, on the other hand, dialogue is to remain an accompaniment to visual scenes, there will be tensions between scene and dialogue: a scene involving lies or half-lies where the dialogue does not square with the observable scene; a scene in which the gap between image and words stems from the fact that one character sees or imagines the visual scene while another speaks, and so forth. All of this can be seen in contemporary films. The novel will no doubt also follow this path in an appropriate way; and the reader will not so much have to ask himself (as does Vernier in *Degrés*) Who is speaking? but rather, Who sees, imagines, or recalls this?

Each modality of point of view refers to an ontology. The central problem will remain the same that has always existed: What justifies or explains the existence of a narrative text, this lying text that claims to be truthful, that comes to us from somewhere, from someone who is speaking to us from a hidden or ambiguous place, and that offers us an increasingly alien novelistic universe structured along the perspectives of an increasingly polymorphous point of view?

8
THE ALIENATED "I"

The mode of first-person narration, as I have pointed out, is commonly considered to be one that involves the reader in a sympathetic way with the point of view, emotions, and experiences of the persona who speaks through the "I" pronoun of the text. At the same time, the first person is generally looked upon as an automatic solution to the structural problem of the "justification" of a given narration; that is, as an answer to the always implied question, Who is speaking? or Where does this text come from? The illusion of justification is usually buttressed by additional structural devices, such as the pretense that the text is written as a diary or memoirs, recounted to someone who later sets it down, or otherwise explained in an ostensibly realistic fashion, so that the reader may assume it is in some way attached to, or extracted from, life itself. In its purest form, first-person narration dissimulates the origin of the narrative text, creates an illusion of reality, and allows or causes the reader to project himself to the utmost into the situation of the narrator, sharing not only his thoughts and feelings but his very language, since the "I" who speaks becomes, in theory, the "I" of the reader, creating such strong identification with the narrator-protagonist that the reader succumbs to the illusion that he is himself experiencing the events and emotions his mind apprehends through the intimate connivance of the first-person mode.

In many early examples of first-person fiction, the conscious or unconscious search for the most complete kind of justification for the existence of the written or printed text leads to the allegation by the "I" protagonist of one or more compelling motives for setting down his story. This "pretext" becomes in some cases an organizing principle: in the Spanish classic picaresque novel *Lazarillo de Tormes*, for example, Lázaro insists on the purpose of his recital of events, which is, after first establishing the proper background in the earlier episodes of his life, to explain to the mysterious "Vuestra Merced" to whom the text is addressed, and above all to reveal the exact nature of the protagonist's present domestic situation with respect to the virtuous or nonvirtuous conduct of his wife. Channeling all the narrative currents in the direction of a central purpose not only contributes to the unity of the work but reinforces the reader's sympathetic assimilation of the text. In other words, first-person narration, in its earliest and simplest form, seems to stand at the opposite pole from any notion of alienation; and its protagonists appear to the reader not as exiles or outsiders, but as alter egos whose experiences are shared in an illusory state of almost complete reader identification. To this, first-person narration adds the advantage of banishing authorial omniscience, or narrative perspectives lying outside the frame of reference of the protagonist's own mentality, thus appearing "hypermodern" from the outset. And since the early "I" narrators were mostly "reliable," telling all they knew and never lying about their actions or motives, fiction in the first-person mode seemed to attain a kind of harmonious perfection denied to novels cast, for example, in the competitive third-person mode with its problems of omniscience, authorial intervention, and attendant complexities.

But the illusion of self-contained unity and sufficiency of first-person narration begins to break down under scrutiny. Examination of its structures shows them to be less stable than they seemed. Even the simple, almost naive narratives of the first-person *picaro*, like Lazarillo, raise structural problems related to the "double register" of their ostensible chronology. Nearly all the recounted episodes exist in an incompletely fused merging of two distinct systems of time: the time of the event being related, which is the time of the protagonist-in-action, and the time of the actual writing or narration, which is usually after the last of the narrated events. The interplay of the two times leads to a dilution of the "solid reality" of the narrated events through interventions of the narrator commenting on past actions from his present vantage point, as well as through anticipatory phrases such as "little did I suspect," "had I known," and the like, alluding to developments the protagonist, in "real" time, could not have foreseen. These commentaries, intrusions, and judgments made from a later viewpoint closely resemble the intrusions of the traditional third-person omniscient author and produce in the reader corresponding effects of aesthetic or projective distancing. Thus problems of chronology, theoretically nonexistent in straightforward first-person narration, are far from absent from such texts, whose earliest examples show evidence of the same difficulties with time structures that will affect such modern counterparts as, for example, Camus's *L'Etranger* (1942).

As important as time may be as a source of perturbations in the mode of the first person, we must look at other aspects to search out the development of features that work against the original function of this mode as a technique of justified realism and against its traditional status as the mode par excellence of reader identification. This analysis requires questioning the fundamental assumption that empathy and self-projection are necessarily enhanced by the use of the set of first-person terms "I," "me," "my," and the like. In theory these terms acquire in the reader's mind the force of his own ego, so that when the narrator or protagonist says "I" the reader assumes the identity and the responsibility of the personal pronoun, thus validating the text in a way impossible with other modes. Analysts of first-person narration, like Bertil Romberg,[1] have expressed little doubt concerning the psychological truth of such an assumption. What is overlooked is that in assuming the reader will identify the "I" of the text with his own psychic "I," a serious error results if the reader, instead of adopting a *speaking* stance with respect to the words of the text, instead adopts a *listening* stance. Each of us is in fact surrounded in real life by a chorus of first-person narrators all addressing us with "I," "me," and so on, yet most often, as I have already said, we do *not* project ourselves fully (if, at times, at all) into the outlook of the narrator or speaker. Frequently, instead of sympathizing with him, we find his constant self-reference increasingly distasteful and alienating. Pascal's dictum "Le moi est haïssable" ("the 'I' is hateful") applies not only to one's own egotism, but also to that of those we listen to. Such considerations come prominently into view when we reach the stage of development in first-person fiction at which a clash develops between the moral outlook of the narrator and that of the reader. Of this, more shortly.

A corollary problem to that of first-person reader projection is the degree of projection created or allowed by the traditional third-person narrative mode. According to usual theory, it must be less than that afforded by the first person. But is this always true in practice? Does the use of "he" or "she" establish and maintain aesthetic or psychic distance by virtue of its "otherness," or does the reader in some cases bypass the third-person pronoun and associate himself just as closely with the subject as in first narration, or even sometimes more closely, since the ego barrier is now absent? No doubt an analysis of the question from the viewpoint of the third person would reveal a situation as ambivalent as that of the first person. Structurally, the third-person mode develops its own perturbations, so that it is rarely if ever found in the pure, "behavioristic" form that Claude-Edmonde Magny described in the chapter on the objective

---

1. Bertil Romberg, *Studies in the Narrative Technique of the First-Person Novel* (Stockholm, 1962).

novel in her study *L'Age du roman américain* (1948). Nearly all third-person novels teem with "bridging" techniques used to shift the viewpoint to the first person: self-quotations to represent thoughts, *discours indirect libre*, interior monologue or stream-of-consciousness soliloquies, and the like. Even passages that constitute modulations between two third-person sequences relating to two different characters (as so often found in Flaubert's *Madame Bovary*, for example) are connected by "subjective" bridges (such as the use of the verb *voir* in Flaubert) that depend for their effectiveness on intense reader projection into first one, then the other of the third-person subjects. It is as if the reader makes little distinction in his psychological reaction between an "I" and a "he" or "she" passage; in fact, how many readers can be sure of recalling correctly whether a given novel was written in the first or third person? Just as first-person discourse cannot guarantee identification, so third-person style cannot prevent it or maintain psychic distance. The study of distance and identification in film fiction, where a true first person or "subjective camera" mode is rarely if ever sustained (compare the great polemic over Robert Montgomery's *The Lady in the Lake*), may yet shed light on this issue.

Setting aside the important but difficult question of the role of projective psychology as it may affect in either a general or a specific sense the operation of the first-person as opposed to the third-person narrative mode, we may isolate certain technical features in "I" narration that serve to undermine its establishment of intimacy or sympathy in the reader's response. One of these, related also to the fundamental question of what Wayne Booth in *The Rhetoric of Fiction* (Chicago, 1961) calls the "unreliable narrator," is ellipsis, or suppression of information by a first-person narrator, whether to conceal actual events (as in the famous example of the first-person murderer in Agatha Christie's *The Murder of Roger Ackroyd*, who relates everything *except* his own guilty act), or to cover up or avoid explaining motives, as in the case of Camus's Meursault. At times the opposite of ellipsis may occur, that is, deliberate lies or inventions that replace the truth not with a void (always suspect to an alert reader), but with a false and misleading virtuality concealing something quite different. It appears, in fact, that ellipsis leads to one of two main lines of evolution in first-person narration, both producing a type of alienation. In ellipsis, the protagonist or narrator estranges himself from the reader by baffling him as to the reasons for his conduct (as in *L'Etranger*), and finally eliminates even the pronominal system that attaches him to the reader (as in Robbe-Grillet's *La Jalousie*). In the other line of development, which reaches its climax in a number of premodern masterpieces, alienation is achieved by widening the psychological and moral gap separating the personality or character of the narrating "I" from that of the normal or nominal reader (against whom the narrator often measures himself, vaunting the difference between his own value system and that of his reader). A classic example of this type of narration is Dostoyevski's *Notes from Underground*, distant echoes of which may still be heard in such twentieth-century works as Jerome Weidman's *I Can Get It for You Wholesale* or John O'Hara's *Pal Joey*, wherein the reader's projective sympathy is contested at each moment by his moral rejection of what he reads.

Analysis of technical and structural features such as time or ellipsis would lead to an incomplete appreciation of first-person narration if we were to leave out the basic question of the appropriateness of such devices to the basic theme or themes of the fiction involved. Here one of the earliest and greatest manifestations of the first-person novel provides a fertile field of exploration: the aforementioned Spanish picaresque novel, so thoroughly studied by scholars and yet still so productive of new insights into the art of fiction, as demonstrated by a brilliant scholar, Francisco Rico, in *La novela picaresca y el punto de vista* (Barcelona, 1969). The relation to the theme of alienation is obvious: the *pícaro* is, by definition, a social exile, even if he later rejoins society and is reconciled to its values. What is the role of narrative mode in this "literature of the delinquent," as it is termed in A. A. Parker's well-known study?[2]

The three great *pícaros*, Lazarillo de Tormes, Guzmán de Alfarache, and Pablos the "Buscón," all narrate in the first person. Lazarillo relates what he does, what he thinks (or, strictly speaking, what he did and what he thought), but analyzes himself little or not at all. The beginnings of ellipsis may be seen in passages where the protagonist's intentions are already known to him at the moment of the event being narrated but are not revealed in the text until later, as in the famous episode of his inducing the blind master who has tormented him to jump against a stone column. The sudden shock caused in the reader by the unexpectedly cruel outcome of such an action provides a good example of the generation of identificative tension within the first-person mode: we share, to some extent, Lazarillo's gleeful revenge and even laugh with him from the first-person vantage point; yet another side of our being senses that the incident is not really humorous, and we are to some extent outraged by Lazarillo's cruel trick and ashamed of our own collaboration with his act. Moral distance divides us from the projective sympathy created by the narrative mode, and we are, for a time at least, estranged from the hero.

2. A. A. Parker, *Literature of the Delinquent: The Picaresque Novel in Spain, 1599–1753* (Edinburgh, 1967).

At the same time, the double temporal register (Lazarillo the protagonist seen in retrospect by Lázaro the narrator), reinforced by the explanatory attitude of the author-narrator (which at another level serves as a unifying compositional principle for the novel), gives a curious split first-person effect that, by establishing a kind of inner distance between Lazarillo and Lázaro, tends to alienate one from the other and to drive a wedge between both and the reader.

Francisco Rico points out (in the aforementioned study) a number of ways first-person viewpoint affects the structure and meaning of *Lazarillo de Tormes*. In this "novela . . . sometida a un punto de vista" ("novel subordinated to one point of view"), it is "el *yo* quien da al mundo verdadera realidad" ("the 'I' that gives the world its true reality"), since the things and acts of this world have no importance until they are incorporated into the protagonist's subjective apprehension. A third-person mode would have implied a stable, consistent universe whose meaning is given once for all time by the equivalent of an invisible, omnipresent deity represented metaphorically by the Flaubertian conception of the artist. In Rico's view, it is precisely the use of the first person that allows us to accept without indignation the suspension of ethical imperatives and social conventions, that permits us to laugh when Lazarillo plays his trick on the blind man: "Cuando Lazarillo *mata* al ciego (o poco menos) nos reimos, en vez de indignarnos (como hariamos—hay que suponer—en la vida ordinaria)" ("When Lazarillo *kills* the blind man [or nearly does so] we laugh, instead of becoming indignant [as we would—one must suppose—in real life]"). Moreover, for Rico, there can be no doubt about "la caracterizacion del autor como *outsider*, en que insiste L. Lázaro Carreter" ("The character of the *pícaro* author as outsider, as alienated observer").

Guzmán de Alfarache adds to his first-person narrative a large number of moral reflections, calculated to enlist the reader's comprehension and sympathy; since the underlying value system is close to that of a presumed norm shared with the reader, little tension or alienation is engendered. There are, however, many passages of what Rico calls "superficial narration," a kind of objective presentation of bare events "de forma idéntica a tantos *thrillers* de hoy . . . limitándose a la acción, a la intriga interesante, a lo seductor de la trama" ("identical in form to many thrillers of today . . . limited to actions, to the interest of the story line, to the seduction of plot"). The resulting objectivity puts a kind of glass wall between protagonist and reader. In addition, the split between Guzmán the actor or protagonist and Guzmán the author or narrator finds expression in a new stylistic technique, a use of second-person soliloquy with anticipatory suggestions of the device of narrative "you" as developed by

Michel Butor and a number of contemporary novelists (see the next chapter). A. A. Parker discusses Guzmán's use of ellipsis in the suppression of the information "that it is a repentant and not a hardened sinner who is talking." This is a form of unreliability in that the first-person mode is manipulated to deceive the reader. On becoming conscious of the deception, the reader has a reaction of mistrust, uncertainty, or alienation from the *yo* narrator.

In the case of Pablos in Quevedo's *El Buscón*, we find first-person narration used to a great extent in an almost entirely objective or behavioristic manner, limited to the presentation of facts. "Pablos," writes Francisco Rico, "apenas tiene . . . 'vida interior'" ("scarcely has any . . . 'inner life'"). Yet this ostensible objectivity is accompanied by a wholly subjective phenomenon: elaborate wordplay indulged in by Pablos, casting over fictional reality a veil of linguistic inventions that the reader must constantly penetrate. Distance becomes a verbal phenomenon masking (or perhaps indirectly explaining) Pablos's unavowed motive for writing the text. As in so many modern first-person novels, psychological or motivational suppression occurs; the reader must himself supply the missing psychic force that has caused the narrator to narrate; the text becomes a datum to be accepted or rejected by the reader himself, in accordance with his own contribution to the work, as described by José-María Castellet in *La hora del lector* (Barcelona, 1960).

In sum, the picaresque novel in Spain uses first-person narration both structurally and thematically as an alienation device, involving suppression, unreliability, temporal and pronominal double registers, and other techniques producing tensions between narrator and reader, between identification and rejection, between sympathy and alienation.

It is in the nineteenth-century novel that the current of evolution of the alienated first person depending upon a widening gap between the narrator's moral values and those of the reader, rather than upon primarily technical features such as ellipsis or double register, reaches its peak of development. As the gap widens, new tensions are created, since the ostensible difference between outlook of narrator and reader nearly always conceals (by statement or implication) a secret identity between speaker and listener. This powerfully ambiguous author/reader relationship is found not only in fiction but in other genres, such as lyric poetry. When Baudelaire, after depicting the perverse pleasure that the monster Ennui takes in the contemplation of suffering and evil, says to his reader, "Tu le connais, lecteur, ce monstre délicat, /—Hypocrite lecteur,—mon semblable,—mon frère!" the poet makes explicit the principle that the reader's moral rejection of evil is only a hypocritical avoidance of self-realization. Even the guilt-ridden and obsessed "I" narrators of Edgar Allan Poe imply indirectly that their idiosyncrasies are only extensions of qualities that the reader himself possesses. Nevertheless, the first-person protagonist in some works bases his whole raison d'être on strangeness and alienation from his fellowman. An outstanding *cas limite* of this genre is the novel by Dostoyevski mentioned earlier, *Notes from Underground*.

Everyone familiar with the work will recall the aggressiveness with which the anonymous narrator of *Notes from Underground* challenges mankind and separates himself from the "gentlemen" to whom he addresses his text, depriving the reader himself of his identity through the pluralizing form of the "you" he frequently employs. Here are some characteristic utterances:

> I am a sick man . . . I am a spiteful man. I am an unattractive man . . . I was a spiteful official. . . . But do you know, gentlemen, what was the chief point about my spite? Why, the whole point, the real sting of it lay in the fact . . . that I was not only not a spiteful but not even an embittered man. . . . That was my way. I was lying just now when I said I was a spiteful official. I was lying from spite.

And so on. Later, in the great scene of abuse and repentance during his confrontation with the prostitute Liza, the narrator uses the word that by implication underlies his whole being, speaking of himself as "me, an *outsider*." Throughout, the *shame* the protagonist feels for himself, which serves almost as a shield between himself and the reader, ostensibly prevents any sympathetic identification an unwary reader might be inclined to feel through the normal functioning of the first-person mode. In a sense, Dostoyevski was using Brecht's *Verfremdungseffekt*, or a variation of it; if the reader begins to project himself into the narrator's situation and emotions, his empathy is immediately checked by some hostile remark, some new shameful thought or action on the part of the narrator-speaker, so that the reader is constantly thrust back into a stance of moral judgment based on aesthetic or ethical distance.

Nevertheless, there is reason to think that Dostoyevski counted on a secret identification between readers and his spiteful narrator. Critics have written of the similarity between events and ideas in *Notes from Underground* and aspects of the author's own life and personality; but even without this, Dostoyevski's own footnote to the novel shows clearly that he considered his protagonist not only psychologically plausible, but even necessary in the society of his time:

> The author of the diary and the diary itself are, of course, imaginary. Nevertheless, it is clear that such persons as the writer of these notes not only may, but positively must, exist in our society. . . . He is one of the representatives of a generation still living.

In this fragment, entitled, "Underground," this person introduces himself and his views, and, as it were, tries to explain the causes owing to which he has made his appearance and was bound to make his appearance in our midst.

We see from the foregoing that the author first employs an alienated first-person narrator to establish and emphasize that his protagonist is a social and psychological outsider or exile, or even rebel, while at the same time counting on an eventual recuperation of his hero into the human family through a higher recognition of the presence in any reader, if not in all readers, of all the shameful, guilty, ignoble thoughts and impulses that the writer of the "notes" discovers in himself and to which, with an openness that the reader would perhaps be incapable of sharing, he confesses. In such a strategy Dostoyevski employs with consummate skill the one narrative mode best suited to his dialectic of identification/repulsion: the first person.

The case of Franz Kafka illustrates to what extent twentieth-century fiction mixes narrative modes in a significant new way. George Szanto has discussed this admirably in his book *Narrative Consciousness* (Texas, 1972), bringing out that although most of Kafka's works are written ostensibly in the third person, the tone of the narrative voice remains that of an implied first person, distinct from the tone of an observer or omniscient author. Writing of Kafka's "The Judgment," Szanto says:

> That it is not third person point of view should by now be obvious; the story cannot be understood from outside itself. That it is not first person is also obvious—not only is the "I" of such narration absent, but empirical, "realistic" first person narration is also undiscoverable. . . . One knows what is happening only according to the narrator's subjectivity; the external world is rendered incomplete, edited by the narrator's eye. Consequently, the events that shape Kafka's fiction can be comprehended only if one remembers that their significance derives from point of view. (pp. 46–47)

This tendency of modern novelists to use mixed or contaminated modes has become so widespread that some theorists, like Wayne Booth, now consider that too much attention has been paid to identification of viewpoint: "Perhaps the most overworked distinction," Booth writes in *The Rhetoric of Fiction* (p. 150), "is that of person." This is certainly true if analysis is limited to a mechanical identification of mode; but without mode as a point of departure we cannot, as Booth would have us do, "become more precise and describe how the particular qualities of the narrators relate to specific effects," an aim shared by most, if not all, critics of the contemporary novel.

We may now consider the most striking case of first-person narration so far produced in our century, that of Albert Camus's *L'Etranger*, whose title became *The Stranger* in the United States and *The Outsider* in England. (Let us not forget that Camus is also the author of *L'Homme révolté*, translated as *The Rebel.*) The novel's relation to the *theme* of alienation is therefore self-evident, and all readers of the book will recall how Meursault is condemned to death not really because he has murdered an Arab on an Algerian beach, but because his life and personality are considered alien to the society he lives in, an intolerable challenge to its bourgeois values, all the more so because his defiance, as Camus says in one of his prefaces, involves a refusal to lie and an insistence (somewhat as in the case of the narrator of *Notes from Underground*) on telling no more or less than the truth.

Setting aside the moral issues thus defined (about which a great deal could be said), how does first-person point of view fit into the design of a novel that openly proclaims itself a study in alienation? First of all, Camus eliminates most if not all of the protagonist's subjectivity in a way reminiscent of the more objective passages referred to earlier in certain Spanish picaresque novels. Where the narrative mode might invite the reader to expect, as we find in Dostoyevski, an outpouring of inner feelings and thoughts, we encounter only a curious opacity. A persistent suppression occurs behind the "I" and other first-person forms Meursault uses to recount his life. Sometimes this stubborn blankness is brought out in the answers he gives to specific questions put to him about his motives or feelings. When the concierge at the home where his mother has died asks him why he does not wish to see her body in the coffin, which has been opened so he may look at her a last time, he replies, "Je ne sais pas," I don't know, as he does later to Marie when she asks whether he loves her. When his friend Salamano conjectures that he must be unhappy over the death of his mother, Meursault states merely, "je n'ai rien répondu," I did not answer. When he sees that the threatening group of Arabs has observed his own group taking a bus to the shore, he adds, "mais je n'ai rien dit," I said nothing. The reader, frustrated and perhaps irritated by this uncommunicative *je*, is thus made to share the sense of the protagonist as a "stranger" that the jury itself later feels when Meursault is unable or unwilling to explain why he shot the Arab.

Even when Meursault is not refusing or failing to answer questions put to him by others, he remains silent about the important workings of his mind. When he expresses interest in something, it is usually in a commonplace or banality; he finds "intéressant" what the concierge has to say about burials, or the comments of his friend Raymond, or even the courtroom spectacle of his own trial. Never, until the last pages of the novel, where the tone changes abruptly, does Meursault express any serious concern over his own fate, and when at last he does, he seems to betray his own identity.

What is Camus's artistic purpose in this applying to the first person the outward techniques of the objective or behavioristic third-person mode? It is perhaps, first of all, to destroy the "projective illusion" that causes readers to inject empathically into fictional heroes a set of plausible motives, even if none are given. Readers do this habitually in third-person narration, and normally in the first-person accounts the speaker or protagonist himself provides the necessary clues or information. But when the first-person narrator sets up between himself and the reader an opaque screen that prevents the latter from seeing into the mind of the narrator, the tension created by this purely technical device serves to emphasize to the reader the "strangeness" of the narrator and his alienation from the norm. The reader's reaction is typically either to insist on putting motives into Meursault's mind despite what he says or does not say (as W. H. Frohock does when he explains the murder as an act of self-defense),[3] or to conclude that these curiously disturbing blanks in fact conceal nothing at all, constituting instead a radical rejection of all relationships of cause and effect in the psyche of a person like Meursault. (In this connection we should recall Sartre's analysis of the present perfect tense in which the novel is cast as a syntactical equivalent of causal rupture.) It is Meursault's subjective opacity in the first part of the novel that has most interested other writers; when later he launches into pseudophilosophical diatribes against society, the work becomes a more conventional embodiment of moral views expressed by Camus elsewhere, as in *Le Mythe de Sisyphe*.

Nowhere has suppression in the first-person mode been carried out more brilliantly, from both a technical and a thematic viewpoint, than in Alain Robbe-Grillet's novel *La Jalousie*. Since I have written extensively about this work, I may be permitted to summarize here a number of my observations. First, I found it expedient to invent a special term, the *je-néant* or absent I, to describe the innovative narrative mode created by Robbe-Grillet in this striking novel. Without going into the metaphysics of Sartrian *néantisation* as part of the process of the perceiving consciousness, the *je-néant* may be defined as a technique of the suppressed first person in which all pronouns or forms associated with it, such as "I," "me," "my," "mine," and the like, are eliminated. The protagonist of the novel is, of course, a jealous husband whose close surveillance of his wife and her probable lover, a planter on a nearby banana plantation, consti-

3. W. H. Frohock, "Camus," *Yale French Studies* 2 (Fall 1949): 91–99.

tutes the basis of the "narrative," which is expressed without any immediately discernible reference to self. The inner ellipsis that removed from
Meursault's narration all personal avowal is extended here to the apparatus of first-person language itself to such an extent that some early critics actually failed to realize that there was a central narrator, going so far
as to wonder where the husband was. Robbe-Grillet has spoken of a
creux, or hole (as in *Le Voyeur*), at the center of the narrative. It is here
that the reader installs himself and, seeing, hearing, witnessing what the
husband perceives, is obliged to assume the narrator's vision of things
and to create without verbal clues or instructions his own interpretation
of scenes and events. If the scene suddenly "shifts" from a description of
the wife's writing at a small table—as seen through her bedroom window
from the veranda of the tropical house—to an account of the quincunx
arrangement of banana trees in a certain sector, the reader must sense
that this veering of the text is the outward manifestation of the husband's
quickly diverting his glance from his wife as she turns to look toward the
window outside which he is standing.

If only the immediate dynamics of the husband's perceptions were involved, the mode would even so appear highly original; what lends it
added force and interest is the mental content of the hidden or opaque
first-person narrator; that is, the text itself contains all sorts of secondary,
associative materials, such as memories and imaginations. These subjective "visions," expressed in the same pseudo-objective way as the nominal action—by means of close descriptions of things, gestures, and events
as "seen" by the narrator—are always deformed, to a greater or lesser
extent, by the implicit emotional tensions of the jealous husband. Often
they are erotic or paranoid visions, as in the series of increasingly paroxysmal images of the *mille-pattes* or centipede whose crushing on the
wall by Franck, the other man, becomes a supercharged objective correlative for the husband's dread of his wife's being possessed by another.
At times purely hypothetical scenes develop within the seemingly objective text, revealing a murderous, imaginary wish fulfillment, as in the false
scene of the crash and burning of the car containing the wife and her
presumed lover. I have had a number of occasions to refer to Robbe-
Grillet's invention of the *je-néant* or absent I. Should we view this late
form of first-person narration as essentially different from the alienated
"I" of, for example, Camus's Meursault? For some readers it indeed produced estrangement: for them the husband's implied passivity—his failure either to take direct action *or* to express his jealous resentment in
conventional commentary—made of him not only an unsympathetic but
even an incomprehensible character. But it appears evident that Robbe-
Grillet intended, and successfully so, to erase the narrational separation

that all modes of narration, even the first person, inevitably create through the intrusion of pronouns and direct reference to the guiding consciousness behind the narrative. By transcending the opacity of Meursault's *je*, by turning the subjective vision of his narrator outward to real (or inward to imaginary) perceptive fields, Robbe-Grillet forces the reader not only to accept, but to reinforce with his own projective empathy the unexpressed inner feelings of a man who, hypostatized into a virtual personality, would undoubtedly appear as an implausible, alienated case history from some manual of psychopathology. In a sense, Robbe-Grillet has succeeded in a new and different way of achieving what Dostoyevski sought to do in *Notes from Underground*: to create an exceptional outsider whom the reader comes to accept, finally and for the duration of the narrative, as a possible form of himself. On the other side of alienation lies recuperation and reconciliation, neither of which occurs unless there is first the essential separation embodied in a particular technique of narrative mode.

It would be a mistake to suggest that the evolution of first-person narrative forms has ended or that it has reached a definitive stage. New experiments are in progress, most notably in the multiple, fragmented "I" forms in novels by practitioners of the *nouveau roman*, not only Robbe-Grillet, but also Claude Simon and Robert Pinget. Critics and historians of literary techniques will need to pay continuing attention to narrative modes and to examine at each stage the dialectic relationships that work for and against reader projection and reader rejection, leading to unforeseen and original syntheses of empathy and alienation.

9
NARRATIVE "YOU"

As I have noted, it is characteristic of the evolution of the art of fiction that from time to time a new, or apparently new, technique is launched involving narrative mode. The disappearing narrator of Flaubert and Maupassant, the post-of-observation narrator of James, the "double I" of Proust, the laconic/elliptical first person of Meursault in Camus's *L'Etranger* (reinforced by the systematic use, in French, of the *passé composé* to fragment the presentation of time), the unreliable narrator of Svevo's *The Conscience of Zeno*, the inarticulate idiot's voice of Benjy in Faulkner's *The Sound and the Fury*, the *je-néant* or "absent I" of Robbe-Grillet's *La Jalousie*: all these and many others are cases in point. The impact of such innovations and devices is doubtless due in large measure to the not always apparent fact, first enunciated by Sartre, that every novelistic technique implies a metaphysical attitude on the part of the author. The choice of narrative mode, far from being a mere "formal" feature of fiction, conditions its whole structure and determines to a great extent the receptive stance and aesthetic involvement of the reader.

Perhaps the best-known modern case of excitement provoked in readers and critics by a seemingly new technique of narrative mode is that of Michel Butor's *La Modification*, first published in 1957. The novel's large circulation (aided by its Prix Renaudot and no doubt by its "poetry of adultery" story of a weak Parisian who gives up his Roman mistress to return to his wife) focused attention abroad and in the United States on its use of narrative "you," widely regarded as "l'innovation de Butor" (Paul Delbouille) and subjected to elaborate critical analysis. In France the *vous narratif* of *La Modification* has been studied at greater or lesser length by Bernard Pingaud, Roland Barthes, Michel Leiris, Pierre de Boisdeffre, Paul Delbouille, Luc Estang, and numerous others.[1] In the

---

1. See below, notes 39 and following, for specific references.

United States the observation of W. M. Frohock may be considered typical: "Manipulation of the point of view—through the introduction of Butor's famous use of *vous* which attempts to implicate the reader in the action—produces a novel narrational dimension."[2] Oddly enough, none of these critics remembered previous uses of narrative "you" or sought to link it to the various forms of the second person employed by other genres in the past.[3]

In this examination of the problem I shall present a certain amount of historical background, through a survey of samples that cannot hope to be exhaustive; I shall trace the evolution of narrative use of "you" in the twentieth century and analyze the structural, aesthetic, and metaphysical significance of the second-person technique. Far from constituting a technical "trick" (though it could degenerate into exactly that, as certain later examples would indicate), narrative "you," although of comparatively late development, appears as a mode of curiously varied psychological resonances, capable in the proper hands of producing effects in the fictional field that are unobtainable by other modes or persons. Narrative "you" generates a complex series of perspectives whose multiple angles deserve to be explored.

How old is the use of narrative "you"? In earlier literature, especially in English or English translations of foreign works, "you" had a wide use as a generalized pronoun with a meaning roughly equivalent to "one" (or, often, as a rendering of the French *on*). The very existence of a widely used pronoun of the third person with a general meaning in French (*on*) has no doubt retarded the proliferation of the second person in that language (where the additional complication arises of the existence of *tu* as well as *vous*) and has caused the systematic use of narrative *vous* to seem more radical than "you" in English.

Leaving aside the imperative or command uses of "you," which appear to have little relation to the mode in question (though something of the psychology of the imperative undoubtedly tinges modern uses of "you"), we find a family of cases in which "you" invites the reader to place himself in the position of the writer, with the clear implication that *anyone* who so places himself will witness the identical scene or perform the same action. This is, for example, the "you" of guidebooks: as early as

2. W. M. Frohock, "Introduction to Butor," *Yale French Studies*, 24 (Summer 1959): 54–61. No survey of reviews of the English translation (entitled *A Change of Heart*) has been attempted; in general, Anglo-Saxon comment on such "technical" novelties tends to be superficial and summary.

3. See chapter 5, "International Aspects of the *Nouveau Roman*," in which I cited a few earlier appearances. I also made passing reference to the problem in "The New Novel in France," *Chicago Review* 15 (Winter–Spring 1962): 14–15.

Pausanias, we find: "If you get farther away, you seem to see a woman bowed down and weeping" (*Description of Greece*, 1, 21, 3). Note that such remarks hold a certain implication of the imperative: that is, "you" are instructed, if not ordered, to move farther away and look. Cookbooks frequently employ "you" in a similar manner; a passage of this kind that I have quoted elsewhere (and that was picked up with great glee by *Le Figaro Littéraire*) has Madame Express (a sort of French Julia Child) address her readers as "you": "Vous faites durcir 4 oeufs. Vous les plongez ensuite dans l'eau froide. . . . Vous nettoyez et lavez les champignons; vous les coupez en morccaux. . . . D'autre part, vous préparez une béchamel."[4] We approach here a whole group of "you" modes related to publicity, advertising, and journalese. These are related (as all modes of writing are) to literature and constitute deliberate stylistic tricks or mannerisms, borrowed consciously or unconsciously from writers of fiction or essays of more serious intent.

Newspaper columnists are predisposed to such tricks. Doris Lilly in the New York *Post*, while casually plagiarizing material from a London paper, couches her scene in a pseudonarrative "you" form: "With only these few things to clutter up your mind, you listen to a spot of conversation that an outsider would find impossible to translate. You mention this phenomenon to Abe Burrows and the two of you create a glossary of phrases heard at every party."[5] Note that the verb tense in such uses is almost invariably the *present*, thus further generalizing the action into something the reader not only *might have done*, but might conceivably *do*. Sometimes the thinly concealed autobiographical first person implied beneath the "you" of such passages betrays itself and breaks forth inconsistently but revealingly as "I." Thus another columnist, Whitney Bolton:

> MIDNIGHT MEANDERS: *You* leave a dinner given in honor of the men and women who have worked 25 years or more for one of the corporations whose payroll *you* infest and decide to walk up Park Avenue. . . . *You* look in a store window. . . . *You* decide that if you had $83,600 all in one piece, *you'd* retire to Mexico. . . . *I* have often wondered why people treat animals this way. . . . Then *you* remember a passing-by conversation. . . . *I* assumed. . . .[6]

The angry and sometimes irrational M. Etiemble of *Parlez-vous franglais?* has underscored the insidiousness of the meretricious appeal of

---

4. See the comment thereon in *Le Figaro Littéraire*, 5 August 1961, 3 ("Les Recueils de recettes de cuisine n'ont-ils pas inspiré certains romanciers?").

5. See *The New Yorker*, 20 February 1961, "Funny Coincidence Department."

6. Whitney Bolton, "New York Street Scene after Dark," from the Saint Louis *Post-Dispatch*, 27 November 1961 (italics supplied).

the first- and second-person pronouns employed by advertising in its constant assault—through self-identification—on the reading public. In one of the few relatively sound passages of a work strongly contaminated by anti-American bias and full of illogicalities, Etiemble writes:

> Reine du monde libre, du monde de la libre entreprise, la publicité . . . a fort bien compris qu'il n'y a de publicité payante que celle qui personnalise l'individu inconnu en client, en acheteur éventuel.
>
> Elle a donc transfiguré deux pronoms . . . celui de la première personne du singulier et celui de la seconde personne du pluriel. [Voici] des titres qui préfigurent prospectivement l'avenir du pronom *je: Je cuisine vite, Je nettoie tout, J'élève mon chat, Je me maquille, Je connais tous les vins, Je conduis mieux.* . . .
>
> Les spécialistes US du marketing ont depuis longtemps compris que, pour vendre à un particulier un produit standard tiré à des millions d'exemplaires, il faut que le vendeur valorise le pronom de la seconde personne et, ce faisant, personnalise l'acheteur du point de vue du vendeur: *English is good for you* [*sic*]. C'est pourquoi un journal soucieux de beauté, de produits de beauté, doit s'appeler *Votre Beauté*; une rubrique publicitaire de *Marie-France* s'intitulera donc *Choisi pour vous*: "Waterman a créé, spécialement pour *vous*, la plus grande cartouche du monde."
>
> En personnalisant par l'emploi systématique du *je* et du *vous*, chacun de objets jetés sur le marché, le sabir atlantique contribue, et non médiocrement, à rendre au monde actuel, robotisé qu'il est, nivelé, bulldozerisé, le "supplément d'âme" qui lui manque en français. . . .
>
> [C'est à tout ceci] que nous devons le soutien-gorge à *vos* mesures, parce que "sur mesures" ne personnalise ni *vos* seins, ni *votre* soutien-gorge.

Queen of the free world, of the world of free enterprise, advertising . . . has well understood that there is no profitable advertising other than that which makes the unknown individual into personal client, a potential buyer.

It has thus transfigured two pronouns . . . the first-person singular and the second-person plural. Here are titles that foreshadow the future of the pronoun *I: I Cook Quickly, I Clean Everything, I Raise My Cat, I Put on Makeup, I Am a Connoisseur of All Wines, I Drive Better.*

The American marketing specialists have for a long time understood that in order to sell to an individual buyer a standard product made millions of times over, a seller must enhance the second-person pronoun, and as he does so, give the buyer a personality with respect to the seller: *English is good for you.* [*Sic*] That's why a magazine that is concerned with beauty, beauty products, must be called *Your Beauty*; a publicity column in *Marie-France* will be called *Chosen for You.* "Waterman has created, especially for *you*, the biggest ink cartridge in the world."

By personalizing through the systematic use of *I* and *you*, each of the products launched onto the marketplace, Atlantic pidgin English contributes in no small way to give the present-day world, robotized as it is, leveled off, bulldozed, the additive of soul that is missing in French.

It is to all this that we owe the bra according to *your* measurements, because "customized" does not personalize either *your* breasts or *your* bra.[7]

It seems obvious, then, that "you" (as well as "I" itself) can be a dangerous pronoun that advertising and journalism may corrupt so badly as to render it virtually useless to "literature." If "you" is captured by professional copywriters, it will not be the first serious device to be thus kidnapped and violated.

The use of "you" in narrative appears to have been preceded by the use of "you" by lyric poets. The context, however, is usually narrative, though perhaps somewhat generalized: a description of a typical event or one so characteristic of a given situation that the reader can well imagine its appropriateness. Take Robert Browning's piece in stylized conversational tone entitled "How It Strikes a Contemporary," where the interchange with "I," far from identifying the poem as one of those Brownian monologues like "My Last Duchess," in which the speaker addresses the poet-listener, tends to give to the pronoun "you" a distinct first-person tonality. Notice that the verbs here are not in the present tense, but in a past corresponding to the French *imparfait* for repeated or customary action. This is another important aspect of a "you" that is not quite, in the strictest sense, narrative, since the true narrative action must necessarily be a single, unique past or present action. (For example, "You could look out of your window and see . . ." is not narrative "you." "Attracted by a sudden noise outside, you went to the window and saw . . ." *is* narrative "you.") Here is Browning:

> I only knew one poet in my life:
> And this, or something like it, was his way.
>
> You saw go up and down Valladolid,
> A man of mark, to know next time you saw. . . .
> You'd come upon his scrutinizing hat. . . .

7. Etiemble, *Parlez-vous franglais?* (Paris, 1964), 168–69, 250. Everyone has heard store clerks say the equivalent of "This is your Dacron and wool model."

> If any beat a horse, you felt he saw. . . .
> Yet stared at nobody, —you stared at him,
> And found, less to your pleasure than surprise,
> He seemed to know you and expect as much. . . .
> But never a word or sign, that I could hear. . . .
>
> I found no truth in one report at least—
> That if you tracked him to his home, down lanes
> Beyond the Jewry, and as clean to pace,
> You found he ate his supper in a room
> Blazing with lights, four Titians on the wall,
> And twenty naked girls to change his plate![8]

The only action here that could be interpreted as having occurred only once is "you stared at him," but even this is ambiguous. Incidentally, one of the appearances of "I" is accompanied by a typical hypothetical-general use of "you," as in conversation ("*I* found no truth in one report . . . that if *you* tracked him to his home"). Browning's lyrical "you," like the dramatic "you" of the monologues, is not yet narrative "you."

The closeness of lyrical "you" to the impersonal third person is illustrated by a Rimbaud poem of 1870, entitled "Roman." Here *vous* obviously stands for the poet as a generalized spokesman, not as Rimbaud in a particular or unique event, and the transition to *on* shows that the poet is "the" seventeen-year-old:

> Ce soir-là . . . vous rentrez aux cafés éclatants,
> Vous demandez des bocks. . . .
> On n'est pas sérieux, quand on a dix-sept ans.
>
> That evening, you go back to the brightly lit cafés,
> You ask for some beers. . . .
> One isn't serious when one is seventeen.

More varied, more intimate and personal, so that it almost, but not quite, becomes a true autobiographical-narrative use of "you" is the set of three pronouns (*je-tu-vous*) with which Guillaume Apollinaire projects both ideas and past actions in "Zone" (1913):

> A la fin tu es las de ce monde ancien
> Bergère ô tour Eiffel le troupeau des ponts bêle ce matin
> Tu en as assez de vivre dans l'antiquité grecque et romaine . . .
> J'ai vu ce matin une jolie rue dont j'ai oublié le nom . . .
> Ta mère ne t'habille que de bleu et de blanc

---

8. *The Complete Works of Robert Browning* (New York, 1899), 5: 3–6.

Tu es très pieux . . .
Vous n'aimez rien tant que les pompes de l'Eglise . . .
Vous priez toute la nuit dans la chapelle du collège . . .

Maintenant tu marches dans Paris tout seul parmi la foule . . .

Je suis malade d'ouïr les paroles bienheureuses
L'amour dont je souffre est une maladie honteuse
Et l'image qui te possède te fait survivre dans l'insomnie et dans
    l'angoisse . . .

Te voici à Marseille au milieu des pastèques . . .

Tu es à Paris chez le juge d'instruction
Comme un criminel on te met en état d'arrestation

Tu as fait de douloureux et de joyeux voyages . . .
J'ai vécu comme un fou et j'ai perdu mon temps
Tu n'oses plus regarder tes mains et à tous moments je voudrais
    sangloter.

In the end you are tired of that ancient world
Shepherdess oh Eiffel Tower the herd of bridges bleats this
    morning
You've had enough of living in Greek and Roman antiquity . . .
I saw a street this morning a pretty street whose name I have
    forgotten . . .
Your mother dresses you only in blue and white.
You are very pious . . .
You like nothing so much as the pomp of the church . . .
You pray all night in the school chapel . . .

Now you walk in Paris quite alone in the crowd . . .

I am sick of hearing the blessed words
The love I suffer from is a shameful sickness
And the image that possesses you makes you survive in
    sleeplessness and anguish . . .

Here you are in Marseilles among the watermelons . . .

You are in Paris with the examining magistrate
They put you in jail like a common criminal

You made painful and joyous trips . . .
I have lived like a madman, and I have wasted my time
You no longer dare to look at your hands and at every moment I
    want to sob . . .

Even admitting that the occasional *vous* of this poem may be a plural,
applying to the poet and his early companions, we are left with a shifting

movement between first and second persons that greatly enriches the lyrical mood of self-analysis and autobiographical recapitulation and evaluation. (The place names, the incident of Apollinaire's arrest in the affair of the theft of antique objects from the Louvre, and the frequent and tightly linked transitions to *je* leave no doubt that *tu* in "Zone" is Guillaume himself, and not some muse or other real or imaginary listener.)

Apollinaire's "you" has been much imitated in the twentieth century. An example will illustrate this influence, the case of Archibald MacLeish, who in "Cinema of a Man" closely suggests the French poet, and who writes in a similar vein in "Memory Green":

> Or you in Paris on the windy quai . . .
> You will stand in the June-warm wind . . .[9]

Of some interest here is the use of the future tense: not only does "you" generalize the past, but it may invite the future presence of the reader at an as yet unreal, but still typical, event.

In at least one well-known poem, "you" appears as a lyric-narrative pronoun used *on behalf* of the subject, whose actions are expressed as it were from without, as if contemplated by the poet who makes a portrait of and for the subject. Thus T. S. Eliot's depiction of the sordid quarters of a prostitute, to whom he says in *Prelude 3*:

> You tossed a blanket from the bed,
> You lay upon your back, and waited.

Curiously enough, only our external knowledge that this poem is written by a man permits us to identity it in an absolute sense as a genuine second-person poem of address *to* its subject. We experience a double tug of identification in reading, not only toward the woman described, but also toward the poet who speaks. If we did not know who wrote the poem, we might believe that it came from the subject herself and that the "you" was indeed not only lyrical but narrative.

Turning to prose, we find a more complicated situation. Obviously, we must eliminate all uses of "you" in oratory or elsewhere that are addressed frankly to an audience. Moreover, "you" as a substitute in English for "one" gives rise to all sorts of proverbial statements or maxims ("You don't have to be a chicken to recognize a bad egg," etc.) that have little or nothing to do with our subject. The conversational modalities of "you" include various devices, such as the use of "you" to avoid the appearance of excessive egotism or self-reference ("When you meet the president, you find him very friendly," etc.). Occasionally in writing we encounter an editorial "you," comparable to editorial "we" in that the egotistical "I"

9. Archibald MacLeish, *Collected Poems, 1917–1952* (Boston, 1952), 45, 47.

is softened and generalized, but much more directed to involving the reader, particularly when an evaluative judgment is to be provoked. An example is Somerset Maugham's essay "The Beast of Burden," in which the author tries to communicate to the reader a sense of participation in the scene, as if he were standing in the author's shoes. The effect is not unlike that of the Browning poem quoted above. Maugham writes:

> At first, when you see the coolies on the road . . . You watch their faces . . . and when you see them lying down . . . If you have tried to lift their bales . . . But you will be thought somewhat absurd if you mention your admiration . . . You will be told . . .
> You are filled with a useless compassion.[10]

Note that if reference is made to what must have been a *specific* past action (the author's mentioning, by implication, his admiration), this action is immediately generalized by the combination of "you" with the future tense ("you will be . . .") into something standard or typical and thus rendered nonnarrative.

It is difficult to say precisely when "you" first appeared in fiction as a narrative or quasi-narrative pronoun, as it is difficult to establish at this time a firm chronology of its modes. So far as I have been able to determine, few if any analysts of fiction have seriously considered the second-person narrative form. Percy Lubbock, the pioneer of point-of-view studies, neglects it; Joseph Warren Beach devotes a paragraph to it; Cleanth Brooks and Robert Penn Warren write as if only first- and third-person modes existed; E. M. Forster says nothing about it; the two chapters of Thomas Uzzell's treatise (which work begins, oddly enough, in the "you" mode: "If you have arrived and your novels are moving happily off the bookstore shelves and viewpoint has never haunted your sleepless nights") contain only a passing mention of the device, regarded as a curiosity.[11] Wayne Booth, in his voluminous and authoritative work *The*

10. Somerset Maugham, "The Beast of Burden," in *Selected Modern English Essays* (New York, 1940), 312–14.

11. Percy Lubbock, *The Craft of Fiction* (New York, 1947 [originally pub. 1929]); Joseph Warren Beach, *The Twentieth Century Novel* (New York, 1932), 280; Cleanth Brooks and Robert Penn Warren, *The Scope of Fiction* (New York, 1960)—see below for Warren's own *use* of the "you" mode in the novel; E. M. Forster, *Aspects of the Novel* (London, 1927); Thomas H. Uzzell, *The Technique of the Novel* (New York, 1959). On p. 219 of Uzzell's book "omniscience . . . mingled occasionally with a *second* person angle" is mentioned in connection with Lillian Smith's novel *Strange Fruit* (New York, 1944). Much of this novel does employ narrative "you," especially in the reflective-didactic mode (cf. p. 81: "You wonder why a man is like that. . . . You think of a preacher as soft-fleshed"), which sometimes shades off into preterite "you" narration (cf. p. 83: "What made you lose your head, what made you—you stood there staring at your mother, shocked at what you had said—").

Rhetoric of Fiction, referring to Butor's second-person novel, states in a footnote that "Efforts to use the second person have never been very successful" but cites no other illustrations.[12] Edouard Dujardin, in the study of the origin and development of the interior monologue that he published in 1931, after Joyce's recognition of Dujardin's role as precursor in the use of that technique, spoke of dramatic and fictional monologues in which "le personnage se dit TU, comme on le fait couramment dans certaines provinces," though he cited no examples, and he expressed the opinion that "la seconde et la troisième personne, en réalité, ne sont là qu'une première personne déguisée."[13]

Narrative "you" may be used intermittently and sporadically or consistently and systematically. Since Butor's *La Modification*, which first focused wide critical attention on the mode, is one of the relatively few works to use the second person in a systematic way and thus appears as a sort of summa of the problems involved, it seems logical to investigate first the nonsystematic appearances of narrative "you" in a sampling of authors. Can one determine what, if anything, causes "you" thus to appear? And when it does so appear, has it one or more identifiable fictional functions?

Perhaps the earliest use, however brief, of the narrative second person is found in Valery Larbaud's story "Mon plus secret conseil" ("My Most Secret Advice"), from the collection *Amants, heureux amants* (*Lovers, Happy Lovers*) of 1921. Most remarkable is the fact that, along with the second person, we find other elements similar to those of Butor's novel of 1957 (the Paris-Rome express and a lover with a sentimental problem concerning his mistress). Here is an excerpt from Larbaud:

> Monter, en gare de Naples, dans le Paris-Rome; arriver à Paris, gare de Lyon. La grille du Jardin des Plantes. Vous passerez par le Boulevard Saint-Michel et vous vous arrêterez devant le bureau de tabac de la place Médicis. . . .
>
> Lucas, il faut vous habituer à cette idée: vous vous attendiez à décrire, à partir de Salerne, une courbe inclinée vers la droite et suivant le rivage de la mer, mais c'est vers la gauche que vous serez entraîné. . . . Depuis que je suis dans ce pays les mathématiques m'attirent. . . . Mais tu es devenu paresseux; tu ne lis pas tes dix vers de Virgile tous les matins. Tu as beau dire, tu t'es rangé. Isabelle a fait de toi un bon citoyen.

12. Wayne C. Booth, *The Rhetoric of Fiction* (Chicago, 1961), 150n.

13. Edouard Dujardin, *Le Monologue intérieur* (Paris, 1931), 39. Although Dujardin held *tu* to be the natural form of self-address, critics who interpreted the *vous* of Butor's *La Modification* as self-address pointed out the damaging alteration of the novel's tone and effect that they think would have occurred had *vous* been changed to *tu*!

To get into the Paris-Rome in the Naples station; to arrive in Paris at the gare de Lyon. The gate of the Botanical Gardens. You will take the Boulevard Saint-Michel, and you will stop in front of the to-bacco shop on the Place Médicis. . . .

Lucas, you must get used to this idea. You were expecting to trace, from Salerno, a curve inclined toward the right following the seashore, but it is toward the left that you'll be carried away. Since I have come to this country mathematics draws me, but you have be-come lazy; you don't read your ten lines of Virgil every morning. Whatever you say, you have settled down. Isabelle has turned you into a good citizen.[14]

Clearly, although we are here precisely in the domain of the interior monologue described by Dujardin, where both *tu* and *vous* are a "dis-guised first person," we begin to sense the moralizing, self-evaluative tone of such a second person. Merely setting up a second person within the first person allows the text to give, as it were, moral orders and to pass judgment on the self. Or is it the author who is directly or indi-rectly haranguing his character? Is it Lucas speaking to himself, or is it Larbaud who says, "Lucas, il faut vous habituer à cette idée"? Such distinc-tions will take on considerable importance among the critics of Butor's *La Modification*.

Faulkner's extremely ambiguous use of narrative "you" (or something closely resembling it) in *Absalom, Absalom!* (1936) is difficult to ana-lyze exactly. At the start we seem to have a case of one character telling another's story to him. In Quentin's recollections, related to his friend Shreve, Quentin's father speaks of "your grandfather," saying, "you had an aunt once," and so on. Then, curiously, Shreve takes over the narration and relates "for" Quentin's father, still addressing Quentin: "And yet this old gal, this Aunt Rosa, told you that some one was hiding out there and you said it was Clytie or Jim Bond and she said No and you said it would have to be." Later Shreve's monologue is converted into a paraphrase, in the midst of which occur sentences in the "you" form detached from any spoken passages, constituting a deeply intimate mode: "But you were not listening, because you knew it already, had learned, absorbed it already. . . . No, you were not listening, you didn't have to." The text later points up the symbiotic ambiguity of the Quentin/Shreve narrative relation in a passage that may explain why the pronoun "you" in earlier pages may be identified as uttered sometimes by one, sometimes by the other:

14. Valery Larbaud, *Œuvres*, Pléiade edition (Paris, 1961), 649, 664. The use of second-person narration in this work was first pointed out in Melvin Friedman's study *Stream of Consciousness: A Study in Literary Method* (New Haven, 1955), 172. Cf. also note 3 above.

It was Shreve speaking, though save for the slight difference which the intervening degrees of latitude had inculcated in them . . . it might have been either of them and was in a sense both: both thinking as one, the voice which happened to be speaking the thought only the thinking became audible, vocal.[15]

Faulkner's use of "you" thus constitutes a conscious, and internally necessary, method of mixing personalities and viewpoints within the narrative field, in order to secure an overlapping of identities and to enhance, as it were, the archetypic or mythic aspect of the story.

The intrusion of second-person passages into "normal" novelistic practice is well illustrated in the novels of Ernest Hemingway. In most instances, if not in all, it is possible to discern the stylistic intention involved and to detect the underlying psychological basis for each transition. Far from constituting inadvertencies on Hemingway's part, his shiftings from first or third person to second person and back have a definite aesthetic function. The case is somewhat parallel to the same author's "inconsistent" uses of Spanish or pseudo-Spanish vocabulary and syntactical forms in such works as *For Whom the Bell Tolls*, which at first glance seem chaotic but on close analysis prove to be a deliberate and systematic manipulation of mood and tone by stylistic technique.[16] In *A Farewell to Arms* (1929) we are introduced to such shifts in one of the earliest of Lieutenant Henry's interior musings:

> *I* would like to eat at the Cova and then walk down the via Manzoni in the hot evening and cross over and turn off the canal and go to the hotel with Catherine Barkley. . . . *I* would put the key in the door and open it and go in and then take down the telephone and ask them to send a bottle of capri bianca in a silver bucket full of ice and *you* would hear the ice against the pail coming down the corridor and the boy would knock and *I* would say leave it outside the door. . . . And when it was dark afterward and *you* went to the window. . . . That is how it ought to be. *I* would eat quickly and go and see Catherine Barkley.[17]

Though these alternations may at first seem haphazard, like those of the journalist Whitney Bolton quoted earlier (a writer who undoubtedly knew Hemingway's works), we may note certain distinctions. The whole

15. William Faulkner, *Absalom, Absalom!* (New York, 1951), 191 ff., 211, 216, 303.

16. Edward Fenimore, "English and Spanish in *For Whom the Bell Tolls*," *Journal of English Literary History* (June 1943): 73–86; reprinted in J. K. M. McCaffery, *Ernest Hemingway: The Man and His Work* (New York, 1950), 205–20. Here a new problem arises, that of shift between "you" and the pseudo-Spanish "thou" and "thee."

17. Ernest Hemingway, *A Farewell to Arms* (New York, 1929), 40 (italics supplied).

passage appears as a hypothetical projection, not a report on specific past action. The reader, therefore, is invited to share the experience by the momentary, almost subliminal, use of "you" (a "you" that obviously is not to be misread as applying to Catherine). Later, Henry does narrate a definite action (his wounding), but again the "you" embedded in the otherwise first-person account suddenly generalizes the situation and constitutes almost a maxim of behavior, guiding the reader to prepare, as it were, for an identical or similar event:

> then there was a flash . . . and a road. . . . *I* went out swiftly, all of myself, and I knew *I* was dead and that it had all been a mistake to think *you* just died. Then *I* floated . . .[18]

The force gained by "you" in this case, rather than "one," is evident. When Henry describes the effect of shells coming over, the repetitive verb tense leads to "you" transitions:

> *I* would recognize them because of their flat trajectory. *You* heard the report and then the shriek commenced almost immediately.
>   . . . *I* watched the sudden round puffs of shrapnel smoke in the sky . . . soft puffs with a yellow flash in the centre. *You* saw the flash, then heard the crack.[19]

Elsewhere, an "I" may change to "you" through a kind of categorical imperative (*my* feelings ought to be *your* feelings):

> now, for a long time, and *I* had seen nothing sacred, and the things that were glorious had no glory and the sacrifices were like the stockyards at Chicago if nothing were done with the meat except to bury it. There were many words that *you* could not stand to hear and finally only the names of places had dignity. Certain numbers were the same way and certain dates and these with the names of the places were all *you* could say and have them mean anything.[20]

In the famous "small rain" passage, a "you" surges into the interior monologue, mixed with the hero's "I" and the "I" of the old English poem as well, another call to sentimental identification:

> In bed I lay me down my head. . . . Maybe she was lying thinking about me. Blow, blow, ye western wind. Well, it blew and it wasn't the small rain but the big rain down that rained. It rained all night. You knew it rained down that rained. Look at it. Christ, that my love were in my arms and I in my bed again.[21]

18. Ibid., 58 (italics supplied).
19. Ibid., 193, 197 (italics supplied).
20. Ibid., 196 (italics supplied).
21. Ibid., 210.

Frequently, Hemingway's "you" cannot be said to apply completely to either the protagonist or the reader but represents the author's didactic or moralizing merging of the two: "You could not go back. If you did not go back what happened? You never got back to Milan" (p. 231). "You do not know how long you are in a river when the current moves swiftly. It seems a long time and it may be very short. The water was cold" (242). "You did not love the floor of a flat-car nor guns with canvas jackets . . . but you loved some one else whom now you knew was not even to be pretended there. . . . You were out of it now" (247). "So now they had got her in the end. You never got away with anything" (342). "Now Catherine would die. That was what you did. You died. . . . They threw you in and told you the rules and the first time they caught you off base they killed you" (350). In almost each case, Henry's experience, or Catherine's, becomes the basis of an empirical maxim, and "you" enhances the change from individual event to moral conclusion.

Not even the third-person mode that predominates in *For Whom the Bell Tolls* (1940) prevents Hemingway from turning to uses of "you" ranging from frankly avowed self-address on the part of the hero to appeals to that "you" persona—part protagonist, part reader, part author— we have identified in his earlier work. Particularly interesting from the technical viewpoint is the appearance of certain syntactic clues ("he told himself," "he thought," and the like) as to the narrative center involved, devices that Hemingway rarely employed earlier and that indeed seem superfluous here, perhaps marking a tendency on the part of the author. to conventionalize his style and render it more traditional, more accessible to the general public:

> But I must go back, he told himself. . . . I think that we are born into a time of great difficulty, he thought. . . . We fight to live. But I would like to have it so that I could . . . see the chicks of the partridge in my own courtyard. I would like such small and regular things.
>
> But you have no house and no courtyard to your no-house, he thought. You have no family but a brother. . . .
>
> . . . You, you, he raged at himself. Yes, you. You told yourself the first time you saw him that when he would be friendly would be when the treachery would come.[22]

In all this proliferation of "you" forms, few if any can be called strictly narrative; all have a rhetorical cast, which never in fact disappears entirely from the mode, even when it becomes unmistakably narrative. Some other examples from American authors will show how a first or

22. Ernest Hemingway, *For Whom the Bell Tolls* (New York, 1940), 366–71.

third persion is at times blended with the second person in effects similar to Hemingway's, with an occasional close approach to a real narrative "you." The frequentative tense gives rise to "you" in a first-person Salinger story:

> Some afternoons she met the bus on time, some afternoons she was late. Sometimes she talked a blue streak on the bus, sometimes she just sat and smiled. . . . When you sat next to her on the bus, she smelled of a wonderful perfume.[23]

Many passages in the "Camera Eye" sections of Dos Passos's *U.S.A.* are couched in a kind of lyrical-reminiscent style studded with "you" forms that invite the reader to imagine himself in the narrator's place:

> when you walk along the street you have to step carefully . . . easier if you hold Mother's hand . . . you're peeking out of the window [of a train] into the black rumbling dark . . . you were scared . . .
>
> . . . an address you don't quite know you've forgotten the number . . . somewhere a steamboat whistle stabbing your ears . . . that time you leant from a soapbox over faces . . . while I go home.[24]

Here "that time you leant from a soapbox" is, of all the "you" phrases cited, the most clearly narrative, since it is attached to a specific past action of the speaker, or thinker, or vehicle (or persona).

Robert Penn Warren makes extensive use of "you" in *All the King's Men.* The novel begins with a passage in the pseudoguidebook "you" mode, in which "you" is gradually transformed into the dominant narrative "I" and what could be a generalized experience is suddenly fixed in a specific first-person preterite framework:

> MASON CITY.
>
> To get there you follow Highway 58, going northeast out of the city, and it is a good highway and new. . . . You look up the highway and it is straight for miles, coming at you. . . . You'll go past the little white metal squares set on metal rods. . . .
>
> You come in on Number 58, and pass the cotton gin and the power station and . . . you hear the July flies grinding away in the verdure.
>
> That was the way it was the last time I saw Mason City.[25]

---

23. J. D. Salinger, "The Laughing Man," in *Nine Stories* (New York, 1954), 51.

24. John Dos Passos, *U.S.A.* (New York, n.d.). The first quotation is from *The 42nd Parallel*, 5, 25; the second, from *The Big Money*, 149–50.

25. Robert Penn Warren, *All the King's Men* (New York, 1953 [originally pub. 1946]), 3–5. The serviceability of the initial "you" of arrival devised by Warren is shown by its imitation in many quarters, including the mystery story: cf. the same sort of text in Bart Spicer's *Act of Anger* (New York, 1963), 1–2: "You drive in a long tight curve around the

Aiding in the shift of narrative focus from general to particular is, again, the use of tenses: future and present with "you," to show typical or probable action, imperfect and past with "I," once the plot begins to unfold. Nevertheless, the dominant "I" is not quite stable and at times yields to "you" in phrases of genuine narration, applicable to definite actions or single past events:

> then he gave his head a twitch, and his eyes bulged wide suddenly. . . . *It's coming*, I thought.
> You saw the eyes bulge suddenly like that, as though something had happened inside him, and there was that glitter. You knew something had happened inside him, and thought: *It's coming*.

Here the unmistakable narrative "you" leads, as if by rhetorical contamination or association, to a regeneralizing of the pronoun, and we shift to an exemplary mode introduced by a comparison and couched in the universal present tense. The passage continues:

> It was always that way. There was the bulge and the glitter, and there was the cold grip way down in the stomach as though somebody had laid hold of something in there, in the dark which is you, with a cold hand in a rubber glove. It was like the second when you come home late at night and see the yellow envelope of the telegram sticking out from under your door and you lean and pick it up.

Then an action occurs, and with it "you" reverts to its narrative function, from which it is again released in a momentary decline in tension that allows "I" to resume almost as if in a refrain:

> There's the cold in your stomach, but you open the envelope, you have to open the envelope, for the end of man is to know.
> The Boss stood up there quiet, with the bulge and glitter in the eyes, and there wasn't a sound in the crowd. You could hear one insane and irrelevant June fly sawing away up in one of the catalpa trees in the square. . . .
> But the glitter was still there, and I thought: Maybe it's coming.[26]

It should be fully apparent from these examples that the various modes of "you" that modern novelists have developed have been employed with a certain amount of conscious technical intent. But in none of the works examined so far is the entire fictional structure created around a methodical armature of second-person narration. We may now turn our attention to an interesting example of this comparatively rare procedure.

Cobra range. . . . The low white-plastered adobe building . . . is not enough to block your view." Having set the scene, the author completely abandons his "you" of invocation.

26. Warren, *All the King's Men*, 11–12.

Apparently, the first thoroughgoing second-person novel (it was in any case not Butor's *La Modification*) was the mystery-story writer Rex Stout's early "serious" work entitled *How like a God*, which appeared in 1929. Though its unusual technique was noticed at the time by critics, it seems that in the furor over Butor's novel of 1957 no one recalled Rex Stout's much earlier venture into the use of narrative "you." It is worth recalling here. It was the antagonistic suggestion of that then-eminent critic Clifton Fadiman that the novel ought to have been "reworked so as to fall into the straightforward pattern of a direct third-person narrative," so that it would "lose some of its sensational aspect" and "gain in genuineness." [27] Just why the "you" mode should have "sensational" aspects was not made clear. In general, the reviewers of 1929 found the "you" mode distasteful: the critic of *Outlook*, for example, commented on the "difficulty the author must have found in having Bill tell his story to himself," a phrase that reveals its writer's conception of the technique as leading merely to an impression of overhearing someone talking to himself.[28] Stout's novel is also structured according to a nonchronological, associative patterning of events stretching over many years, a fact that caused one reviewer to praise its author as a "moulder of new forms," while another complained of the "lack of sequence in the narrative." [29]

How like a God has sixteen chapters, in each of which narrative "you" is strictly adhered to. Separating the chapters are bridging passages in italics, in the third person, describing the protagonist's slow progress up two flights of steps to the room where he will kill the woman whose existence has poisoned his life. It is in the italic sections that the associative jumps occur that link the chapters in a psychological rather than a chronological design, though there is in general a gradual movement from past to present throughout the novel. Despite the seeming implausibility of this arrangement (a whole life recollected while going up to a third-story room), the effect sought—that of imparting depth of memory to a developing present action—is on the whole successful. In the main text, narrative "you" functions both with and without rhetorical overtones of generalizing, moralizing, or axiomizing; it is an insistent, harsh pronoun carrying a tonality of bitterness and self-reproach. Some sample passages will show the effect:

> You are timid and vengeless.
> When you first saw that word you were in short pants and numberless words in the books you read were strange and thrilling.

27. Clifton Fadiman's review in the *Nation*, 25 September 1929, 329.
28. Unsigned review in *Outlook*, 11 September 1929, 70.
29. Review in the New York *Herald Tribune*, 8 September 1929, 4; the critic of the *New York Times*, 15 September 1929, 8. Joseph Warren Beach, *Twentieth Century Novel*, 280, calls *How like a God* an "interesting recent example" of second-person technique, in

. . . Blindly you slapped him in the face and as he leapt out of his chair a dozen restraining hands clutched him . . . with your face a mass of pulp . . . you still poked your bruised fists somehow at that gigantic shape which must be annihilated before you went down to stay. . . .

. . . You lay for hours, recalling and analyzing, objectively and dispassionately, these familiar phenomena. At times you had hated it. . . . Now that you had seen her again, it struck you as amazing that not once in all the years you had thought of trying to find her. . . .

And then, yesterday, like a lousy coward you didn't go to the office at all. . . . You found the revolver and sat on the edge of the bed for an hour, holding it in your hand and looking at it.[30]

The bridging passages, written in the third person, contain various devices for penetrating the psychology of the protagonist, mostly conventional in nature: interior monologue, *discours indirect libre*, and the like. Not infrequently a phrase or theme introduced in a bridging passage reappears in the following narrative "you" chapter, with an effect of liaison and modulation of mode. This procedure occurs from the outset. The first (italicized) text of the novel begins:

He had closed the door carefully, silently, behind him, and was in the dim hall with his foot on the first step of the familiar stairs. His left hand was in his trousers' pocket, clutching the key to the apartment two flights up; his right hand, in the pocket of his overcoat, was closed around the butt of the revolver. Yes, here I am, he thought, and how absurd! He felt that if he had ever known anything in his life he knew he would not go up the stairs, unlock the door, and pull the trigger of the revolver.
She would probably be sitting in the blue chair. . . .
His mind seemed suddenly clear and intolerably full. . . . A vast intricacy of reasons, arguments, proofs—you are futile, silly, evil, petty, absurd—he could not have spoken in all his years the limitless network of appeals, facts, memories that darted at him and through him as his foot sought the third step.[31]

The interior monologue passage "you are timid and vengeless" becomes the first sentence of the body of the text, transformed entirely into narrative "you." Other transitions take this form:

---

which the leading character is "talking to himself, as it were . . . through the body of the story . . . [and thus] is always 'you.'"

30. Rex Stout, *How like a God* (New York, 1961 [originally pub. Vintage Press, 1929]), 8, 12, 180, 246.

31. Ibid., 7 (italics in the original).

> *He stopped, and again stood still, and his lips moved as though*
> *he were talking. . . .*
> *You counted on, a bitter voice said to him; yes, you might count*
> *on that, you might count on anything except yourself.*[32]

The "bitter voice" (whose ambiguity is the very basis of the effect of narrative "you") then continues in the "you" text that follows:

> You have always betrayed yourself, most miserably at those moments when you most needed the kind of fortitude. . . .[33]

In summary, *How like a God* rigorously applies a predetermined pattern of narrative "you" in which the pronoun, while retaining its moralizing tonality in a rhetoric of self-judgment (or judgment by an outside "voice" that must nevertheless be *audible* to the narrator or hero), is used to recount individual, specific past actions devoid of any general or typical implications.

This is precisely the mixture of modes found in Michel Butor's *La Modification*, though the French novel contains additional complexities. The *récit* is structured on many chronological levels, involving flashbacks in associative rather than linear order, dream sequences, and imaginary passages in the future tense. The initial present perfect, *vous avez mis*, with its momentary stasis, becomes a true present as the action begins:

> Vous avez mis le pied gauche sur la rainure de cuivre, et de votre épaule droite vous essayez en vain de pousser un peu plus le panneau coulissant.
>
> Vous vous introduisez par l'étroite ouverture en vous frottant contre ses bords, puis, votre valise.

> You have put your left foot on the brass groove, and with your right shoulder you have tried in vain to push the sliding door a little farther open.

---

32. Ibid., 87 (italics in the original).

33. Ibid., 88. My colleague Elder Olson has brought to my attention an interesting short story that appeared some years after the Stout novel and in which the author consistently addresses the *reader* as "you," stating that he proposes to relate something that "actually happened to you." He continues: "And when I say 'you,' I mean *you*—now reading these very words. For I know something about you—something deeply personal—something which, however, I am afraid that you have forgotten." The "you" text that follows, involving an impotent, sadistic, *voyeur* hypnotist, one of his beautiful girl victims, and "you," is cleverly explained at the end by having "you" left hypnotized with all his (your) memory of the events narrated erased. With the "frame" of amnesia (posthypnotic) removed, a story would be left in the purest "you" mode. This ingenious piece of *curiosa* is Ralph Milne Farley's "The House of Ecstasy," which originally appeared in a 1938 issue of *Weird Tales Magazine* and was reprinted in *Suspense Stories Collected by Alfred Hitchcock* (New York, 1945), 88–97.

You slip through the narrow opening, rubbing yourself against the edges, afterward, your suitcase.[34]

Shortly the protagonist, settled in the train to Rome and musing over his troubled situation, reverts to the very recent past (6:30 A.M. of the same morning, two hours before train time). The verbs shift to the imperfect and present perfect (the preterite or *passé défini*, by reason of its restricted use in "printed" context, is automatically eliminated): "Tournant vos yeux vers la fenêtre, vous avez vu les cheveux autrefois noirs d'Henriette" ("Turning your eyes toward the window, you saw the once black hair of Henriette"; p. 17). As the hero looks forward to his arrival in Rome and his reunion with his mistress Cécile, the tenses shift to the future:

> Une fois que vous aurez pris votre espresso dans le bar qui lui, s'il n'est déjà ouvert, s'ouvrira à peu près à ce moment-là, que vous serez descendu à L'Albergo Diurno au sous-sol pour vous y baigner, vous y raser, vous y changer, que vous en serez remonté. . . . il vous restera encore près de deux heures à flâner avant que soit venu le temps opportun pour surprendre Cécile au bas de sa maison.

> Once you have drunk your espresso in the bar that, if it is not already open, will open about that time, when you have gone down to the basement of the Albergo Diurno to take your bath, have a shave, change your clothes, when you have come up again. . . . you will still have nearly two hours to wander about before the time is ripe to go and surprise Cécile at the entrance of her house.[35]

In some dream passages, a sort of detached objectification of the protagonist is obtained by comparatively short sections in third-person narrative form, perhaps as if the "narrator" or *récitant* hero, alienated from his central personality in a dream state, could watch himself from the outside (or perhaps as if the narrative "voice" assumed an exterior viewpoint). Little critical attention has been paid these passages, whose syntactic relation to the rest of the text is not dissimilar to that of the italic passages in Stout's novel, establishing from time to time a sort of pronominal perspective. Here even the literary *passé défini* appears, and the incidents of the legend of the "Grand Veneur" associated with most of the dream sequences take on an added literary tone of irreality:

> Or comme il écoutait depuis longtemps prostré le tumulte de cette rivière encaissée sur les vagues de laquelle brillaient maintenant de minces éclats de lune . . . il crut distinguer de l'autre côté de la

34. Michel Butor, *La Modification*, ed. 10/18 (Paris, 1962 [originally pub. Editions de Minuit, 1957]), 9.
    35. Ibid., 44–45.

rivière comme le galop d'un cheval et même un cri, quelques syl-
labes . . . "Qui êtes-vous?"

Now, as he had been listening for a long time on his stomach to the
tumult of this deeply embanked river on whose waves slender
shimmerings of moonlight were now visible . . . he thought he
heard on the other side of the river a galloping horse and even a cry,
a few syllables . . . "Who are you?" [36]

Even more curious is the intrusion into the text of a certain number of
je and *moi* forms (as well as first-person possessives). These, in my opinion, do not constitute "mistakes" or *bévues* (like the dozen or so *passés
définis* in Camus's *L'Etranger*, in the opinion of many critics) but are directly related to the author's conception of the function of narrative
vous. They permit us to arrive at a consistent, logical answer to the question "Qui parle dans *La Modification*?" ("Who is speaking in *The Modification*?") and prove that the explanation of Butor's narrative *vous* as
the voice of the protagonist addressing himself in an interior monologue
(as seems to be the case in Stout's novel) is probably only partially correct. The first of the passages in question does indeed attribute *first-
person pronouns* to the inner voice of the protagonist:

Alors terrorisée s'élève en vous *votre propre voix* qui se plaint: ah,
non, cette décision que *j*'avais eu tant de mal à prendre, il ne faut
pas la laisser se défaire ainsi; ne suis-*je* pas dans ce train, en route
vers Cécile merveilleuse? *Ma* volonté et *mon* désir étaient si forts.
. . . Il faut arrêter *mes* pensées pour *me* ressaisir et *me* reprendre,
rejetant toutes ces images qui montent à l'assaut de *moi*-même.

So, in terror, there rises in you *your own voice* that complains: oh
no, that decision that *I* found so hard to make musn't be allowed to
undo itself; am *I* not in this train, going toward marvelous Cécile?
My will and *my* desire were so strong. . . . I must stop *my* thoughts
in order to regain my self-control and recover, rejecting all those
images that rush to attack *my*self. [37]

And the paragraph that immediately follows has the sound of a *reply* to
this voice:

Mais il n'est plus temps maintenant . . . et malgré tous *vos* efforts
pour *vous* en dégager, pour tourner *votre* attention ailleurs, vers
cette décision que *vous* sentez *vous* échapper, les voici qui *vous*
entraînant dans leurs engrenages.

36. Ibid., 211. Cf. also 206, 214, 218, 222, 230.
37. Ibid., 163 (italics supplied). Cf. also 189, 190, 191, 196, 210, 211, 272, 274, 276.

But the time has passed now . . . and in spite of all *your* efforts to get *yourself* free, to turn *your* attention elsewhere, toward that decision *you* feel to be slipping through *your* fingers, now they are drawing *you* into their mesh.

In a passage that establishes the relation of observed events in the novel to the psychological "modification" the hero undergoes and makes of the exterior decor and action a series of objective correlatives, Butor again allows his protagonist to speak in the form, significantly, of a first-person soliloquy:

Vous vous dites: s'il n'y avait pas eu ces gens, s'il n'y avait pas eu ces objets et ces images auxquelles se sont accrochées *mes* pensées de telle sorte qu'une machine mentale s'est constituée . . . *mes* illusions auraient-elles pu tenir encore quelque temps?

You say to *yourself*: if there had not been these people, if there had not been these objects and these images to which *my* thoughts fastened in such a way that a mental machinery was constituted . . . would *my* illusions have been able to hold out much longer?[38]

Michel Butor has commented at some length concerning his intentions in constructing *La Modification* with narrative *vous*. His earliest comment leaves much unclear and suggests, without actually stating flatly, that the *vous* represents the character addressing himself:

Il fallait absolument que le récit soit fait du point de vue d'un personnage. Comme il s'agissait d'une prise de conscience, il ne fallait pas que le personnage dise *je*. Il me fallait un monologue intérieur en-dessous du niveau du langage du personnage lui-même, dans une forme intermédiaire entre la première personne et la troisième. Ce *vous* me permet de décrire la situation du personnage et la façon dont le langage naît en lui.

The narration absolutely had to be written from the point of view of a character. As it was a question of a realization, the character could not say *I*. I had to have an interior monologue beneath the level of the character's language, in a form halfway between the first person and the third. The *vous* allows me to describe the situation of the character and the way language arises in him.[39]

38. Ibid., 274 (italics supplied). The passage abounds in *je* and *moi* forms as well. A curious parallel example of a shift from first to second person may be found in an interior monologue in *Tirez sur le pianiste* (Paris, 1957), 136 ff. This work was based on David Goodis's *Down There* and was subsequently adapted for film by Truffaut. Looking backward, the protagonist refers to his present self in the first person and to his previous self in the second: "Si *mes* souvenirs sont exacts, *tu* as fait toutes sortes de besognes" (italics supplied).

39. Quoted from Paul Guth's portrait-interview in *Le Figaro Littéraire*, 7 December 1957.

What troubles us here is that, at crucial moments of his "prise de conscience," the protagonist docs, as we have shown, say *je*. Furthermore, it is far from evident that the first-person mode is incompatible with such a design or that *vous* permits the author to describe "la façon dont le langage naît" in his personage. Some four years later, Butor returned to the subject of narrative pronouns, and his declaration concerning the second person appears not only to better fit his procedure in *La Modification*, but also to better explain the real force of the technique:

> C'est ici qu'intervient l'emploi de la seconde personne que l'on peut caractériser ainsi, dans le roman: celui à qui l'on raconte sa propre histoire.
> C'est parce qu'il y a quelqu'un à qui l'on raconte sa propre histoire, quelque chose de lui qu'il ne connaît pas, ou du moins pas encore au niveau du langage, qu'il peut y avoir un récit à la deuxième personne, qui sera par conséquent toujours un récit didactique.

> Here the use of the second person intervenes, which can be characterized in the novel in these terms: the one to whom his own story is told.
> It's because there is someone to whom his own story is told, something about him that he doesn't know, or at least not yet on the level of language, that there can be a narrative in the second person, which will consequently always be a didactic narrative.[40]

Butor goes on to compare the second-person text to the words of a *juge d'instruction* addressing an accused man or a witness who "ne veut pas ou ne peut pas . . . raconter" ("who will not or cannot . . . tell"), saying to him: "Vous êtes rentré de votre travail à telle heure; nous savons . . . à quelle heure vous avez quitté votre domicile" ("You got home from work at such and such a time; we know . . . at what time you left your place of residence"). Strikingly (though he does not mention their presence in *La Modification*), Butor also explains why there should be also, in a *vous* narration, some first-person passages. The *vous* narrator may be lying, hiding something, or simply unaware (this seems to be the case in *La Modification*) of the true pattern or import of the elements of his narration. When he does speak on his own behalf, his words "se présenteront comme des îlots à la première personne à l'intérieur d'un récit fait à la seconde et qui les provoque" ("will appear like isolated outcrops in the first person within a narrative in the second that gives rise to them"). Thus we see the importance of the phrase, "à qui l'on raconte sa propre histoire" ("to whom his own story is told"). The voice that says *vous* is

40. Michel Butor "L'Usage des pronoms personnels dans le roman," *Les Temps Modernes*, no. 178 (February 1961): 936–48, esp. 941.

less that of the character than of the author or, better still, that of a persona, invisible but powerfully present, who serves as the center of consciousness in the novel.

It is a measure of the sophistication if not the perceptiveness of contemporary literary critics that, although in 1929 Rex Stout's novel provoked only the most superficial comment on its unusual pronominal form, Butor's *La Modification* in 1957 was subjected to exhaustive and subtle analysis, especially with respect to its narrative mode. Luc Estang saw the *vous narratif* as expressing "l'ambiguïté 'sujet-objet' du personnage" ("the subject-object ambiguity of the character") and raised the question, "Qui dit 'vous'?" ("Who says 'you'?") Perceptively, he replied:

> Le romancier à son personnage? Sans doute. Mais pour autant ce romancier ne joue pas au dieu omniscient qui—comme il arrive dans des récits à la troisième personne (c'est la fameuse querelle de Sartre contre Mauriac)—en sait plus long que sa créature. Nous collons à la conscience du personnage, ne connaissant rien qui n'appartienne à ses pensées, à ses souvenirs, à ses sentiments. . . . A croire qu'il s'interpelle lui-même. Mais alors il se dirait "tu." Et pourquoi pas "je"? Ambiguïté voulue, certes.

> The novelist to his character? Certainly, but inasmuch as this novelist doesn't play at being the omniscient god who—as happens in third-person narratives (that's what the famous quarrel of Sartre with Mauriac was about)—knows more about him than his creature. We stick to the consciousness of the character, knowing nothing that is not pertinent to his thoughts, his memories, his feelings . . . as if he were addressing himself. But then he would say "tu." And why not "je"? A willful ambiguity, no doubt.[41]

Yet Butor himself, as we saw above, believed that the justification of *vous* is precisely that something is to be revealed to the character that he "does not know, at least at the level of language." Nor does the use of *vous* necessarily exclude the theory of self-address; even French critics, such as Paul Delbouille, have accepted the *vous* rather than Dujardin's *tu* as the character speaking to himself.

A probing evaluation of Butor's *vous*, relating it skillfully to the structure of the novel, came from Roland Barthes, who, contrasting the non-symbolic use of objects in Robbe-Grillet with the deliberate symbolism of Butor, argued that Butor's *vous* sets up a metaphysics of creator/creature full of humanistic, if not religious, meaning. Barthes wrote:

> Le symbole est une voie essentielle de réconciliation entre l'homme et l'univers. . . . Or *La Modification* n'est pas seulement un roman

41. Luc Estang, "Couronnes et bandeaux," *Pensée Française* (January 1958): 56.

symbolique, c'est aussi un roman de la créature, au sens pleinement *agi* du terme. Je ne crois nullement . . . que le vouvoiement employé par Butor . . . soit un artifice de forme . . . ; ce vouvoiement me paraît littéral: il est celui du créateur à sa créature, nommée, constituée, créée dans tous ses actes par un juge et générateur. Cette interpellation est capitale, car elle institue la conscience du héros: c'est à force de s'entendre décrire par un regard que la personne du héros se modifie, et qu'il renonce à consacrer l'adultère dont il avait initialement le ferme projet.

The symbol is an essential way of reconciling man and the universe. . . . Now, *The Modification* is not only a symbolic novel, it is also a novel of the created being, in the fully *acted upon* meaning of the term. I do not at all believe that the *vouvoiement* used by Butor . . . is a formal device . . . ; this *vouvoiement* seems to me literal: it is that of the creator to his creature, named, constituted, created in all his acts by a judge and procreator. This interpellation is crucial, for it establishes the consciousness of the hero: it is by dint of hearing himself described by a glance that the person of the hero is modified, renounces the adultry he had in the first place firmly planned to commit.[42]

That narrative *vous* holds a strong implication of judgment, of moral or didactic address, is a frequent theme of the critics. Butor himself says as much; but before he expressed that view, Barthes in passages like the above and Bernard Pingaud in an article devoted to the problem of "*je, vous, il,*" as well as other writers, had stressed the point. The hero of Butor's earlier novel *L'Emploi du temps* had written, according to Pingaud, not so much a journal as a detailed inventory of acts whose meaning escaped him, the manuscript destined to be read by a suspicious and invisible *juge d'instruction.* Now, in *La Modification*, Pingaud finds that Butor inverts this perspective:

C'est le juge, cette fois, qui parle, mais nous ne nous en apercevons pas tout de suite. . . . "Vous," c'est quelqu'un que l'on voit, que l'on touche. . . . Mais c'est aussi l'autre, l'étranger, celui qu'on regarde du dehors. . . .
En réalité, Michel Butor renouvelle les données du problème bien plus qu'il ne les résoud. Si l'on se demande qui est le "vous" auquel le romancier s'adresse, l'ambiguïté du procédé apparaît tout de suite. Ce "vous," c'est le personnage principal du roman, mais c'est aussi le lecteur. Racontant son histoire à la deuxième personne, Butor retrouve l'attitude spontanée qui est la nôtre lorsque nous voulons montrer le caractère exemplaire d'une aventure qui

---

42. Roland Barthes, "Il n'y a pas d'école Robbe-Grillet," *Arguments* (February 1958): 7.

nous est arrivée ou qui est arrivée à quelqu'un que nous connais-
sons. "Vous avez mis le pied gauche . . . ," cela veut dire: "Imaginez
que vous mettez le pied gauche sur la rainure de cuivre. Placez-
vous un instant dans la situation de celui qui. . . ." . . . Cette sorte
d'objectivité-subjectivité qu'institue le "vous" est en réalité un ré-
quisitoire sans appel.

It is the judge this time who speaks, but we don't realize it immediately. . . . "You," is someone seen and touched. . . . But it is also
the other person, the stranger, he who is seen from the outside.

In reality, Michel Butor renews the givens of the problem much
more than he resolves them. If one asks who is the "you" the novelist addresses, the ambiguity of the process immediately becomes
apparent. This "you" is the main character in the novel, but it is also
the reader. Telling his story in the second person, Butor finds the
spontaneous attitude that is ours when we wish to show the exemplary character of an adventure that happened to us or to someone
we know. "You have put your left foot . . . ," which means: "Imagine
that you put your left foot on the brass groove. Put yourself for
a moment in the situation of someone who. . . ." . . . This kind of
objectivity-subjectivity that the *vous* introduces is in reality a final
indictment.[43]

Pingaud goes on to modify his assumption that it is a real or imaginary
judge speaking; this first person (who says *vous*), implied everywhere in
La Modification but never seen, "refuse de s'incarner dans aucun indi-
vidu déterminé" ("refuses to be incarnated as a specific individual"), being fundamentally "la voix de la conscience, la mienne, la vôtre, la sienne,
celle du héros" ("the voice of the conscience, mine, yours, his, that of the
hero"). The result is that it is the *vous narratif* that gives the work its
"éclairage moral" ("moral illumination"), its moral tone.

Michel Leiris in a substantial study of *La Modification* published in
1958, and now reprinted as a postface in the "10/18" paperback edition
of the novel, pointed out that the second person constituted an immediate invitation to the reader:

C'est vous-même, lecteur, que le romancier semble mettre poli-
ment en cause. . . . Ce procédé inusité vous incite à vous demander
(gageons-le) à quel type particulier de lecture vous êtes ici convié.

It is you yourself, reader, that the novelist seems to implicate po-
litely. This unusual process urges you to ask yourself (let us wager)
to what particular type of reading you are being invited.[44]

43. Bernard Pingaud, "Je, vous, il," *Esprit* 7–8 (July–August 1958): 91–99, esp. 98.

44. Michel Leiris, "Le Réalisme mythologique de Michel Butor," *Critique* (February
1958). See the "10/18" edition of *La Modification*, referred to in note 34, 287.

More important, the novel is constructed in this way so as to provoke a "prise de conscience" ("a realization") in the reader (as one might say is supposed to occur, though Leiris does not draw the parallel, at the end of Camus's *La Chute*):

> la chose se passe—de l'écrivain à vous, lecteur—comme si l'emploi comminatoire du *vous* y était une effective incitation à prendre conscience vous aussi et à entrer en action de manière que l'histoire . . . devienne (si elle ne l'est déjà) un équivalent de votre propre histoire.

> the thing happens—from the writer to you, reader—as if the threatening use of *you* were an effective incitement to become aware also and to act in such a way that the story . . . becomes (if it has not already done so) an equivalent of your own story.[45]

Implicated in the narration, the reader, summoned by *vous*, joins the protagonist as if "arrêté et amené devant un commissaire de police" ("arrested and taken before a police magistrate"). For *vous* is the person par excellence of interrogation and the imperative. Leiris calls attention to the hero's speculations in the course of the novel as to the Jesuit father's possible writing assignments to his pupils, including one saying "Imaginez que vous voulez vous séparer de votre femme" ("Imagine that you want to separate from your wife"), the theme not only of the novel itself, but also of the other novel that the hero, Léon Delmont, will ostensibly write as *La Modification* comes to an end.

Pierre de Boisdeffre, using terms from Leiris's article, relates the *vous* mode to the questions uttered by the infernal boatman of the protagonist's dream, by the customs inspector, and (Boisdeffre might have added) by the "Grand Veneur" whose legend appears sporadically throughout *La Modification*:

> Le *vous* comminatoire au rythme duquel se déroule toute l'action souligne l'interrogation métaphysique qui s'adresse au personnage comme au lecteur: *d'où venez-vous? que voulez-vous? où allez-vous?*—questions posées à la fois dans un rêve par le nautonnier fantôme d'un Styx imaginaire et par le douanier trop réel qui s'étonne de son sommeil.

> The threatening *vous*, to the rhythm of which all the action unfolds, underlines the metaphysical questioning addressed to the character, as it is to the reader: Where do you come from? What do you want? Where are you going?—questions that are asked both in a

---

45. Ibid., 307. Incidentally, Leiris is one of the few critics to notice the third-person passages of *La Modification* (cf. ibid., 301), though he says nothing of those in the *je* form.

dream by the ghostly pilot on an imaginary Styx and by the all too real customs officer who is surprised at his sleep.[46]

The critic who has reacted most strongly against thus interpreting Butor's *vous* as addressed to the reader is Paul Delbouille. Delbouille cites Pingaud's statement that "Ce 'vous,' c'est le personnage principal du roman, mais c'est aussi le lecteur" ("This '*vous*' is the main character of the novel, but it is also the reader") only to reject the claim that the second-person pronoun can have any special power to cause reader identification. He writes:

> La question que je me pose . . . est seulement de savoir si ce "vous" s'adresse réellement, ou peut s'adresser, au lecteur du roman. . . . Pour ma part . . . je vois tout de suite que l'historie n'est pas la mienne; je ne puis l'endosser parce qu'elle n'est pas à mes mesures. Partant, il faut bien que j'imagine quelqu'un qui ne soit pas moi. . . . Or, si ce héros existe en dehors de moi, c'est évidemment à lui et à lui seul que s'adresse ce "vous" qui est un singulier. Bernard Pingaud a beau dire que celui qui dit "vous" est quelqu'un "qui refuse de s'incarner dans aucun individu déterminé, qui est, en somme, la voix de la conscience, la mienne, la vôtre, la sienne, celle du héros," il ne peut pas faire que ma conscience me dise des choses qui ne nous concernent directement ni elle ni moi.

> The question I ask myself . . . is simply whether this "vous" really speaks, or can speak, to the reader of the novel. . . . As for me . . . I immediately see that the story is not mine; I can't assume it because it doesn't fit me. Therefore I must imagine someone who is not I. . . . Now, if this hero exists outside myself, it is clearly he and he alone who is addressed by this "vous" that is singular. Bernard Pingaud can insist that the person who says "vous" is someone "who refuses to be incarnated in any single individual, who is, in short, the voice of conscience, mine, yours, his, that of the hero," he cannot make my conscience tell me things that don't concern us directly—either my conscience or myself.[47]

For, the critic argues, "le seul emploi d'un pronom personnel ne peut suffire à donner la direction du dialogue" ("the use of a personal pronoun is not in itself sufficient to set the direction of the dialogue"). Then what is the significance of the innovation? Delbouille reverts to the simplest explanation: the hero of *La Modification* is literally speaking to himself in a variant type of interior monologue:

46. Pierre de Boisdeffre, *Où va le roman?* (Paris, 1962), 252.
47. Paul Delbouille, "Le *vous* de *La Modification*," *Cahiers d'Analyse Textuelle* 5 (1963): 84.

Au total, il est sans doute beaucoup plus enrichissant, et beaucoup plus juste en même temps, de considérer le "vous" de *La Modification* comme s'adressant exclusivement au héros lui-même. La question reste alors de savoir par qui ce "vous" est prononcé. Il pourrait s'agir, peut-être, d'un romancier qui aurait pris, vis-à-vis de son héros, l'attitude d'un juge d'instruction, mais ici encore il faut imaginer une continuelle intrusion de l'auteur dans l'univers qu'il crée. Ne s'agit-il pas, plus vraisemblablement, du héros lui-même, qui soliloque en quelque sorte, mais dans un monologue très différent du "monologue intérieur"? Se dédoublant et se parlant à lui-même, il a l'avantage de se voir réellement de l'extérieur.

All in all it is doubtless much more profitable and at the same time more correct to consider the "vous" in *La Modification* as addressed directly to the hero himself. The question remains then to know by whom this "vous" is uttered. It could perhaps be a novelist who has taken, with respect to his hero, the attitude of an examining magistrate, but here again one must imagine the continual intrusion of the author into the universe he is creating. With greater likelihood, may it not be the hero himself, who talks to himself in a way, but in a monologue that is very different from interior monologue? Splitting into two personalities and speaking to himself, he has the advantage of seeing himself really from the outside.[48]

But as I have shown, the appearance of first-person passages at certain key moments, as well as the expressed views of Butor himself, all tend to exclude this interior monologue interpretation. Without accepting Pingaud's argument that *vous* is addressed to the reader, we can readily understand it as addressed to the hero and as uttered by the "voice" or persona detected and analyzed earlier.

Several partial parallels may be cited. Readers of Joyce will recall the "Ithaca" section of *Ulysses* in which a long series of impersonal questions (uttered by one kind of authorial voice) are replied to with equal impersonality by another. Robert Pinget has utilized a kind of extension of this technique in *L'Inquisitoire* (1962), where, throughout, questions emerge from an ambiguous interrogator ("votre secret dites-le," "poursuivez," "dites exactement ce que vous savez," "quels étaient vos rapports avec eux," etc.) ("tell your secret," "continue," "tell exactly what you know," etc.), provoking the replies that constitute the novel.

Butor juggles both personae and narrative pronouns, including the second person, in the novel *Degrés* (*Degrees*) of 1960: the ostensible nar-

48. Ibid., 87. Cf. also Pierre Deguise, "Michel Butor et le *nouveau roman*," *French Review* 35 (December 1961): 155–62. For Deguise, the *vous* of Butor is author, character, *and* reader and is hence a "*vous* synthétique."

rator of one section addresses the "real" author of that portion of the text as *tu*:

> Le soir, tu as commencé à rédiger ce text que je continue, ou plus exactement que tu continues en te servant de moi, car, en réalité, ce n'est pas moi qui écris mais toi.

> That evening, you began to write the text that I am continuing, or more exactly, that you are continuing through me, for in reality it is not I writing, but you. (p. 149)

Here we leave the domain of narrative "you," strictly speaking, and enter that of interchangeable personalities and other ambiguities.

Although Butor's *La Modification* of 1957 exerted its influence on the use of narrative pronouns, narrative "you" had already proliferated not only in the novel, but elsewhere. Mary McCarthy organized into a "novel" a number of her pieces from the late thirties and forties under the title *The Company She Keeps* (Dell, 1955). The chapter "The Genial Host" illustrates how the frequentative "you" mode can blend into, if not actually generate, the pure narrative mode of "you." The frame is repetitive: "When he telephoned to ask you to do something he never said baldly. . . . Whenever you really noticed Pflaumen, you became aware. . . . If you were in a sympathetic mood you might think. . . ." Then the events of a specific evening, out of many similar ones (hence the frequentative), lead to the preterite tense and genuine narrative "you": "Suddenly you knew that you must cut yourself off from these people. . . . You took a deep breath and leaned across the table. . . . 'God damn you,' you said in a very loud voice." But at the chapter's end the "you" again becomes frequentative, at least in prospect, as the heroine has obviously not succeeded in cutting herself loose from the habit of this environment: "The time after next, you promised yourself, you would surely refuse" Pflaumen's invitation (pp. 103–22). Curiously, in her preface Mary McCarthy, referring to "points of view" revisited, calls the "you" mode "affectionate, diminutive," two adjectives whose pertinence seems at best doubtful.

William Styron placed at the beginning of his novel *Lie down in Darkness* (1961) a second-person text reminiscent of Butor (even the setting of the train is the same), and John Ashmead in *The Mountain and the Feather* (1961) used "you" exclusively, except for short linking passages in italics, similar to those in Stout's *How like a God* (though functioning more in the manner of the "historical" insertions in Dos Passos's *U.S.A.*). That Ashmead's novel lacks the context of *crise de conscience* or moral struggle of *La Modification*, or that of self-reproach and retrospective self-judgment of the Stout work, may account for the unsatisfactory effect of the "you" mode in *The Mountain and the Feather*. As Pierre Delbouille argued in the passage quoted earlier, the use of "you" alone is no guarantee of reader projection; the point is well illustrated by Ashmead's novel, of which Gerald Walker wrote in the *New York Times*, "One doesn't really get to know Monty, the you-narrator." Sporadic appearances of short passages in pure or pseudonarrative "you" mode characterize contemporary fiction generally, from the lowest to the highest levels. As a rule, a frequentative basis or point of departure is involved: a present experience recalling similar ones in the past, for example. Popular and commercial writers constantly use this device. Ian Fleming has the heroine of his James Bond episode *The Spy Who Loved Me* (Viking Press, 1962) narrate:

> I suddenly wanted to go to the john, and I smiled to myself. It was the piercing tickle that comes to children during hide-and-seek-in-the-dark . . . when, in your cupboard under the stairs, you heard the soft creak of a floorboard, the approaching whisper of the searchers. Then you clutched yourself in thrilling anguish and squeezed your legs together. . . . Standing there, a "big girl" now, I remembered it all. (p. 22)

In France, one may cite *vous* passages in Nathalie Sarraute (*Le Planétarium*, 1959), in Jean Thibaudeau (*Une Cérémonie royale*), and in works like Jean Cau's *La Pitié de Dieu*, of which André Billy wrote that one cannot know "exactly who is speaking": "La première et la deuxième personne . . . du pluriel sans qu'on sache exactement qui parle." Even the art of criticism has turned to "you" and *vous*, and not solely for purposes of ironic parody: Michel Leiris's article on Butor, quoted earlier, made meaningful use of *vous*, and John Kneller wrote a witty review of a novel by Roger Vailland in which the critic imitated the "you" of *La Modification*.[49]

Finally, in recent years, as the sound track has come to be used less

49. Styron's use of "you" in *Lie down in Darkness* was pointed out by Melvin Friedman in *Configuration critique de William Styron* (Paris, 1967); later, Styron himself stated that his source was Robert Penn Warren's *All the King's Men* (cf. my discussion and note 25). Styron mentions this both in *Sophie's Choice* (New York, 1979) and in his collection of essays *This Quiet Dust* (New York, 1982). Kneller's review of Vailland's *La Fête* (Paris, 1960) is in *French Review* 34 (April 1961): 499–500. Using as his pretext resemblances he detects between *La Fête* and *La Modification*, Kneller transforms Vailland's third-person mode into the second person in this manner: "Your name is Duc. You are a novelist about fifty years old. . . . You are writing a novel."

Also, Philip Thody in *Un Nouveau Roman?* ed. J. H. Matthews (Paris, 1964), 67–73, published a critical piece entitled "Michel Butor: La Rectification" in which, following the lead of Michel Leiris no doubt, he discusses *La Modification* in a text couched in the *vous* mode. Thody expresses surprise that "no one had previously thought" of using the second person and foresees no future for it. The only antecedent he finds is a single lyric occur-

literally, films have proved a fertile field for the development of various "you" modes of narration. In Jules Dasin's *Naked City* (story by Malvin Wald, scenario by Albert Maltz), an unidentified voice (actually Mark Hellinger's) addresses various characters in the film, including a released criminal ("Now you are free to go, Niles, but what you don't know is that two men will be following you around the clock. That makes six men a day." Then, as another man appears, "Or is it seven?"), a character to whom the "you" remarks are not even supposed to be audible. Note also that, like the "you" mode described by Butor, this "you" narration hinges on something not known by the person it is ostensibly addressed to. Sometimes hypothetical questions are put to one character or another ("Here, Halloran, here's a question for you"); sometimes the commentary comes from an imaginary observer gifted with both curiosity and omniscience, who gives instructions, makes inquiries, promises revelations ("Ask your question, Halloran. . . . How are your feet holding out? You'll be interested to know there's been a development in the Dexter case"). Not infrequently, a "you" mode passage on the sound track serves as a bridging device between episodes or sequences ("You've lost him, Halloran, haven't you?")—and then we follow the criminal who has escaped Halloran's watchful eyes.

In the film *Slattery's Hurricane*, Herman Wouk's hero, a disgraced airplane pilot, recalls the past as he battles his way toward a hurricane whose course over the sea he seeks to plot in order to save lives ashore. The film is a montage of flashbacks, each separated from the next by a shot of the pilot, accompanied by the pilot's voice on the sound track setting the scene through use of a narrative "you" passage. The film *The Bribe* has roughly the same structure, as have doubtless many others. Typically, the "present" moment (that of the film's beginning) is reached at about the two-thirds point of the flashback series, following which the film progresses into the "real" present or future.

An unusual case of "you" narration occurs in the film *Man in the Dark*

---

rence (the seventeenth stanza of Valéry's "Le Cimetière marin"). Thody adopts the view that *vous* represents a "trouvaille stylistique . . . où le narrateur se parle à la deuxième personne du pluriel" and that it constitutes a "*vous* de complicité qui mène le lecteur à se voir lui-même," leading the reader to "see himself" in the hero's role.

Michel Zéraffa's novel *L'Histoire* (Paris, 1964) seems to further the exploitation of second-person modes in French. It is entirely couched in narrative *tu*, addressed to a nameless, almost Beckettian "prisoner" in a fortress cut off from the world. Several critics at the time of its publication argued that Butor's *vous* would be inconceivable as *tu*, despite the ostensibly greater appropriateness of the familiar form, correctly sensing that *vous* placed the narrative on a higher level than that of mere self-address. Zéraffa's *tu* is not self-address either, but the *tu* that one uses toward an unfortunate inferior. This aspect is emphasized by subtle, scattered intrusions of a *nous* as impersonal and elusive as the disappearing *nous* of the first chapters of *Madame Bovary*.

(1953). A gangster who has undergone a brain operation (performed experimentally in prison, on condition that if he lives he will earn his liberty) is returned to his former haunts with a complete loss of memory and an accompanying change in personality. Before his imprisonment he had hidden a large amount of loot, and other gangsters now attempt to evoke his memory of the hiding place. One of them starts to narrate the protagonist's past life to him, using the "you" form. This starts a train of pseudoflashbacks in which the narrative voice is still heard saying "you," while the hero, played by Edmund O'Brien, relives the scenes described. Narrative distance is preserved in these flashbacks through the ingenious device of letting us hear everyone's speech *except* the protagonist's, which is suppressed and assimilated into the "you" narration, as if the protagonist were not remembering at all, but only visualizing in accordance with the instructions he receives from the other gangster. Here the manifest impossibility of construing the "you" mode as representing the hero "talking to himself" (as in *Slattery's Hurricane*, for example) emphasizes aspects of my earlier analysis of *La Modification* and other works.

Another example of a character within the work using narrative "you," though quite different in nature from the foregoing, is found in one of the climactic scenes of Marguerite Duras's film *Hiroshima mon amour* (1960). As the heroine narrates (almost as if commenting on the scenes we witness on the screen) her past love in Nevers, the *il* that she uses to refer to her German lover suddenly becomes a *tu* seemingly addressed to the Japanese who is her present lover and to whom she is relating her past. Here confusion of identity, with its symbolic implications of exchange of roles, brings to second-person narrative new psychological overtones.[50]

It appears evident, then, that contemporary literature (including films) has developed both consciously and unconsciously a narrative mode based on second-person forms, related to certain lyrical antecedents and to some habits of everyday speech but containing subtle and far-reaching implications and conveying a unique tonality. One may doubt that novelists will ever adopt the "you" mode as their general practice; but even if it occurs only occasionally (as in Hemingway and Butor) or is used only as a framing device (as in the flashback sequences described above), it seems destined to persist. Its very ambiguity, emphasized by the fact that critics are far from agreement on its true import, favors its retention. Whether it will undergo further evolution is uncertain, but it seems safe to state that it is already a mode that rhetoricians of fiction must take into account.

50. Marguerite Duras, *Hiroshima mon amour* (Paris, 1960). Cf. p. 90.

10
INTERIOR DUPLICATION

I shall be forgiven, I hope, a brief allusion to my own role in one restricted domain of recent criticism of the novel. In 1961, at a meeting of the Association Internationale des Etudes Françaises held in Paris at the Collège de France, I delivered a paper on the new novel in which I indicated the presence in many novels of this "school" of reduced models, or *mises en abyme*, of the narrative's subject itself, such as myths or legends, portraits, paintings, inner plays, and novels read by one or more of the characters. Naturally, I quoted the key passage from André Gide, which I will shortly discuss in detail. Since that time I have found my examples and observations echoed more or less everywhere, and I note with interest that the subject is gaining wide respect, as revealed in L. Dällenbach's extensive study *Le Récit spéculaire; Essai sur la mise en abyme* (Paris, 1977). In the *Entretiens sur André Gide*, published in 1967 as a compilation of the lectures and commentaries presented at the 1964 André Gide colloquium of Cerisy-La-Salle, Claude Martin discusses "Gide and the New Novel" and, quoting me, further develops certain points I made; his interesting comments had the additional merit of eliciting some remarks by Jean Ricardou on the *mise en abyme*, which represent a considerable advance in the research of the aesthetic and even metaphysical bases of this Gidian structure. Unfortunately, *mise en abyme* runs the risk of becoming a catchall formula in the hands of other critics who use it at every turn in their analyses, and who nowadays reinforce their arguments with quotations from Claude Lévi-Strauss and structuralist criticism on the role of reduced models. An example of this can be seen in John Sturrock's treatment of the works of Michel Butor in *The French New Novel* (Oxford, 1969). Sturrock expands the *mise en abyme* to include not only interior duplications, such as the stained glass windows or the detective novel of Butor's *L'Emploi du temps* (1956), but

141

also a symbolic action like the fact that the protagonist, Revel, upon arriving in Bleston, is confused about which railway station he is in!

What I propose to do here is first to situate Gide himself with respect to the historical development of interior duplications, then to examine the considerable effect that his example and thought on the subject have had on subsequent writers and critics. In the course of what follows, I will try to bring out once more, and more thoroughly, the various meanings of the *mise en abyme*.

Here, to begin with, is the text by André Gide, as it appeared in his *Journal* of 1893:

> J'aime assez qu'en une oeuvre d'art, on retrouve ainsi transposé à l'échelle des personnages, le sujet même de cette oeuvre. Rien ne l'éclaire mieux et n'établit plus sûrement toutes les proportions de l'ensemble. Ainsi dans tels tableaux de Memling ou de Quentin Metzys, un petit miroir convexe et sombre reflète à son tour, l'intérieur de la pièce où se joue la scène peinte. Ainsi dans le tableau des Ménines de Velasquez (mais un peu différement). Enfin, en littérature, dans *Hamlet*, la scène de la comédie; et d'ailleurs d'autres pièces. Dans *Wilhelm Meister*, les scènes de marionnettes ou de fête au château. Dans "La Chute de la Maison Usher," la lecture que l'on fait à Roderick, etc. . . . Aucun de ces exemples n'est absolument juste. Ce qui le serait beaucoup plus, ce qui dirait bien mieux ce que j'ai voulu dans mes *Cahiers*, dans mon *Narcisse* et dans la *Tentative* c'est la comparaison avec ce procédé du blason qui consiste, dans le premier, à en mettre un second "en abyme."

> In a work of art I quite like to find the very subject transposed onto the level of the characters. Nothing lights it better and establishes more surely the proportions of the whole. Thus, in some paintings by Memling or Quentin Metzys, a small, dark convex mirror reflects in its turn the interior of the room where the painted scene is depicted. Thus in *Las Meninas* of Velasquez (but in a slightly different way). Finally, in literature, the play scene in *Hamlet*; and other plays too. In *Wilhelm Meister* the marionette scenes or those of château festivities. In "The Fall of the House of Usher" the passage read to Roderick, etc. . . . None of these examples is absolutely correct. What would be much more so, and would express much better what I purposed in my *Notebooks*, my *Narcissus*, and the *Tentative amoureuse*, is the comparison with the heraldic technique that consists of placing a second blazon, *en abyme*, in the first.

Without getting involved in a detailed "explication de texte," let me nevertheless stress certain essential points of this rich passage and provide several lexicographical details that should contribute to a clear understanding of the question:

1. Gide recognizes that the process is already an old one.

2. He attributes to it the function of *clarifying* the work and of establishing its *proportions*.

3. The examples of the paintings Gide cites would require a study on their own account, since, apart from the faces reflected in the mirror (in Memling, for example), the images reflected in the convex mirrors that Gide is referring to come from the *outside* (of the painting) and in no way reflect the interior of the scene (except in very rare cases, such as Van Eyck's *Giovanni Arnolfini and His Bride*, in which the mirror reveals to us the backs of the onlookers, with the face of the painter-spectator in the middle). As for *The Maids of Honor* (*Las Meninas*) of Velasquez, the interior canvas represents nothing at all, since we see only its completely white back, and the mirror in the background reflects the royal couple that does not otherwise appear in the painting itself. The book to consult for all of this is the excellent *Zauber des Spiegels* by Gustav Friedrich Hartlaub.

4. Gide makes the point that interior duplication exists in at least two art forms, painting and literature. He thus draws from this a principle of general structure, admitting, no doubt, its eventual applicability to music, cinema, and so on. The first literary example he mentions, the inner play of *Hamlet*, is actually an example of a *double* duplication, since the mimed and silent prologue duplicates the spoken play that follows, both actions duplicating, naturally, the otherwise unrevealed action of an earlier event in the tragedy in which the *mise en abyme* is embedded. It is easy to understand why Gide does not judge any of his examples to be "absolutely correct," although one may wonder why he could not accept the inner play (or plays) of *Hamlet*. It is a pity indeed that Gide does not fully express himself on this point.

5. Finally, as for the fundamental metaphor of the *abyme* (or *abîme*), the center of the *blason* or coat of arms: Littré tells us that it is the "center of the escutcheon" and offers, as a model, this sentence: "Il porte trois besans d'or . . . avec une fleur de lis en abîme" ("it bears three golden bezants . . . with a fleur-de-lis *en abîme*"). The phrase "mise en abyme" does not literally appear in the passage from Gide; it is an invention of Gidian criticism, together with its extension, "construction en abyme," which also retains the *y* (Gide says "mettre . . . en abyme"). Now the works on heraldry that I have been able to consult contain numerous illustrations of blazons placed in the center of the principal blazon but never give an example of an *identical* central blazon, one that would re-

produce the surrounding shield. On the contrary, the inner blazon, placed "en abîme" according to heraldic terminology, always represents the coat of arms of *another* family branch, especially the wife's. Although Gide does not in fact say that the second blazon, placed "en abyme," must be a duplication of the first, larger blazon, he does suggest as much. The whole theory of the *mise en abyme* therefore is based on a false metaphor or a defective analogy. (One of Gide's principal critics, Pierre Lafille, writes unhesitatingly in his *André Gide romancier* (Paris, 1954, 25) that "Gide often had recourse . . . to composition 'en abyme,' in accordance with the heraldic terminology 'inescutcheon' that designates the reproduction, in the center of the shield, and in reduced dimensions, of the shield itself." But is there a single example of this anywhere?[1]

If the point of departure of André Gide's theory is painting, it can be rather quickly stated, without claiming a profound knowledge of the history of art, that as early as the beginnings of pictorial representation inner duplication was almost exclusively limited to the inclusion, in the painting, of a mirror that sometimes—but not always, since the mirror is often turned away or obscured—reflects a face, a back, the hair of a figure contemplating herself: a woman busy at her toilette, or the like. Many examples can be found on Greek vases and in the mural paintings of Pompeii. The artists of the early Italian Renaissance refined the use of the mirror; a 1402 illustration to Boccaccio's *De claris mulieribus* shows a lady in the process of painting her own portrait while looking in a mirror, and we see three facial images: the lady's face, its reflection in the mirror, and the portrait she is painting on the canvas.

Later, Michelangelo and others produced a quantity of paintings of Narcissus (that preeminently Gidian character), in which reflection begins to suggest intellectual or psychological values. During this period there appeared the procedure so admired by Gide (but which, as we have seen, often does not support his theory) of including a small convex mirror, which provides the viewer with a distorted image either of the scene itself (as in the paintings of Van Eyck) or, in most cases, of a scene supposedly situated outside the painting, in the viewer's space, as in the paintings of Quentin Metzys or Petrus Christus. These images can be considered more as attempts to introduce hypothetical or virtual places and scenes into the painting, in defiance of traditional laws of perspective, than as true *inner* duplications.

The great painters of the classical age and of the Enlightenment added

1. Some additional information: the Huguet, Nicot, and Cottgrave dictionaries do not attribute the heraldic meaning "center of the blazon" to the term *abîme*. The English term seems to be "innerscocheon" or "inescutcheon." There are also the French expressions "brochant sur le tout" and "sur le tout du tout."

almost nothing to the evolution of these inner pictorial images, which were repeated throughout the nineteenth century, with slight variations, in the creations of Gavarni, Böcklin, Grandville, and Beardsley, for example, and which in the twentieth century can be found in the paintings of Max Beckmann, Braque, Picasso, and others. There is no doubt that on the optical level of illusions there exists among "op" artists an effort to renew visual ambiguities, or "topological impossibilities," as in classical uses of the mirror, in a way that connects with certain procedures of the modern novel. In general, however, in the twentieth century the pictorial art of the mirror is lacking.

Can similar observations be made in the field of music? I am unaware whether anyone has spoken, to date, of interior duplications in music, but conspicuously analogous structures could certainly be seen (or rather, heard) in the fugue, not to mention the "leitmotifs" and overtures that, like prologues in plays, announce in a reduced form what will follow. But the pursuit of structural analogies often presents great dangers of exaggeration and paralogism; I shall be content, for the time being, to point out possible parallels between reentry, repetition, variation, and inversion in musical composition and certain literary procedures, although I will not attempt to develop these parallels fully here. Let us say in passing that the analogy with music can become, as it does in *La Jalousie* of Robbe-Grillet (in which a native song is described in terms that obviously apply to the novel itself), a totally conscious use of the *mise en abyme*.

"The renowned *mise en abyme* can be found more or less everywhere through the centuries," declared Claude Ollier during the discussion at Cerisy-La-Salle in 1964, without specifying whether he meant the general existence of this structure or its purely literary usage. Indeed, one can recognize in certain classical literary works incidents that seem to be related to the *mise en abyme* and that serve as precursors. The way these episodes or incidents are attuned to the very texture of the work reflects a procedural conception that is so to speak pragmatic or operational, since interior duplication, or its prototype, almost always functions to move the narrative forward and justify the transition to other matters— as can still be seen, moreover, in a number of contemporary novelists. In the case of at least one ancient work, Longus's *Daphnis and Chloe*, a painting constitutes the point of departure that by the rhetorical process known as "ecphrasis" engenders the entire story: it is a description of a painting, as Claude Simon would say. In book 8 of the *Odyssey*, a bard begins to sing the story of the wooden horse; Ulysses, who has already experienced this episode, listens and then himself resumes the narration of his own past. Aeneas sees the paintings of Troy on the walls in Carthage, and these images of his past thereby enter the narrative of the present. Other examples like Apuleius's *Golden Ass* illustrate in one way or another the use of duplication. Let me note in passing that in the classical period the duplicating image is always the image of the same thing, not of a parallel or similar thing or event: this important notion of duplication by analogy appears only later in the evolution of *mise en abyme* processes.

A first example is perhaps the interior book that Dante attributes to Galeotto, and whose reading by Paolo and Francesca engenders their great passion: "on that day, they no longer read from this book." Even if Dante does not reveal the book's content to us, he lets us understand what it is about and gives a perfect illustration of the *mise en abyme* that involves ellipsis. If we wished to expand our research to include the larger theme of the *mirror* (as should perhaps be done, in view of the emphasis on the mirror in Gide's passage), the medieval period would provide a rich mine of examples, with its *Speculum mundi*, *Speculum doctrinale*, *Speculum morale*, its *Miroir de l'âme pécheresse*, *Miroir de vie et de mort*, and all the variations on the theme of the mirror that Jean Frappier has studied, extending from Bernard de Ventadour to Maurice Scève (*Cahiers de L'Association Internationale des Etudes Françaises*, 1959). Just as in the history of painting, the personage of Narcissus plays a major role in this evolution, especially in the Renaissance. Narcissus's contemplation of his own image, duplicated in a literary mirror, constitutes a philosophical and moral *mise en abyme*—one that can almost be called an independent subgenre—up to the time of Gide himself. Last, it is in the Middle Ages that collections of *framed* tales begin, such as *The Decameron* and *The Heptameron*, in which each of the intercalated or narrated stories reflects the same theme, treated as a parallel or contrasting story. However, a tale told to illustrate a theme announced by the narrator or his party, as in Boccaccio's *Decameron*, must be distinguished from an intercalated story whose plot evokes thematic resonances for the reader alone, if not exclusively; such is the case, for example, in the brief episodic narratives illustrating the dangers and disorders of love in Madame de Lafayette's *La Princesse de Clèves*, or the overlapping stories in Cervantes' *Don Quixote*, now recognized by critics as having a structural or duplicative function with respect to the work itself.

During the baroque period, the interpenetration of parts in the literary work begins to abound: inner plays (*Hamlet*, *Célinde*, *Saint-Genest*), intercalated stories (*L'Astrée*, the heroic novel, *La Princesse de Clèves*), inner books (*Don Quixote*), allusions to the author in his work (Cervantes, Molière) or to former exploits of a character in a drama (Corneille), interior spectacles whose relation to their framework breaks with any spatial or temporal logic (Corneille's *L'Illusion comique*, Schelandre's *Tyr et Sydon*), "Pirandellian" parades of actors in the process of putting on their plays (Buckingham's *The Rehearsal*, *La Comédie des comédiens*), allegorical works in which life itself is presented as a theatrical play in the process of being duplicated (Calderón's *El gran teatro del mundo*, as well as the same author's *La vida es sueño*).

Above all, it is in the drama of the baroque period that the greatest development of duplication occurs. This phenomenon has at least been partly studied by scholars of seventeenth-century theater such as Lancaster, Allewyn, Livingstone, and Nelson. Often, in the most baroque of these works, interior duplication involves actions hidden from the audience as well as from the characters of the drama before they are revealed at the moment when the illusion is shattered, as happens in *A Mad World, My Masters* by Middleton, or in Corneille's *L'Illusion comique*, in the scene where Pridamant's son "dies" before being resuscitated in order to receive his actor's wages for having performed in an inner play. Although this kind of duplication or rather interpenetration is without a doubt linked to the *mise en abyme* procedure, it represents a special aspect of the principle, since in most cases it is less a matter of the presence in the work of a reduced or analogical model than it is of a lateral current, or sidestream, that manages to connect, in a surprise junction, with the main river of the principal action. If Rotrou's Adrien the actor plays the role of Saint-Genest in a religious tragedy that reflects his own crisis of conscience, it is in order to recognize himself in Saint-Genest at the moment he steps out of the inner play to proclaim himself a Christian and become a martyr. References are frequently made to the inner play enacted by "professional" actors in *Hamlet*, cited by Gide among his examples of the *mise en abyme*: a small model on the scale of the characters that directly contributes to the principal action. Let me point out, however, that it is Hamlet himself who has the idea of putting on this play, who appoints himself to write its scenario, and who articulates the theory that justifies and explains it. We are still far from modern duplications in which the parallel is only implied and the irony of contrapuntal allusions is recognized exclusively by the reader or spectator.

If the baroque period abounds in duplications and interpenetrations of the works' reciprocal parts, it does not, as far as I know, produce theories or commentaries on the procedure. In that preeminently creative age, style prevails over criticism: neither the Abbé d'Aubignac nor the more subtle Tesauro of the *Téléscope aristotélicien* takes it upon himself to identify or explain the phenomenon. One has to wait for the end of the eighteenth century to find, in Goethe, the first *theory* of inner duplications. As for works of the Enlightenment, I have asked colleagues who are well informed on this period for examples of duplications, but with relatively meager results. The baroque current of illusory *dédoublements*, or duplications, continues with Destouches and Marivaux. In the domain of the philosophy of that preeminently philosophical century, the great mystic Swedenborg (whose later influence on Baudelaire and the symbolists is well known) seems to have modified the hermetic principle of Paracelsus (everything below reproduces what is above) for the purpose of extracting from it a principle of identical interior structures: each object is made of an infinity of small identical objects, language is composed of a multiplicity of little languages, and so on. Obviously I could also cite the old theory of the homunculus in the sperm, a reduced analogue of the embryo in the body of the pregnant woman, but let us move on to other matters.

It is Gide himself who points out the interest of interior duplications in the works of Goethe, but the French author does not seem to be acquainted with the passages of his German predecessor's diary where the process is commented upon and an attempt is made to draw a kind of aesthetic theory from it. Professor Liselotte Dieckmann has done a fine study of Goethe's ideas and procedures,[2] but, curiously, she does not mention Gide and even speaks of "the uniqueness of Goethe's technique." To justify such duplications as the performance of *Hamlet* in *Wilhelm Meister* (in which there also appears the portrait of a sick prince who resembles Wilhelm), or the insertion in *The Sorrows of Young Werther* of a young peasant lad whose story duplicates, in a certain way, Werther's own, Goethe presents us with his ideas on what he calls "repeated mirror reflections" in the form of a list involving approximately ten paragraphs. For example, says Goethe, the writings of genius are none other than reflections of images from memory, which become a new reality, and so forth. The scientific or pseudoscientific explanation of this phenomenon that Goethe offers is very curious: "optical effects, when reflected from mirror to mirror, rather than becoming dim progressively increase in brilliancy." Now this is certainly not the case with images that are mutually reflected by mirrors facing each other: on the contrary, everyone has noticed the progressive dimming or darkening that occurs in facing-mirrors. Thus, just as Gide a hundred years later was to propose a faulty analogy with interior blazons to illustrate his conception, so did Goethe, the first theorist of duplications, choose a scientific analogy that does not hold physically. The theorists themselves are duplicated in their errors.

The nineteenth century would surely furnish researchers with numer-

2. "Repeated Mirror Reflections: The Technique of Goethe's Novels," *Studies in Romanticism* 1 (1962): 154–74.

ous modalities of interior duplications before Gide. Comparatists would especially find material to their hearts' content. Emma Bovary's novels and keepsakes, the tapestry representing Pyramus and Thisbe in Maupassant's *Une Vie*, the use of Shakespeare's *As You Like It* to parallel the characters and incidents of Gautier's *Mlle de Maupin*, the performance of *Phèdre* in Zola's *La Curée*, the interior novel in Jorge Issac's *Maria*, Novalis's novel in which Heinrich von Ofterdingen finds a book that already illustrates his entire life, the inner paintings of Melville's *Moby Dick* and *Pierre*, the statues and portraits in the novels of Hawthorne, from *The House of the Seven Gables* to *The Marble Faun*, the inner portrait of Dorian Gray that becomes tainted with the moral degradation of Wilde's protagonist. All of this barely scratches the surface of an abundantly rich mine of examples.

It would be superfluous to retrace the numerous *mises en abyme* of the Gidian opus: they range from *Paludes* (where an author is in the process of writing *Paludes*) and *L'Immoraliste* (wherein Michel rediscovers his immoralism in the history of the Goths, which he is studying) up to *Les Caves du Vatican* (in which the novelist Julius discusses the notion of *mise en abyme* with Lafcadio) and especially *Les Faux-monnayeurs* (in which the novelist Edouard is in the process of writing a novel bearing the same title, centered on the same characters, and we are given portions of the text to read). This latter novel is, in turn, duplicated so to speak in *Le Journal des faux-monnayeurs*, which again multiplies the perspectives. Both Pierre Lafille and Claude-Edmonde Magny have thoroughly examined these duplications; and Lafille in particular has extensively compared *Les Faux-monnayeurs* with Aldous Huxley's well-known novel *Point Counter Point*, which picks up the principle and extrapolates it into a pattern involving ten overlapping novels, similar to the interior figures on Quaker Oats boxes or in Dubonnet advertisements. (Gide's silence in his comments on Huxley's novel concerning this aspect of Huxley's work remains a mystery in Gidian studies.)

Among those works that are more or less contemporary with Gide's and in which the *mise en abyme* or similar procedures can be found, let me draw attention to Lacretelle's *Le Pour et le contre*, in which—just as in group therapy sessions of today—a number of characters together "compose" a novel that is revealed to be the very image of their situation. Let me also indicate some paths that remain to be followed, adding Shean O'Brien's novel *Swim Two Birds*, the use of portraits as characters' models in Henry James's *The Real Thing* and *The Wings of the Dove*, the parable of the church keeper in Kafka's *The Trial*, and all of Pirandello's theater. The question of the existence of a *mise en abyme* in the work of Proust, which inspired considerable discussion at the André Gide colloquium in Cerisy, would in itself merit a separate study; in my view, it is less a question of a *mise en abyme* with Proust than of a process that could be labeled "infolding": the novel that the narrator projects at the end of *Le Temps retrouvé* is supposedly the very novel we have just read; literally, or textually, however, at this point in the text the novel is supposedly not yet written. The *mise en abyme* connects here with the notion of fictional *circularity*, or the return to the point of departure; other comparable though not identical examples might be Joyce's *Finnegans Wake* or even Beckett's play *En attendant Godot*, in which the circular song of the dying dog can be seen, in turn, to be a true *mise en abyme*.

If interior duplications can therefore be said to exist more or less everywhere and to have existed for a very long time, the example of Gide and especially his theory and *mise en abyme* formula now suffice to attribute to him the mastery, if not the origin, of the procedure. Gide is unanimously referred to by novelists and critics of the new novel; the numerous variations on the technique of the reduced model can be discerned not only in the new novel itself, but also in the new cinema and in the structural ideas of an author like Jean Ricardou. Ricardou, who is above all a practitioner and theorist of the most advanced modes of the *mise en abyme*, recognizes, in *Le Nouveau Roman* (Paris, 1973, 47 ff.), the importance of Gide's influence. Let me quickly review the most typical and striking examples of the use of interior duplication or *mise en abyme* in the works of the new French novelists.

First, what may be termed a "classic" example: in *Portrait d'un inconnu* (1956), a museum painting that bears the same title as the novel is subjected to an analytic commentary in which Nathalie Sarraute brings out the parallels with her own central character, without openly identifying the analogies. The role of paintings is generally rather obvious in the new novel: in *La Route des Flandres*, Claude Simon describes for us the portrait of another de Reixach whose life prefigures that of the protagonist; Claude Ollier in *La Mise en scène* gives a minute description of a primitive drawing on the walls of a cave that sums up the story of Lassalle (the hero) as well as the quasi-identical story of his predecessor Lessing. The picture on the post office calendar in Robbe-Grillet's *La Jalousie* reflects a phantasm-fear of the husband, while the print of the *Défaite de Reichenfels* in *Dans le labyrinthe* not only literally duplicates a principal scene of the novel, but comes to life as it fuses with the text that frames it. Other duplications drawn from the fine arts can be seen in the stained glass and tapestries of Butor's *L'Emploi du temps*, the "legendary" statue of *Le Voyeur* and the one of *Marienbad*, and to some extent in the scenes of statues and wax figures in the gardens of the "Villa Bleue" of *La Maison de rendez-vous*.

The use of the literary texts inside a novel for the purpose of reflecting or duplicating the principal work is also found pretty much everywhere. The "classic" example this time could be the "African novel" of *La Jalousie*, whose reading and commentary by A. . . and Franck, together with the distorted image the husband creates of the inner novel that he himself has not read, allow for the only intrusions of psychological terms, which may be applicable to a situation of infidelity or jealousy, in a text that is otherwise strictly "objectal" or phenomenological. The role of the detective novel *Meurtre de Bleston* in Butor's *L'Emploi du temps* is a little more complicated: the interior text describes a *possible* aspect of the action that surrounds Jacques Revel, but this text functions above all to establish parallels between the very structure of detective novels and the structure of the diary, and with it the search for self-knowledge in which the hero is involved. As for novels projected by novelistic protagonists themselves, they are not, strictly speaking, interior duplications: I have in mind those novels proposed by Roquentin of Sartre's *La Nausée*, by Léon Delmont in *La Modification*, and by others as well. An interesting case of ambiguous connections between a written text and the novel being read can be found in *Eté indien* by Claude Ollier (1963): the protagonist, in search of exotic places to use as settings for a movie scenario his company wants to shoot, envisions possible versions of this scenario that vary according to all the places he visits: New York, Mexico, and so on. Moreover, Ollier introduces (as he does again in *L'Echec de Nolan*, 1967) a very elaborate system of verbal and visual correspondences between different parts of the novel: descriptions of New York skyscrapers using the same vocabulary as that used to describe the pyramids of Yucatán, for example.

The novelist who has pushed the domain of the literary *mise en abyme* the furthest is Jean Ricardou. (I have covered much of Ricardou's role in chapter 1, "Postmodern Generative Fiction," so that some overlapping here is inevitable.) In *La Prise de Constantinople*, whose back cover bears the "reflected" title *La Prose de Constantinople*, there is first of all a creative process based on Roussel's "generative" principle: from the interplay of eight letters, Ricardou extracts several groups of characters whose names (using these letters) are plays on words or resonances linked to other parts of the novel. In the unnumbered pages of the book, the characters are in a library, reading another book with unnumbered pages that contains, if not the same story, then at least an altogether parallel one. Certain pages of the interior book are identical to pages of the principal text, and from time to time one comes upon the same paragraphs or entire pages without knowing which "text" is being read. A letter Jean Ricardou sent me at the time *La Prise de Constantinople* came out contains the following remarks that prove how conscious the author is of the influence of Gide: "il me semble qu'on peut insister . . . sur un principe de *création par la structure*: le problème étant: comment composer un livre tel que l'une ou plusieurs de ses pages seraient dédoublées (photocopiées en quelque sorte) et reproduites ailleurs dans le livre avant ou après. Vous voyez qu'il s'agit d'une sorte de *mise en abyme* textuelle. . . . Le livre à faire est 'impossible'—paradoxal à tout instant. Il faut inventer un *nouvel espace romanesque*" ("it seems to me that a *principle of creation by structure* can be stressed, the problem being: How could one so compose a book that one or more of its pages could be duplicated [photocopied, as it were] and reproduced elsewhere in the book before or after. You see that it has to do with a kind of textual *mise en abyme*. . . . The book to be written is 'impossible'—paradoxical at every instant. A new fictional space [*espace romanesque*] has to be invented").

Is this new fictional space too "formalistic," indeed baroque or manneristic? Perhaps. In any case, I view this tendency of Ricardou and of others (let us say those of the Tel Quel group) as the consequence of a reaction against the politically committed ("engagé") novel of Sartre and his disciples; an effort, in other words, to disengage the novel on the one hand and to engage it in an aesthetic independence on the other. During the 1971 discussion at Cerisy, Ricardou presented the following argument: "Je crois que la plupart des livres du Nouveau Roman contiennent, d'une façon ou d'une autre, une *mise en abyme* ou plusieurs, ou même, de continuelles *mises en abyme*. Cette réduction, cette image du livre dans le livre . . . a donc, je crois . . . la singulière fonction de souligner que le roman n'a de rapport avant tout qu'avec lui-même. Au lieu d'attirer l'attention vis-à-vis du monde quotidien dans lequel nous sommes, il semble qu'il y ait là comme une volonté extrêmement concertée d'attirer l'attention vers le centre secret du livre" (*Nouveau Roman: Hier, aujourd'hui*, Paris, 1972) ("I believe that most books of the new novel contain, in one fashion or another, one or more *mises en abyme*, or even continual *mises en abyme*. This reduction, this image of the book within the book . . . therefore has, I believe, the singular function of emphasizing that the novel primarily relates only to itself. Instead of drawing attention to the daily world we are in, it seems that there is in this procedure a sort of extremely concerted will to draw attention toward the secret center of the book"). The *mise en abyme* therefore becomes a facet of the looping or infolding of the modern work that like the famous "Sonnet en -*yx*" of Mallarmé (an author whose traces are everywhere to be found in Ricardou's *La Prise de Constantinople*), causes the work to turn in upon itself.

In his *Problèmes du Nouveau Roman* (1967), Jean Ricardou recapitulates these same ideas (especially in the chapter "L'Histoire dans l'histoire"), and after astute analyses of Poe's "The Fall of the House of Usher," the book within the book of Novalis's *Heinrich von Ofterdingen*, the sadoerotic paintings of Robbe-Grillet's *Le Voyeur*, and the "central *mise en abyme*" of Butor's *L'Emploi du temps* (the outbreak of fire, according to Ricardou), he moves on to a distinction between the metaphorical or fictional *mise en abyme* and the one he himself uses in an original way, that of textual duplication or repetition of passages already read, a new means of "contesting" the very principle of novelistic chronology. These remarks, together with the study of Poe's *The Adventures of Arthur Gordon Pym*, which Ricardou considers an immense *mise en abyme* or almost an allegory of the idea of writing or of the written page, completely coincide with the procedures of *La Prise de Constantinople* (even including the suppression of "customary pagination numbers" and the "second title, on the opposite side of the book's cover"). Language, the alphabet itself, engenders the narrative, which in turn brings the reader, or the reading process, back to language.

In his 1969 novel *Les Lieux-dits* Ricardou continued to develop plot, setting, and characters starting from linguistic data: as in *La Prise de Constantinople*, we witness a play of eight place names (made up of eight letters each) serving as titles for eight chapters, recapitulations of identical passages, settings illustrating the named places and relating back to them by means of subtle analogies, numerous reflections, tapestries, and paintings, all of which constitute continual *mises en abyme*. In addition, the author, or rather the very novel, "explains itself," establishes itself as its own guide (as the subtitle of the work indicates: "petit guide d'un voyage dans le livre"), and clears itself up. Does language follow reality (guide) or does it create its universe (novel)? The novel is a mass of anagrams, alphabetical tangles, paradigms, syntagmas, symbolic, allegorical, and thematic reciprocities.

In Robbe-Grillet's *Les Gommes*, the whole action, as I have pointed out in *Les Romans de Robbe-Grillet*, is nothing other than a kind of reversed and parodied duplication of the myth of Oedipus, which is not, however, mentioned in the book. Should one speak of interior or even exterior duplication? What then is the function of the small duplications of certain aspects of Oedipus's story in the conversation of the simple women in the streetcar, the scenes of the ruins of Thebes, and such? Joyce's great book *Ulysses* at least bears a title that tempts one to find parallels with the *Odyssey*. (Would these be found anyway, without the title?) And in Michel Butor's *L'Emploi du temps* the protagonist himself comments at length on the role of reduced models, played by the images of Cain, Abel, Theseus, and once again Oedipus. Almost always, Marguerite Duras inserts reduced actions in her novels, which are more or less separated from the thread or plot of the work and constitute a kind of exemplary provocation for the characters, such as the small passional drama at the beginning of *Moderato cantabile* that represents in advance what the heroine herself will experience.

It would be a mistake to think that the *mise en abyme* appears these days only in France.[3] Obviously, certain novels by Vladimir Nabokov are constructed upon a system of overlapping duplications, the principal example of which is *Pale Fire*—an example that by itself would merit a long discussion—in which the author-narrator is transformed in a poetic duplication (Charles Kinbote and John Shade). John Updike and others ingeminate myths (*The Centaur*), sometimes with painfully obvious parallels. Thomas Pynchon in *V* resorts to interior diaries, corresponding parts, and more or less duplicated characters, any one of which could be the "V" of the title. In Albee's play *Tiny Alice*, a small representation or reduced model of the setting occupies the center of the stage; just as the "true" setting will do later, this simulacrum catches fire. These examples could surely be multiplied.

Finally, the cinema seems to have opened, with its immense visual possibilities, a whole new chapter in the history of the structural *mise en abyme*. The reciprocity of past and present, in the two stories of *Hiroshima mon amour*, plays on duplications; at the beginning of *L'Année dernière à Marienbad* we witness a theatrical performance that already repeats the principal dialogues of the protagonists, whose very voices intervene at the moment of transition to the level of the fictional "reality." Fellini's *8½* presents us with a scenarist who is looking for his motion-picture scenario, and the movie itself is none other than this scenario of a film producer looking for his scenario. Thus, Christian Metz makes the statement that: "the author of *8½* . . . is . . . the first to have constructed his *entire* film and arranged *all* of its elements in terms of the *mise en abyme*."[4] The comic film by George Axelrod, *Paris When It Sizzles*, develops possibilities of multiple solutions, rejected or adopted, of the same principle (a scenarist looking for his text); on a more serious level this principle serves as the basis of the film by Robbe-Grillet, *Trans-Europ-Express* (1967), in which a movie writer on a first-class train "invents"

3. See the review of J. Mitchell's *The Undiscovered Country* that appeared in *Time*, 26 January 1970, 82. Not only the interior novel, but the name and personage of the "true" author reappear "en abyme." And apropos of her novel *In Transit*, Brigid Brophy declares: "I'm playing games, like a painter who includes in his picture a mirror in which he shows himself standing outside the picture painting it" (*Time*, 2 February 1970, 72).

4. Christian Metz, *Essais sur la signification au cinéma* (Paris, 1968), 223.

the scenes that we see, but that seem to escape their "author's" imagination and unfold independently. The movie by Roger Leenhardt, *Le Rendez-vous de minuit*, has us witness the projection of a film in a small neighborhood movie theater; inside are two characters who strangely resemble the stars of the picture (portrayed by the same actors) and whose meeting and adventures mix with what is happening in the "film" to the point that soon we no longer see the latter's image or screen, creating an exceedingly Pirandellian ambiguity in which we no longer know what is the "reality" and what is its cinematographic duplication, as in the Swedish film *I Am Curious Yellow*.

It happens rather often that certain critics, while avoiding the use of the terms *mise en abyme* or interior duplication, refer at length to the procedure itself, which they consider as having a fundamental importance in the structure of the works being analyzed. Thus, René Prédal in his book on Alain Resnais,[5] repeatedly develops the interrelations of interior models, such as the statue of *L'Année dernière à Marienbad*, "which reflects the entire film, and plays the same role as the painting of *Dans le labyrinthe*," the cathedral of Bleston and the detective novel of Butor's *L'Emploi du temps*, and still others, which he associates with "expressionist objects" or "strongly stressed" symbols in modern novels and movies, typical examples of which he says are the "sounds of laughter, broken heel, pistol-range, corridors, labyrinth, strange costumes, mysterious theater or balustrade against which A is often leaning and which collapsed" in *Marienbad*. Jean Rousset's remark concerning Robbe-Grillet's *Dans le labyrinthe*,[6] in which he sees each scene as "referring to all the others" in "a series of internal reflections and mirror effects," leads in the same direction.

Let me point out, finally, that the theory and function of the *mise en abyme* vary according to a rather complicated evolution, one that seems far from having run its course. For Gide, the reduced model "clarified" the work by establishing proportions, especially for the author and the reader; but one of the examples he cited, the inner play of *Hamlet*, has already showed us an "active" duplication at the level of the characters. Awareness or unawareness, within the work itself, of the existence of a duplication (perceived by the reader only or by one or several characters as well) continues to provide an important distinction in the use of this duplicated structure, just as awareness or unawareness of the presence of a myth (implicit in *Les Gommes*, explicit in *L'Emploi du temps*, for example) serves to characterize parallel or analogous techniques.

5. *Etudes cinématographiques*, nos. 64–65 (1968): 58–60.
6. Jean Rousset, *L'Intérieur et l'extérieur* (Paris, 1968), 233.

In passing to its most recent stage (in the novels and theory of Jean Ricardou), the *mise en abyme* seems to function neither to reflect the work as in a small mirror nor to provide the novelistic characters a means, on their own level, of watching themselves act, of judging and understanding themselves (with or without explicit consciousness of the procedure), but rather to allow the text itself to attain new modalities, to distort novelistic space in order to fold it in upon itself, by cutting all the ties between the novel and everyday life. The novel thus becomes more "self-sufficient" by means of reintegrated repetitions, interpenetrated and reciprocal parts, recapitulations, reflections, duplications, and diverse *mises en abyme*, including a new use of "lettristic" correspondences between the names of characters and the texture, or internal structures, of a work like Ricardou's.[7] It remains to be seen whether the reader will in turn find himself "cut off" from the novel or whether this procedure, now transformed into a weapon in the war of "aesthetic" commitment of literary works, will be able to function henceforth so as to create in the reader a new symbiosis with the future novel. In any case, it hardly seems doubtful that some very evolved forms of the Gidian *mise en abyme* will play a significant role in the mirroring processes of novelistic perspectives.

7. Allan Pasco sees an antecedent of this procedure in certain phonetic and etymological resonances already present in the works of André Gide, who, he believes, intended that each detail of the work reflect the whole. See A. Pasco and Wilfrid J. Rollman, "The Artistry of Gide's Onomastics," *MLN* 86 (1971): 523–31.

11
GAMES AND GAME STRUCTURES IN ROBBE-GRILLET

Along with mathematics, games have come to play a considerable role in contemporary literary works and criticism. From the outset, the proliferation of game structures in the works of Alain Robbe-Grillet identifies him as a notable example of *artifex ludens*. Almost all the tendencies that are termed "aspects ludiques" in his novels and films may be uncovered by careful scrutiny of his earliest productions. It is even possible to reduce the numerous game structures to a few basic models, such as the circular or winding path of individual *cases* or rectangles (like those found on board games played with dice and pawns), the maze or labyrinth, and the multiple-solution type of game, such as Clue, in which shuffling the cards or figures representing characters and places allows each separate *partie*, although created out of identical elements, to produce a totally different outcome.

The conception of a fundamentally gamelike structure of the novel would also make specific games mentioned in the works, or specifically played by the characters therein, examples of *mise en abyme* or interior duplication, functioning with respect to the overall structure in somewhat the same way as an "inner novel" (cf. *La Jalousie*) or play (cf. *L'Année dernière à Marienbad*) that duplicates, at the level of the characters and within the fictional field, the general pattern of the novel or film. This integrative principle constitutes one type of "justification" of an actual game (as in *Marienbad*) as coherently incorporated into the aesthetic structure. The literal game may be minimized or may not appear at all, but the "metaphysical" aspect of general game structure cannot, since it is part of the novelistic technique, be avoided. It is in turn this metaphysical implication that protects the work from falling into the gratuity of a neo-Kantian "free play of the faculties" conception of fictional art that might, if pushed to the limit, reduce the creative process to a kind of aesthetic billiard game or acrobatic display. It is also evident that the problem of formalism in the use of game structures in novels and films has its parallels in painting (from abstract expressionism to pop art) and the other arts, especially contemporary music. In order to tie the discussion to the specifics of fiction, however, I will set aside these tempting analogies.

If, as Hjelmslev declares, language itself is "put together like a game,"[1] with a large but finite number of underlying structures that permit a vast repertory of combinations representing the totality of actual practice or usage in all given cases, then by the principle of analogous extension all fiction may be said to be put together like a game, with each specific story or novel constituting merely one of the possible *parties* or individual playings of the game of fictional composition. However, such a broad view, though perhaps sound in theory, fails to distinguish between a novel whose structure bears no identifiable or obvious resemblance to any known *game* (in the usual sense), such as *Madame Bovary*, and one that closely parallels or imitates a known game structure, such as Robbe-Grillet's *Dans le labyrinthe* (1959). Here I am concerned with the latter type of novel, as well as with the playing of games or execution of game-like patterns by characters in the novel, and with specific or hidden allusions to games in novelistic contexts of which the characters (and sometimes the readers themselves) remain unaware.

Puzzles, mathematical games, riddles, paradoxes, topological curiosities (like the Möbius strip), optical illusions (like the pinhole fly image in *Dans le labyrinthe*), and all such pararational phenomena have fascinated Robbe-Grillet since his childhood. I recall his once calculating rapidly and precisely the number of times a single sheet of paper would have to be folded to make it thick enough to reach from the earth to the moon (it is a mathematical possibility). I have described elsewhere his first project for a novel, whose pertinence here justifies repeating the following essentials: this novel, which he never gave a title, was to have its plot organized according to the hermetic series of 108 scales on drawings made by medieval alchemists of the legendary snake Ouroboros. Note that we are dealing from the outset with the combination of an archetype or traditional symbolic representation (the Gnostic snake biting its own tail, symbolizing the Universe in Horapollo's *Hieroglyphics*, Time in Plotinus, and the repeated cycles of metempsychosis among the Ophites) and a mathematical game, depending on the properties of a unique series of the numbers from 1 to 108 (108 being also, Mircea Eliade informs me, a sacred number among certain Hindu sects). If one constructs a mandalalike wheel or circle with 108 spaces around the circumference (a

1. Quoted in Jacques Ehrmann, "Oh Articulation," *Yale French Studies* 39 (1969): 11.

pattern suggestive of board-and-dice games), it is possible, according to a certain formula, to arrange the numbers 1 to 108 in such a way that at any given point the sum of the two numbers on opposite sides of the circle will be 108. No other number will permit such an arrangement. What the "prenovelist" Robbe-Grillet proposed to do was divide his plot chronologically into 108 narrative elements or narremes and put them textually in the order of the spaces around the Ouroboros diagram. "Dechronology" would thus be introduced artificially into the novel's time structure, in a manner directly comparable to the use of external forms or models in determining the order of musical elements in certain compositions of John Cage and others. Also, the novel, however random in apparent structure, would in reality be constructed upon secret inner principles of organization left unrevealed to the reader or critic, a procedure the author was shortly to follow in his first published novel. The effect of such chronological juggling would no doubt have been to some extent comparable to that produced by the ordering of plot elements in such later works as *La Maison de rendez-vous* (1965), especially if Robbe-Grillet, having rearranged his 108 plot elements into his hermetic series, had then established *liaisons de scène* to articulate the whole into an apparent continuity, in defiance of the obvious nonlinearity of the intrigue. At any rate, two fundamental compositional principles, circularity and series, may be seen in their earliest form in the gamelike project for the Ouroboros novel.[2]

In *Les Gommes* (1953) Robbe-Grillet employs myth as hidden structure and establishes ingenious correspondences between myth and the semioccult "game" of tarot cards. Neither the myth (that of Oedipus) nor the tarot is specifically mentioned in the text, and the general recognition now of their presence may be attributed to the publication of various critical essays, beginning with my own.[3] It is now possible to reinforce and extend my original findings, thanks to the unexpected and welcome collaboration of the distinguished surrealist critic Jacques Brunius. I had limited myself to studying more or less separately the systematic correspondences between the Oedipus myth and the plot of *Les Gommes* (in which Wallas, the protagonist, seeks a murderer only to *become* that murderer in the end), reflected in references to an abandoned

2. The public's fascination with such paraliterary matters as this nonexistent "novel" by Robbe-Grillet is shown by the fact that my remarks were seized upon by such reviewers as *Paris-Match*, which delighted in citing such examples of Robbe-Grillet's baroque imagination.

3. See my "Oedipus and Existentialism: *Les Gommes* of Robbe-Grillet," *Wisconsin Studies in Comparative Literature* (Fall 1960), and *Les Romans de Robbe-Grillet* (Paris: Minuit, 1963, 1965, 1971).

child, Thebes, the riddle of the Sphinx, Apollo's oracle, Laïus's chariot, and the like, and to separate parallels between traditional readings of certain tarot cards and the fictional situations in which they occur (in hidden form) in the novel. The reader may recall that the tarot references first appear as the "other protagonist," Garinati, climbs the stairs to Dupont's study, intending to murder him. This stairway consists of twenty-one wooden steps plus one nonconforming stone step at the bottom that "bears a brass column . . . ending in a fool's head capped with a three-belled bonnet." This detail, together with the picture on the wall at the sixteenth step, described exactly in terms of the sixteenth tarot card, the *Maison Dieu*, establishes the parallel without revealing it explicitly: the *Mat* or Fool, which may be card one or twenty-two, has no number in the tarot pack, while the remaining *arcanes majeurs* correspond to the twenty-one wooden steps. I have pointed out that the Fool "upside down" (or in the bottom position) stands in the tarot manuals for the sudden stopping of progress, thus forming a subtle support for the first "frozen" scene in *Les Gommes*, Garinati's motionless pause on these steps. The resonances of the *Maison Dieu* card are more complicated, since what is merely announced in the first stairway passage recurs later with more explicit allusions to the death of a king (Laïus), with the card (or rather its picture image) contributing its traditional meaning of *coup de théâtre, choc inattendu* to reinforce the novel's surprising final twist.

What Jacques Brunius proposed to me, in his letters, was the possibility of discerning in the novel certain cross-correspondences between the Oedipus myth and the tarot pack that would "bring out a troubling parallelism between the two perspectives on Destiny represented by Oedipus and the tarot." The effect of these would be to further integrate the "game" aspect of the tarot into the novel's total structure. For example, Brunius points out that the café where the protagonist Wallas tries to answer the riddles posed by the drunkard (riddles composed of various distorted versions of the Sphinx's riddle about man in Sophocles' play) is at 10, rue des Arpenteurs, and that the major tarot card ten, called the Wheel of Fortune, shows a sphinx seated on the wheel. Moreover, the chariot statue on the square (which I had seen only as a reference to the chariot of Laïus in the scene of the murder at the crossroads in *Oedipus the King*) recalls card seven, showing a king (father image) on such a chariot, cubical like the *gomme* eraser and the basalt cube in Dupont's (the father's?) study; and the Hanged Man of card twelve is suspended by one foot like the infant Oedipus on the mountain. These findings do indeed create a new parallelism within the novel, and they demonstrate conclusively that the notion of game, in the sense of purely formal diversion, carries with it implications reaching all the way into the domains of archetypes and myths. True, the tarot is rarely if ever played as a "pure" game, since it is used for fortune-telling and prophecy. Yet its structure and interpretative systems are gamelike in their organization, and from its minor *arcanes* the pack of cards used in contemporary "empty" games has been derived.[4]

While there are no outright or hidden references to games in *Le Voyeur* (1955) and *La Jalousie* (1957)—if we except such offhand allusions as that to pinball machines in the café scenes of *Le Voyeur*—both novels show serial patternings with analogies to the general conception of game structure referred to earlier. One might, *à la rigueur*, compare some of these patterns to the "game of resemblances" familiar to readers of magazines and Sunday supplements. The entire series of eight-shaped objects and forms in *Le Voyeur* is a case in point, as is the more subtle series of Y-shaped objects and designs that can be discerned in a minute reading of the text, and which are organized around the Y of the pubis and thus brought into the erotosadistic gestalt of the eight-shaped bonds, rings, and the like associated with Mathias's rape and murder of his victim Jacqueline. Similarly, the V series of *La Jalousie*, from the parquet floors to the "accidental" arrangement of logs waiting to be used on the footbridge, as well as the "spot" series (centipede, oil spot, grease spot at Franck's place at the table, defective spot on the window, and the like), may all be seen as an extension of a high-order game of "find the resemblance." Needless to say, this aspect of the novel is subordinated to less gamelike and more "serious" matters; but the games "people play," like Mathias's burning holes side by side in paper (and perhaps a girl's flesh) with his cigarette, or like the husband's testing the mathematical regularity of his trapezoidal banana fields, have easily recognizable psychic meanings and readily find their place in novelistic structures that are far from constituting "mere" games.

It is *Dans le labyrinthe* (1959), which offers, for the first but not the last time in Robbe-Grillet's production, outright analogies with those

4. Jacques Brunius, who has graciously allowed me to use his findings, points out other interesting details. For example, "Note that the 12th letter of the Hebrew alphabet is L (lamed). Garinati wears a raincoat with an L-shaped tear (L is the initial of Laïus), just as the *Mat* or Fool has a tear in his pants. This establishes the identification of a) the murderer to the Fool, and b) the murderer to Oedipus-Wallas." Furthermore, he informs me that in 1947 André Breton had proposed for the surrealist exposition "a stairway of 22 steps of which each step would symbolize one of the major tarot cards," and that this project is mentioned in the text of the exposition, though the stairway was never constructed. If Robbe-Grillet knew this text, which is doubtful, we have another example of surrealist "influence" on his work: if he did not, we still have a fine illustration of *le hasard objectif*. Jacques Brunius wrote to me spontaneously upon reading my treatment of *Les Gommes* in *Les Romans de Robbe-Grillet*, and I here express my appreciation of his contribution.

board games that depend for their effect on multiple attempts, with advances and retreats, with side excursions into dead ends, with repeated efforts to find the "right" path to the center and win the game (in the case of the soldier in the novel, to deliver the box). The title of the work invites the comparison, and the paragraphs of the text itself often give the effect of a throw of the dice permitting no movement ("Non. Non.") or of frantic turnings from right to left (the scenes in the corridor), of arrivals at hopeless impasses. I have suggested that this whole pattern is a metaphor of the problem of writing this or any novel; in this view the "game" aspect of randomness, multiplicity, and alternatives becomes an allegory of the creative process, somewhat in the Mallarméan sense. Every narrative effort, to paraphrase the poet, is a throw of the dice and will never abolish chance.

We now come to *L'Année dernière à Marienbad* (1961), which could well serve as a model of game structure in novel and film. Readers and viewers of the film may recall the worldwide reaction to this game, ranging from articles setting forth its basis in binary mathematics (or contesting this basis) to the distribution in movie houses, in New York and elsewhere, of matchbooks bearing the rules of the game. Alain Resnais, the director, announced after the release of the film that the "Marienbad game" was a variant of the ancient "Chinese" game of Nim; it was also learned that Robbe-Grillet thought that he himself had invented it, and at least one angry French citizen, claiming to have invented and patented the game, threatened to sue the producer, director, and scenarist. *Cinéma 61* and *62* carried a learned debate on the mathematics of Nim, and I myself appended to my study of *Les Romans de Robbe-Grillet* (1963) an explanation with examples of the binary calculations necessary to win in any situation. Following the general impression, I also spoke of Nim as "Chinese" in origin; but later a mathematician, D. W. Bushaw, sent me an article, "On the Name and History of Nim," arguing convincingly that the name derives from German *nimm*, a form of *nehmen*, meaning to take.[5] Aside from the incidental interest of the game itself, the important point suggested by the existence of a mathematical theory is that Nim, both in reality and in the film, is not a "game" in the open sense, but the execution of a predetermined certainty by one familiar with its system. Obviously, only M, the husband figure, is privy to Nim's secrets in the film, and the various remarks heard among the spec-

---

5. *Washington Mathematics* 11 (October 1966): 52–55. Bushaw points out that the game has been known as "Takeaway," and that in the eighteenth century the poet John Byron used "The Nimmers" as the title of a poem on thieves. The first scientific treatment of Nim in print came in C. L. Boulton, "Nim, a Game with a Complete Mathematical Theory," *Annals of Mathematics* (New York, 1902).

tators (such as "It must be a logarithmic series," etc.) reflect the surrounding ignorance on which the power of M's play depends. (In a sense,
the "native song" of *La Jalousie*, described as incoherent only to one not
familiar with its "rules," is an analogous structure.) The antagonists X and
M confront each other in two ways: in the struggle of passion to possess
A, and in the duel of the mind to win at Nim (or at poker, dominoes, etc.).
A certain tonality of playing dice with the devil is sounded in these encounters at the gaming table. M always wins, but he "can lose," as he says,
and in the end he does. Is it deliberately?

It is perhaps unnecessary to do more than refer briefly to the integration of Nim into the visual series of the film, and thus into the implicit
psychology of the characters, especially A: the broken glass, the slippers,
the photographs, the torn pieces of a letter, even the final oblique reference in the pattern of the lighted windows along the facade of the château as the film ends. All the games of the film, including that of the shooting gallery, reinforce the themes of contest, domination, imposition of
one's will upon another, even violence, that form the basis of the main
action of *Marienbad*. Like the play on the château stage, the games of the
film are forms of interior duplication, of *mise en abyme* in the Gidian
sense, which serve not only to permit the characters themselves to take
cognizance of their situations (as the dialogue on the statue does, for example), but also to let the spectator or reader plunge deeper into the
"vertical" significance of the work.

When in the summer of 1967 I mentioned to Robbe-Grillet that I
planned to do a piece on *le jeu* in relation to his work, he replied, "Ah, il
faut parler de *Trans-Europ-Express*. C'est fait comme le *jeu de l'oie*." Indeed, this film (1967) carries to great lengths the "duck game" principle
of starts, retreats, and new starts. A novelist-scenarist on a luxury train
begins to "imagine" a scenario suitable for filming on the train; his first
conjectures, objectified into actual sequences, are broad caricatures of
spy movies and are almost immediately "erased" and replaced by more
"serious" attempts. As this game of improvisation continues, the reality of
the game, though retaining its tendency to proliferate into alternatives,
begins to overwhelm the ostensible reality of the character of the writer,
and his imaginings. In this sense *Trans-Europ-Express* is closer to *Dans
le labyrinthe* than to *La Maison de rendez-vous*, in which the "alternatives" (such as the various forms taken by the murder of Manneret) are
spliced together in an "impossible" topology in which events can occur
in reverse or double order: for example, as I have pointed out in this connection, the protagonist Johnson, fleeing the police who are seeking to
arrest him for Manneret's murder, evades them and proceeds to commit
the murder for which he is being sought. (Note a certain similarity here

to the plot of *Les Gommes*.) As for the other "games" of *La Maison de rendez-vous*—the erotic sketches, the garden of statues—these are mostly examples of interior duplications linked in typically complicated ways to other elements in this work as well as in previous works of the author.

Is the predilection for games and game structures evidence of excessive formalism in Robbe-Grillet? It would be possible to argue that since Raymond Roussel the creation of novels on game premises has given rise to certain tendencies in fiction leading away from the "serious" thematics (such as Sartrian *engagement*, the depiction of contemporary alienation, and the like) associated with the novel in the mind of the public. These tendencies appear not only increasingly in Robbe-Grillet, but also in such works as Jean Ricardou's *La Prise de Constantinople* (1965), one of the most significant and "serious" novels-as-game yet to appear. Meanwhile, game for Robbe-Grillet has come to mean structural freedom, absence of traditional rules of transition, viewpoint, chronology, and other parameters of previous fiction, and, on the constructive side, an invitation to create new models, to develop new combinations, to push ahead even further the aptly termed *nouveau roman*.[6]

6. For the most recent evidence of the continual evolution of game forms in Robbe-Grillet, see my *Intertextual Assemblage in Robbe-Grillet: From Topology to the Golden Triangle* (Fredericton, N.B.: York Press, 1979), passim.

12
THE EVOLUTION OF VIEWPOINT
IN ROBBE-GRILLET

It now appears that Robbe-Grillet, following in the wake of Jean-Paul Sartre, has contributed more substantially than any other contemporary novelist to the evolution of theory and practice of narrative viewpoint. Some decades ago this question seemed quite amenable to critical analysis; yet today it appears as one of the most ambiguous and unresolved aspects of fictional structure. The elimination of the omniscient narrator and his replacement by posts of observation within the fictional field are steps in a well-known history: first, in the English tradition of narrative analysis, James and Lubbock (as stated earlier) argued on aesthetic grounds for observers situated within the framework of the novel; then, in the French tradition, Sartre offered a systematic philosophical defense of internal viewpoints, holding that Einsteinian relativity and existential views of knowledge justify relative "frames of reference" in fiction and the restriction of content to that present in a "framing" consciousness. But the apparent stability of a fictional geometry based on internally justified viewpoints proved illusory, and the prospect of rational coherence was of short duration. Indeed, we can see in retrospect that the novel had already rejected such tidy consistency. Soon it would proliferate with new narrative modalities, to return, astonishingly and unpredictably, to a kind of "omniscient" stance in which the reader himself is placed at the—often shifting—narrational focus.

Some of the main factors of instability that led to the abandonment of the novel of justified viewpoint lay, paradoxically, in the novel of the first person that had always seemed to call for little if any structural defense, because its straightforward and automatically justified recital of events is given by a single character, a central or peripheral observer of the action, whose thoughts, observations, and other direct testimony constitute, in principle at least, an unassailably coherent text. When the mode was further justified by the *cadre* of a diary, letters, or other pretexts of written documents, it seemed to produce the maximum illusion of reality or authenticity, if not with respect to outer reality or the real universe, at least with respect to the fictional field. But already in the case of Proust, the *je* or first-person mode had revealed unsuspected ambiguities,[1] and André Gide in *Les Faux-monnayeurs* had played mirror tricks with the first person by introducing an inner novel or journal, while ironically reserving to himself the supposedly outmoded privilege of intervening as the "real" author. Meanwhile, the urgent claims of interior psychology had led to wide acceptance of interior monologue and stream-of-consciousness techniques, which in most cases found no place within the logical scheme of the novel of justified viewpoint.

To complicate matters further, the example of films and cinematic constructions, which seemed at one time to strengthen the case for the objective novel (see earlier remarks concerning the classic chapter on "Roman et cinéma" in Claude-Edmonde Magny's *L'Age du roman américain*), underwent an abrupt change. With the advent of what Raymond Borde calls the "cinéma de la vérité subjective," subjective viewpoints appeared on the screen with spectacular results (*Les Temps Modernes*, December 1961). In *Hiroshima mon amour* and *L'Année dernière á Marienbad* (not to mention the long prehistory of cinematic flashbacks, camera scenes shot from the viewpoint of a single character, contrapuntal sound-track monologues, and the like), mental content was projected on the screen, and the last bulwarks of justified, pseudo-objective cinematic structure began to crumble. Both films and novels were entering a phase of ad hoc framing and *découpage* wherein each new work would create its own narrative perspective.

No contemporary author's works illustrate these tendencies and techniques more brilliantly than those of Alain Robbe-Grillet, whose ingenious and constantly varying narrative modes cover almost the entire spectrum of current experimentation and practice.

In *Les Gommes* (1953), a pseudo detective story of a protagonist who repeats, without realizing it, an inverted and semiparodied version of the myth of Oedipus as he murders the "victim" whose death he is investigating, Robbe-Grillet set out deliberately to destroy clock time (which he calls "linear and without surprises") in favor of human time, the time that each man "secretes about himself like a cocoon, full of flashbacks, repetitions, and interferences." Consequently, the author seeks also to present the contradictory versions of the same events that exist in a world of observational perspectives that he compares, following Sartre's lead, to Ein-

---

1. See Marcel Muller, *Les Voix narratives dans "A la recherche de temps perdus"* (Geneva, 1965), identifying as many as nine separate modes of *je* in the "narrative voices" of Proust's novel.

stein's universe of multiple frames of reference. Such an intention explains, indeed almost necessitates, the use of a wide range of viewpoints in *Les Gommes*. The characters see the same decor from different angles, observe each other, witness and interpret according to their *situations*. (Robbe-Grillet's quoted comments on *Les Gommes* are preserved in a rare pamphlet, never republished.)

The specific narrative mode of this much discussed novel is in most cases third person, but deepened and extended by use of Flaubertian indirect discourse and passages of interior monologue, as well as pseudo-objectification of conjectures, memories, and even hallucinations. The characters who "see" the scenes number about a dozen; they are, in order of their "appearance," the following: the owner of the Café des Alliés, a focal point in the action; Garinati, the hired assassin; Juard, a shady abortionist who ministers to the "victim"; Marchat, a fearful friend of the intended victim; Laurent, the police chief; Wallas, the "special agent" who has been sent to solve the crime; Anna, the victim's maid; "Bona," Jean Bonaventure, the ringleader of the band of political assassins; Mme Bax, whose apartment overlooks the house of the crime; the drunkard who recites distorted versions of the riddle of the Sphinx; Mme Jean, a postal employee; and Dupont himself, the intended and eventual victim of murder. Some of these "observe" only one or two scenes, but the principal characters, such as Wallas, Garinati, and Laurent, are interwoven into a complex design of different viewpoints.

In the case of the protagonist Wallas especially, radically new techniques of objectifying the character's imaginings cause the ostensibly realistic framework of the third-person mode to collapse suddenly into visionary subjectivity. At times, pure inventions or speculations, such as Laurent's theory of the crime, are described as if actually occurring, as might befit the visualized hypothesis of a trained police chief. Along with the general pattern of rotating viewpoints there exist, consequently, the special techniques of mixed objectivity and subjectivity that Robbe-Grillet will in later novels employ apart from any arrangement involving multiple viewpoints.

One question of theoretical difficulty arising in *Les Gommes* is the following: If, in the novel, everything is seen or described from some particular character's viewpoint, how can such hidden allusions as those to the Oedipus myth, or to the tarot cards, be "textualized," and thus communicated to the reader, if all the characters remain ignorant of them? How can such "metafictional" elements be tolerated at all? The answer must lie close to the basic paradox of all fiction. It should be obvious that the universe "observed" by the characters cannot be their own creation in any real sense but must emanate from the novelist, whether or not he "intervenes" visibly to make his presence known. It is he who determines what kind of universe his characters will observe; he can at will, therefore, hide or partially reveal features recognizable by the reader but not by the characters. This intentionality is essential to the creation of any fictional field, since an opposing theory would necessarily fall into the realistic fallacy of Zola, who tried to persuade himself and his readers that the fictional world he had created was somehow real and subject to the same "scientific" laws as nature or society itself.

One additional narrative mode should be identified in *Les Gommes*. At first it appears to be an anomaly, if not a regression to outmoded omniscience or at least direct authorial intervention. It is the impersonal mode that appears here and there in passages that seem to come from nowhere or no one ("when all is ready, the lights go on"; "Quand tout est prêt, la lumière s'allume," etc.). The explanation, which does not justify the passages in the sense of fitting them into the pattern of observational viewpoints, nevertheless shows them to be structurally related to the conception of the particular novel. They are passages attributable to a "chorus." The work, with its five chapters (acts), prologue, and epilogue, parallels in form the divisions of a Greek tragedy, such as Sophocles' *Oedipus the King*, whose plot is also paralleled. In this regard Robbe-Grillet has allowed formal, aesthetic considerations to outweigh philosophical or metaphysical ideas concerning the relativity of time or viewpoint. Thus, at the outset of his career he reassumes authorial privileges that theoretically should be excluded.

Point of view in *Le Voyeur* (1955) has a paradoxical quality that analysis shows is nevertheless related to the theme and structure of the novel. Some critics have found in the work only a single focus, that of the protagonist Mathias, the traveling salesman who lands on an island to sell wristwatches to its inhabitants and departs several days later after (almost certainly) murdering, in a "suppressed" scene whose content is only gradually revealed, a young girl whose tortured body is thrown over a cliff into the sea. According to the single angle or unified view, the whole text (written in the third person) describes only Mathias's perceptions and outlook on the surrounding world. The third-person form would therefore express only an *internal* view. But, as I have tried to demonstrate elsewhere, there are large blocks of text wherein Mathias is very definitely seen from the *outside*—long, "neutral" passages and developments incompatible with the internal single-viewpoint theory. It is from these scenes that the paradox or ambiguity of narrative mode arises, not from the mixing of real and imagined scenes in the sections of the text that do render the world-view and mind of Mathias through techniques of objectified subjectivity.

Assuming the correctness of this analysis, one may discover, on probing more deeply into the problem, the reason for the paradox as well as its solution. The fundamental structural intention served by the narrative mode of pseudo-objective third person is indeed that of incarnating the world of Mathias, a character "out of phase with himself," a sadistic schizophrenic obsessed with visions (and actions?) of erotic violence. But to present this deformed universe, the author has need of an undeformed background against which the distortions, alterations, and other psychic projections of Mathias may be discriminated, measured, and judged. It is for this reason that Mathias is frequently observed and described from an external *point d'optique* that cannot be his own (as, for example, when he is depicted looking downward) and for this reason that he is seen against a decor presented in a *style Robbe-Grillet* whose objects and other consistent elements (geometrical terms, scientific precision, deceptive qualifiers, and the like) mark the general "manner" of the author (as, for example, in those descriptive portions of the scenario of *Marienbad* designed primarily for the director) and are not a style specifically adapted to a character's mentality. Moreover, when—in a fashion comparable to that of Faulkner when he presents the world through the idiot Benjy's eyes—Robbe-Grillet creates a vision of the world distorted by Mathias's psychopathology, it is this neutral, background universe that is distorted, and the style takes on a deformed, hallucinatory quality only by its relationship to the primary decor.

The well-known figure-eight object series of *Le Voyeur* illustrates how the two worlds—that of the stylized universe in which the protagonist exists and that of the visionary erotic sadist's mind—are linked. In the "background" world the coiled cord, the marks of the iron rings on the quay, the pattern of eyes on the doors, the spirals of cigarette smoke, the adjacent rings left on the bar by wet glasses, and all the other "eights" are coincidental forms such as any attentive observer with an eye for geometrical patterns might discern about him. But as they enter Mathias's mind they become charged with morbid psychological tensions and sinister associations, and the reader begins to feel an upsurge of violent erotic emotion, to recognize in these objects cords that may bind wrists, rings that could hold young limbs apart, bonds, watching eyes, and the whole repertory of obsessive objects found in the novel.

After a certain critical resistance, later studies of Robbe-Grillet came to agree with the analysis that finds *Le Voyeur* "organisé selon deux perspectives," as Jean Alter has expressed it in *La Vision du monde d'Alain Robbe-Grillet* (Geneva, 1966). What is important is to perceive that this dual perspective, that of the author and that of the protagonist, coincides perfectly with the novelist's intention to make the reader experience as directly as possible the disorientation of the schizoid mind, including a "blackout" or period of amnesic repression during which the crime is committed, a "hole" in the text during which, as it were, the viewpoint entirely ceases to exist.

As the novel progresses, the point of view of Mathias (his mental content) occupies more and more the volume of the text, so that the latter sections function in almost pure single-viewpoint mode. Even before that, as we have seen, when we speak of a dual viewpoint in *Le Voyeur* we do not mean one belonging to two narrators or fictional characters, but rather the opposition described between the author's "nominal," stylized decor and the personalized view of that world as apprehended in the mind of a protagonist. In a sense, the remarks made earlier concerning certain details of the author's world in *Les Gommes*, as opposed to the world of the characters themselves, apply also to *Le Voyeur*.

Seeking a term to describe the innovation in narrative viewpoint invented by Robbe-Grillet in *La Jalousie* (1957), I called the new mode that of the *je-néant*, or absent I. Without entering into the metaphysics of Sartrian *néantisation* and its relation to the perceiving consciousness, the *je-néant* may be defined as a technique of the suppressed first person in which all pronouns or forms associated with it (such as I, me, my, mine, and the like) are eliminated. As often stated, even by Robbe-Grillet himself, the perceptions of the protagonist of the novel, a jealous husband who exercises an intense surveillance over his wife, constitute the "narrative," which is expressed without perceptible self-reference. A central focus of vision is created, in a style related to that of the cinematic subjective camera but lacking the first-person commentary on the sound track that typically accompanies the subjective sequences of films made in this mode, such as *The Lady in the Lake*. A hole (Robbe-Grillet calls it a "*creux*," or "hollow") is created at the core of the narrative, and the reader installs himself therein, assuming the narrator's vision and performing, without verbal clues, all the unspoken and implicit interpretation of scenes and events that, in the conventional novel of psychological analysis and commentary, would normally be spelled out by the author or his character. Not only does the text embody the naked dynamics of the husband's perceptions of external events and objects, it also, as the incarnation of the magma of his mental content, contains secondary, associative materials such as memories more or less deformed by emotional tensions, exaggerated visions of an erotic or paranoid nature (such as the paroxysmal image of the enlarged *mille-pattes* or centipede whose crushing carries the weight of the husband's dread that his wife is being possessed by another), and even purely hypothetical scenes of murderous wish fulfillment, such as the crash and burning of the car containing his wife and her presumed lover.

This aesthetically fascinating and powerful effect, arising almost entirely through the special narrative mode employed, seems extraordinarily appropriate to a novel about jealousy. The husband's preoccupation is not with himself; he therefore has little reason for self-reference. What obsesses him is what his wife A. . . is doing, is planning to do, or has done, with the virile and aggressive Franck. The husband returns constantly to past scenes, reexamining them for clues as he visualizes them and simultaneously transforming them and distorting them in line with his mounting suspicions. Sharing these visions through the technique of the *je-néant*, the reader feels, rather than thinks, jealousy. The wiping away of the conventional vocabulary of jealousy, as one would find it in Proust, for example, allows nothing to intervene between the phenomena that give rise to jealousy and the emotion itself. The reader's psychophysical responses take over. We may compare in this sense the text of *La Jalousie* and the essays in the "simulation" of psychopathological states, including paranoia, written by Breton and Eluard in *L'Immaculée Conception* during the surrealist period. The contrast between a novel like *La Jalousie* and a traditional novel of psychological analysis is paralleled by the contrast between the poetic texts of simulation of abnormal mental states and the texts found in conventional manuals of psychopathology, including Freud's and Stekel's, that embed the pathological experience and its visions in the rational context of a psychiatrist's explanatory commentary.

Other writers of the *nouveau roman*, especially Claude Ollier and Jean Ricardou, have used the suppressed first-person mode to good effect. It seems that the *je-néant* will enter the repertory of techniques of point of view (along with Michel Butor's "narrative you") destined for future exploitation by many novelists. Looking back, one may now, as I have pointed out elsewhere, discern a link between Robbe-Grillet's *je-néant* and the partially suppressed first-person mode of the *je* in Camus's *L'Etranger*. While there is in Camus's novel no suppression whatever of the pronoun *je* (on the contrary, it even becomes obtrusive in its proliferation), Meursault's "I" appears as a pronoun of surfaces only, oddly lacking in depth or interiority. The protagonist of *L'Etranger* almost never "thinks" or analyzes, and like the husband of *La Jalousie* he communicates his sense impressions at a more or less objective level. The reader quickly passes over Meursault's repeated *je*, so weightless is it. Suppression takes place *behind* the pronoun. It remained for Robbe-Grillet to erase the pronoun itself and create a wholly new mode.

In the first sentence of *Dans le labyrinthe* (1959), a *je* speaks. No further first-person form appears until near the end, in the phrase "à *ma* dernière visite," and in the last sentence a departing narrator closes his text with the word *moi*. Thus, having announced himself at the outset, the narrator has retired from view (though we sense his presence in passages employing a type of *je-néant* mode), to reappear—but not fully, even then—as the novel closes. Yet as we become sensitive to his presence, we feel that we are near him, in his small author's room, even when the action is taking place outside, in the labyrinthine streets where the soldier-protagonist, ill or wounded, makes his way from café to barracks to ambiguous apartments, carrying his box to a recipient whose identity he cannot remember, toward some forgotten and ambiguous rendezvous.

What has Robbe-Grillet gained by this narrative structure, involving the interior duplication of an author composing a novel? One could easily imagine another version of the novel in which the wanderings of the soldier, described more or less in the third-person style used here, would alone form the text. Even brief reflection shows that such a simplification would not only impoverish the novel, but would in fact negate its meaning. The author is obviously concerned less with the adventures of the soldier, pathetic as they may be, than with the relation between the soldier's feverish story and the concealed inner author whose struggles in the labyrinth of novelistic creation form the most important "subject" of the book.

The title is not "The Labyrinth," but "*In* the Labyrinth." Once the inner author, whose voice creates the novel, may be seen as the real protagonist, the narrative viewpoint becomes clear, and the barely visible first-person frame is justified. As this writer attempts to build from the materials in his room (a steel engraving of a soldier in a café, a shoebox, a bayonet, etc.) a coherent novel, his stops and starts, revisions and alterations, give rise to the textual image of the labyrinth, an image not only of the maze of identical right-angle streets in the story, but also of the labyrinthine verbal style of the text itself. The fact that toward the end of the work this narrator merges with the doctor who treats the dying soldier may be viewed as an effort finally to push the narrator himself into the story, in a fashion somewhat analogous to the reentrant line in certain drawings of Steinberg, which, having emerged from the pen of the artist depicted in the sketch, eventually rejoins the figure of the artist himself. The effect is the opposite of that Camus employed in *La Peste*, wherein Doctor Rieux, hitherto seen only as a third person, suddenly emerges as a first-person narrator, abandoning *il* for an unambiguous *je*.

In *Dans le labyrinthe*, Robbe-Grillet appears to adopt a kind of Mallarméan aesthetics in which the creation of the literary work itself becomes the primary theme, lying beneath the fictional incarnation that may have its own anecdotal or pseudoanecdotal value, as in *L'Après-midi d'un faune* or, more strikingly, in *Un Coup de dés jamais n'abolira le hasard*. Like Mallarmé's "*ptyx*" sonnet, which the poet termed "allégorique de lui-même," *Dans le labyrinthe* is in a sense an analogy of itself. Since the intention was to devise a structure appropriate to a *self-contained* novel, the inner author and inner subject (duplicated in the engraving) seem perfectly justified, as do the pages lying on the table at the end, as the narrative voice leaves the room at last, uttering the final phrase, "derrière moi."

Of particular interest to the study of the evolution of techniques of mode and viewpoint in Robbe-Grillet is the creation in *Dans le labyrinthe* of a new type of authorial intervention that permits, by means of an author placed within the fictional field, the use of free modalities of narration that would be impossible in the system of existentially justified viewpoints. Whereas the passages of abstract intervention in *Les Gommes* had to be explained in terms of formal imitation of the Greek dramatic chorus, such intervention now becomes part of the activities of a "creator" whose operations and maneuvers are at once the subject and the text of the novel itself. The relative "realism" of *Le Voyeur* and *La Jalousie* begins to disappear in favor of a new constructionalism.

The prefaces to the films *L'Année dernière à Marienbad* (1961) and *L'Immortelle* (1963), as well as their structure and the camera angles they employ, show them to be closely related (as far as viewpoint is concerned) to novels of Robbe-Grillet such as *Le Voyeur* and *La Jalousie*. In the preface to *Marienbad*, Robbe-Grillet states that when two people converse, for example, what is present in their minds, as counterpart to the actual words of their dialogue, can only be visual or sensory images related to the topic under discussion. Thus mental content, which in Robbe-Grillet's view is primarily visual, becomes a natural narrative mode for the cinema, which can show the characters' imaginings while retaining the same degree of "realism" in the decor and photography as that used in the "normal" scenes, if indeed any scenes may be thought of as existing apart from the characters' perceptions.

Consequently, if a character in a film remembers or imagines something, especially under the influence of emotion, the scene appears before us as it does in the character's own mind. Sometimes subtle alterations mark such an imaginary scene, but not as an intentional clue to permit any discrimination between the real and the imaginary. The alterations must result from the tensions exerted by the character's emotions: thus the heroine's bedroom in *Marienbad*, recalled in great stress, is visually transformed, and appears in a heightened baroque style. When recalled scenes recur in *L'Immortelle*, they are deformed in accordance with the "narrator's" jealous scrutiny, in a technique comparable to that employed in the written, rather than visual, text of *La Jalousie*.

Neither *Marienbad* nor *L'Immortelle*, however, uses a consistently justified system of viewpoint in the manner just described. In *Marienbad*, in addition to some scenes taken from an imaginary and "impossible" angle high in the air, there are shots where the mingling of two viewpoints occurs, as when the lover X "intervenes" (verbally) in the vision he evokes in the heroine's mind of the seduction scene, which we see through her eyes. In both *Marienbad* and *L'Immortelle*, two or more characters appear twice in different parts of a panoramic camera movement, creating a strange effect of continuity between two moments of time and two spatial locations that on a realistic level could not be proximate. Nor is it always possible to "linearize" such shots by assuming that they consist of memories or imaginings within a single mind. As with the "chronological impasses" of *La Jalousie*, one senses in Robbe-Grillet an impatience with the limitations of the justified system and a tendency to reclaim authorial rights over point of view—to replace the old doctrine of the omniscient author by a new, but in a sense similar, one that would place the point of view not necessarily within a given character, but in the spectator (or author) himself. The novelist demands a creative freedom not possible within the theoretical limits of the James/Sartre system.

The extent to which Robbe-Grillet's ideas and practices had changed about 1963 may be measured against the short article he had published in 1958 bearing the long title "Notes sur la localisation et les déplacements du point de vue dans la description romanesque." Therein we find, as discussed earlier, almost complete support for the visually justified viewpoint, and the cinema is held up as an example to the novel, since the film, "whether or not there is a person from whose viewpoint the scene is shot, must absolutely be shot from some precise point," and this post of observation must be that of a *man*, either one within the fictional frame or one placed at a possible vantage point. But within a few years the early novelist-deity of Robbe-Grillet will compensate in creative freedom for what the old Balzacian author-god had lost in omniscience and protean viewpoint. The justification moves from within the characters to the form or structure of the novel itself.

In *La Maison de rendez-vous* (1965), Robbe-Grillet employs a number of apparently new techniques, not only of viewpoint but also of plot structure. These may, however, be shown to be developments and intensifications of practices already discernible in his earlier works, and they represent outgrowths of tendencies whose evolutionary possibilities may be identified retrospectively, even if they were not clearly predictable.

The common principle uniting these innovations is what may be termed reentry or infolding, a procedure that causes both point of view and story line to turn in upon themselves, with metamorphoses and transfers occurring not only backward and forward in time, but also between characters. Though the closest anticipation of the technique is the inner author's assumption of the role of the doctor mentioned above in *Dans le labyrinthe*, the origins of the mode may be traced back to a work as early as *Les Gommes*, in which the transitions, however, appear more easily detectable, since the viewpoint moves from person to person, and in which the temporal junctions, when nonlinear, involve no serious "dechronology." With *La Jalousie* the viewpoint never changes, but the temporal reversals and impasses, with the altered reiterations of scenes, nevertheless create something of the contradictory quality of the structure of *La Maison de rendez-vous*. An example in *La Jalousie* is the passage in which Franck replaces on an adjacent table a drinking glass in which the ice has completely melted. A few lines farther on, we read that one melting ice cube remains. We soon realize that two different moments of time have merged in the narrator's mind, linked by associative tensions, and the apparent impossibility is resolved. In *La Maison de rendez-vous* no similar resolutions exist for such nonlinear transitions. Thus the fleeing protagonist Johnson, escaping the police by going through a Hong Kong hotel and out the back way, continues on to commit the very crime for which he was being pursued. The crime itself occurs more than once, and each time in different circumstances: not theoretically, as in *Les Gommes* (where several characters visualize the same crime according to their separate hypotheses), or through imaginary projections, like those of Mathias in *Le Voyeur* (as he creates *fantomatique* scenes of selling watches to the same clients, etc.), but literally, or at least textually.

Accompanying this change is an extension of the device of the "initial I" used in *Dans le labyrinthe*. A first person appears and reappears, but the first-person accounts of events merge with virtually verbatim repetitions attributed to another character. Robbe-Grillet progressively establishes what amounts to a *state of viewpoint*; justification is not only abandoned, but distorted and negated so violently that the reader acquires or shares a kind of omnipresence similar to that of certain dreams. If, as its author has stated, "la maison de rendez-vous" is indeed the house of our imagination, it is a domain in which the reader, with the novelist, feels free to create whatever structures of space, time, and action he wishes.

In her excellent analysis of the nonlinear aspects of this novel (see *Etudes*, March 1966), Mme Mireille Latil-Le Dantec quotes from one of my articles my formulation (here translated) of the "eternal question of the novel": "What justifies or explains the existence of a narrative text, this deceitful text that pretends to be plausible, which comes to us from somewhere, from someone who speaks from a hidden or ambiguous place, and who presents us with an ever stranger novelistic universe, structured according to the perspectives of his ever more polymorphous point of view?" Mme Latil-Le Dantec replies that *La Maison de rendez-vous* seems to offer to this basic question of the justification of viewpoint "the proudest of replies," namely, that "Nothing justifies the narrative text other than itself. It seeks no *vraisemblance*, deriving its truth only from itself. It comes from nowhere. It is a mental space, the rendezvous of viewpoints successively adopted or abandoned by an *imaginaire* who has no support other than himself, and who creates his own world."

Must we admit, then, that the omniscient author of Balzac, driven from the house of fiction by a score of novelists from Flaubert and James to Sartre, has returned through the back door of *La Maison de rendez-vous*? Are dechronology, entangled and shared viewpoints, and nonlinear structures only a modern form of the older mode? Careful reflection and analysis will show, I believe, that it is not a case of *Plus ça change, plus c'est la même chose.* The Balzacian omniscient author played his godlike role in a world of characters offered as Aristotelian imitations of life. Even the scientific pretensions of a Zola implied a transfer from fiction to reality itself. But in Robbe-Grillet we enter a domain of psychofiction, akin to that of Mallarméan poetry or the invented novelistic world of Raymond Roussel, with its formal schematics and its principles of self-generating content and self-contained structure. At the height of its popularity, *La Maison de rendez-vous* led all of Robbe-Grillet's novels in sales and public acclaim. Even if some of this popularity could be attributed to erotic elements in the book, or to its pseudo–James Bond atmosphere and plot, we may still detect a willingness to accept, in fiction, some of the same formal liberties and absence of conventional justifications that prevail in modern pictorial styles (from abstract to op) and musical compositional methods (from serial to chance). A McLuhanite or a disciple of George Steiner might argue that the phenomenon is related to the breakdown of language, or at least the breakdown of the old rhetoric of fiction in the direction of the nonrational, if not the nonverbal. To so argue would be in one sense a paradox, since works like *La Maison de rendez-vous* have a stylistic intricacy and polish that set them apart from the "revolution of the word," the syntax of lettrism, beat poetry, post-Joycean free association, syllabic interplay, mangled texts à la William Burroughs, or other symptoms of that retreat from reality which now, according to Steiner, "begins outside the verbal language." One thing at least seems assured:

the *nouveau roman*, in the hands of Robbe-Grillet and other experimentalists, continues to promise evolutionary surprises.

One such surprise has been the use of what I have termed "intertextual assemblage," the polystructured use of earlier texts. Another is the incorporation into the fictional structure of outside elements, especially paintings and etchings, either deliberately composed for such use in the author's work or borrowed from dead contemporaries. Such "assemblage" novels are Robbe-Grillet's *Topologie d'une cité fantôme* (1975), *La Belle Captive* (with reproductions of thirty or more paintings by Magritte, 1975), and *Souvenirs du triangle d'or* (1978).[2]

The three most important evolutionary changes in twentieth-century novel and film have surely been in the basic structural aspects of chronology, narrative mode, and point of view. As we pass from the earlier emphasis on the diegesis and its psychological bases to the exploitation of new structures involving topological forms, Kleinien infoldings, thematic series, and the like, we move from the traditional foundations of the film and novel into the current and future aspects of generative literature and generative art.[3]

2. See my *Intertextual Assemblage in Robbe-Grillet from Topology to the Golden Triangle* (Fredericton, N.B.: York Press, 1979).

3. See chapter 11, note 6, and the articles by Robbe-Grillet, David Leach, Diane Kirkpatrick, Karlis Racevskis, and myself in *Generative Literature and Generative Art* (Fredericton, N.B.: York Press, 1983).

BRUCE MORRISSETTE:
A BIBLIOGRAPHY

Books

Les Aspects fondamentaux de l'esthétique symboliste. Clermont-Ferrand: Bussac, 1933.

The Life and Works of Marie-Catherine Desjardins (Mme de Villedieu). Washington University Studies. Saint Louis: Washington University, 1947.

The Great Rimbaud Forgery: The Affair of "La Chasse Spirituelle." Washington University Studies. Saint Louis: Washington University, 1956. With unpublished documents and an anthology of Rimbaldian pastiches.

La Bataille Rimbaud. Paris: Nizet, 1959. French version of *The Great Rimbaud Forgery*, with some new material.

Les Romans de Robbe-Grillet. Preface by Roland Barthes. Paris: Editions de Minuit, 1963. 2d ed., with new materials, 1965; 3d ed., with new chapters, 1971.

Alain Robbe-Grillet. Columbia Essays on Modern Writers. New York: Columbia University Press, 1965.

The Novels of Robbe-Grillet. Ithaca, N.Y.: Cornell University Press, 1975. English version of *Les Romans de Robbe-Grillet*, revised and expanded by the author, with an additional chapter.

Intertextual Assemblage in Robbe-Grillet from Topology to the Golden Triangle. Fredericton, N.B.: York Press, 1979.

Articles

"*Les Amours des Grands Hommes* of Mlle Desjardins and *Le Docteur Amoureux*." *MLN* 53 (1940): 344–47.

"Scorsonère, Black Salsify." *PMLA* 55 (1940): 602–5.

"Mlle Desjardins and the *Apologie du Luxe*." *MLN* 56 (1941): 209–11.

"Early English and American Critics of French Symbolism." In *Studies in Honor of Frederick W. Shipley*, 159–80. Washington University Studies. Saint Louis: Washington University, 1943.

"The 'Untraced Quotation' of Ernest Dowson's Dedication." *MLN* 58 (1943): 558–59.

179

"French Criticism, 17th Century" and about a dozen shorter entries. In *Dictionary of World Literature*, ed. Joseph Shipley. New York: Philosophical Library, 1943.

"Marcel Langlois' Untenable Attribution of *La Princesse de Clèves* to Fontenelle." *MLN* 63 (1948): 267–70.

"Richard Aldington's Proposed 'Source' for *La Princesse de Clèves*." *MLN* 63 (1948): 164–67.

Articles on Boileau, Chapelain, Cyrano de Bergerac, Mme de la Fayette, La Rochefoucauld, Pascal, Mme de Sévigné, and other topics in various volumes of *Collier's Encyclopedia*. New York, 1950.

"Vance Thompson's Plagiarism of Teodor de Wyzewa's Articles on Mallarmé." *MLN* 67 (1952): 175–78.

"T. S. Eliot and Guillaume Apollinaire." *Comparative Literature* 5 (1953): 262–68.

"A New Document on Rimbaud." *MLN* 72 (1957): 508–12.

"Surfaces et structures dans les romans de Robbe-Grillet." *French Review* 31 (1958): 364–69.

"Naissance d'une citation 'rimbaldienne.'" *MLN* 74 (1959): 328–29.

"Structures de sensibilité baroque dans le roman pré-classique." *Cahiers de l'Association Internationale des Etudes Françaises* 11 (1959): 86–103.

"Lecture de *La Jalousie* d'Alain Robbe-Grillet." *Critique* 146 (July 1959): 579–608.

"New Structure in the Novel: *Jealousy*, by Robbe-Grillet." *Evergreen Review*, no. 10 (1959): 103–7, 164–90. (English version of "Lecture de *La Jalousie* d'Alain Robbe-Grillet.")

"Oedipus and Existentialism: *Les Gommes* of Robbe-Grillet." *Wisconsin Studies in Contemporary Literature* 1 (Fall 1960): 43–73.

"Lettura di *Les Gommes*." *Il Verri* (October 1961): 120–49.

"Roman et cinéma: Le Cas de Robbe-Grillet." *Symposium* 15 (Summer 1961): 85–103.

"Vers une écriture objective: *Le Voyeur* de Robbe-Grillet." In *Saggi e ricerche di letteratura francese*, 267–98. Milan: Feltrinelli, 1961.

"The New Novel in France." *Chicago Review* 15 (Winter–Spring 1962): 1–19.

"Theory and Practice in the Works of Robbe-Grillet." *MLN* 73 (May 1962): 257–67.

"De Stendhal à Robbe-Grillet: Modalités du point de vue." *Cahiers de l'Association Internationale des Etudes Françaises* 14 (1962): 143–63.

"Une Voie pour le nouveau cinéma." *Critique* 203 (May 1964): 411–33.

"Les Idées de Robbe-Grillet sur Beckett." In *Configuration critique de Samuel Beckett*, 55–67. Paris: Minard, 1964.

"*L'Etranger* de Camus." *Revue Belge de Philologie et d'Histoire* 42, 2 (1964): 744–48.

"Clés pour '*Les Gommes*.'" Postface to the 10/18 edition of Robbe-Grillet's *Les Gommes*, 269–314. Paris: Editions Générales, 1965.

"Narrative 'You' in Contemporary Literature." *Comparative Literature Studies* 2, 1 (1965): 1–24.

"Profondeur morale et nouveau roman." In *Métamorphoses du roman*, by R. M.

Albérès, 257–59. Paris: Albin Michel, 1966. Reprinted from its original appearance in *Les Nouvelles Littéraires*, 6 June 1966.

"Last Year at Istanbul: Robbe-Grillet's *L'Immortelle*." *Film Quarterly* 10 (Winter 1966–67): 38–42.

"Cinema and Literature." *Encyclopedia of World Literature*, 1:231–34. New York, 1967.

"The Evolution of Narrative Viewpoint in Robbe-Grillet." *Novel* 1 (Fall 1967): 22–33.

"Problèmes du roman cinématographique." *Cahiers de l'Association Internationale des Etudes Françaises* 20 (May 1968): 277–89.

"Trends in the New French Cinema." *American Society Legion of Honor Magazine* 39, 3 (1968): 153–72.

"Games and Game Structures in Robbe-Grillet." *Yale French Studies* 41 (1969): 153–72.

"Le Visage international du *nouveau roman*." *Actes du vᵉ Congrès de l'Association Internationale de Littérature Comparée* (1969): 391–97.

"Theme and Structure in the New French Film." *Film Review Digest* 1 (Spring 1970): 155–68.

"International Aspects of the *Nouveau Roman*." *Contemporary Literature* 2 (Spring 1970): 155–68.

"Robbe-Grillet as a Critic of Samuel Beckett." In *Samuel Beckett Now*, ed. Melvin J. Friedman, 59–71. Chicago: University of Chicago Press, 1970.

Commentaries in *Positions et oppositions: Le Roman Contemporain*, ed. Michel Mansuy, 40, 55, 197–98. Paris: Klincksieck, 1971.

"Robbe-Grillet's *Project for a Revolution in New York*." *American Society Legion of Honor Magazine* 42, 2 (1971): 73–88.

"Un Héritage d'André Gide: La Duplication intérieure." *Comparative Literature Studies* 8, 2 (1971): 125–42.

"Le Roman, demain." *Marche Romane* 21 (Spring 1972): 65–70.

"Topology and the *Nouveau Roman*." *Boundary 2* 1 (Fall 1972): 45–57.

"Cette gomme multivalante." In *Les Critiques de notre temps et le nouveau roman*, 73–77. Paris: Garnier, 1972.

"Robbe-Grillet Nᵒ 1, 2 . . . X." In *Nouveau Roman: Hier, aujourd'hui*, 2: 119–33. Ed. 10/18. Paris: Union Générale d'Editions, 1972.

"Aesthetic Response to Novel and Film: Parallels and Differences." *Symposium* 27 (Summer 1973): 137–51.

"The Alienated 'I' in Fiction." *Southern Review* 10 (January 1974): 15–30.

"Post-Modern Generative Fiction: Novel and Film." *Critical Inquiry* 2, 2 (1975): 233–62.

"Intertextual Assemblage as Fictional Generator." *International Fiction Review* 5, 1 (1978): 1–14.

"Generative Techniques in Robbe-Grillet and Ricardou." In *Generative Literature and Generative Art: New Essays by Alain Robbe-Grillet, Bruce Morrissette, Diane Kirkpatrick, Karlis Racevskis, and David Leach*, 25–34. Fredricton, N.B.: York Press, 1983.